Two Step

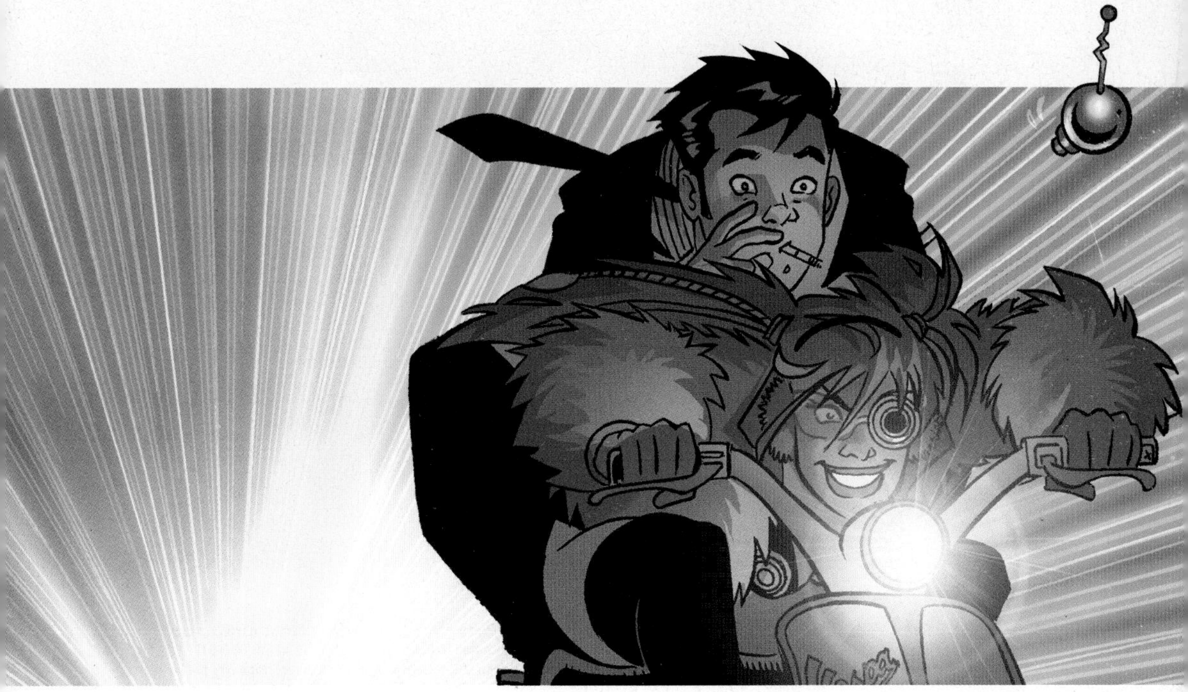

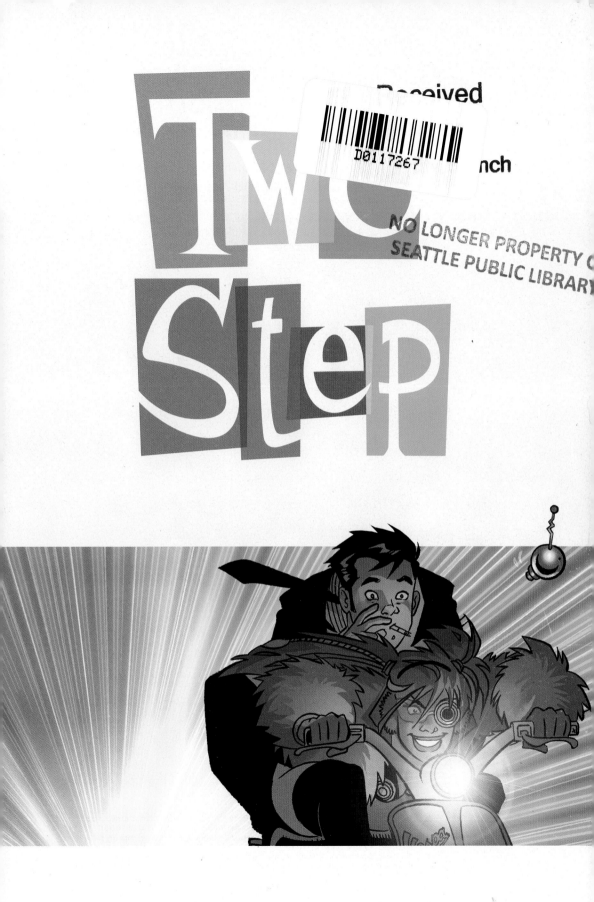

WRITER: WARREN ELLIS
PENCILS: AMANDA CONNER
INKS: JIMMY PALMIOTTI
COLORS: PAUL MOUNTS   LETTERS: KEN LOPEZ

COLLECTED EDITION COVER AND ORIGINAL SERIES COVERS BY
AMANDA CONNER AND PAUL MOUNTS

ALEX SINCLAIR	EDITOR–ORIGINAL SERIES
KRISTY QUINN	ASSISTANT EDITOR–ORIGINAL SERIES
KRISTY QUINN	EDITOR
ED ROEDER	ART DIRECTOR
DIANE NELSON	PRESIDENT
DAN DIDIO AND JIM LEE	CO-PUBLISHERS
GEOFF JOHNS	CHIEF CREATIVE OFFICER
JOHN ROOD	EXECUTIVE VICE PRESIDENT–SALES, MARKETING AND BUSINESS DEVELOPMENT
PATRICK CALDON	EXECUTIVE VICE PRESIDENT–FINANCE AND ADMINISTRATION
AMY GENKINS	SENIOR VP–BUSINESS AND LEGAL AFFAIRS
STEVE ROTTERDAM	SENIOR VP–SALES AND MARKETING
JOHN CUNNINGHAM	VP–MARKETING
TERRI CUNNINGHAM	VP–MANAGING EDITOR
ALISON GILL	VP–MANUFACTURING
DAVID HYDE	VP–PUBLICITY
HANK KANALZ	VP–GENERAL MANAGER, WILDSTORM
SUE POHJA	VP–BOOK TRADE SALES
ALYSSE SOLL	VP–ADVERTISING AND CUSTOM PUBLISHING
BOB WAYNE	VP–SALES
MARK CHIARELLO	ART DIRECTOR

SUSTAINABLE
FORESTRY
INITIATIVE
Certified Chain of Custody
Promoting Sustainable
Forest Management
www.sfiprogram.org

Fiber used in this product
line meets the sourcing
requirements of the
SFI program.

www.sfiprogram.org
PWC-SFICOC-260

TWO-STEP, published by WildStorm Productions. 888 Prospect St. #240, La Jolla, CA 92037. Cover, scriptbook, sketches and compilation © 2011 Warren Ellis and Amanda Conner. All Rights Reserved. TWO-STEP is ™ Warren Ellis and Amanda Conner. WildStorm and logo are trademarks of DC Comics. Originally published in single magazine form as TWO-STEP #1-3, © 2003-2004 Warren Ellis and Amanda Conner. The stories, characters, and incidents mentioned in this magazine are entirely fictional. Printed on recyclable paper. WildStorm does not read or accept unsolicited submissions of ideas, stories or artwork. Printed by Quad/Graphics, Dubuque, IA, USA. 11/17/2010.

DC Comics. a Warner Bros. Entertainment Company.

ISBN: 978-1-4012-2887-3

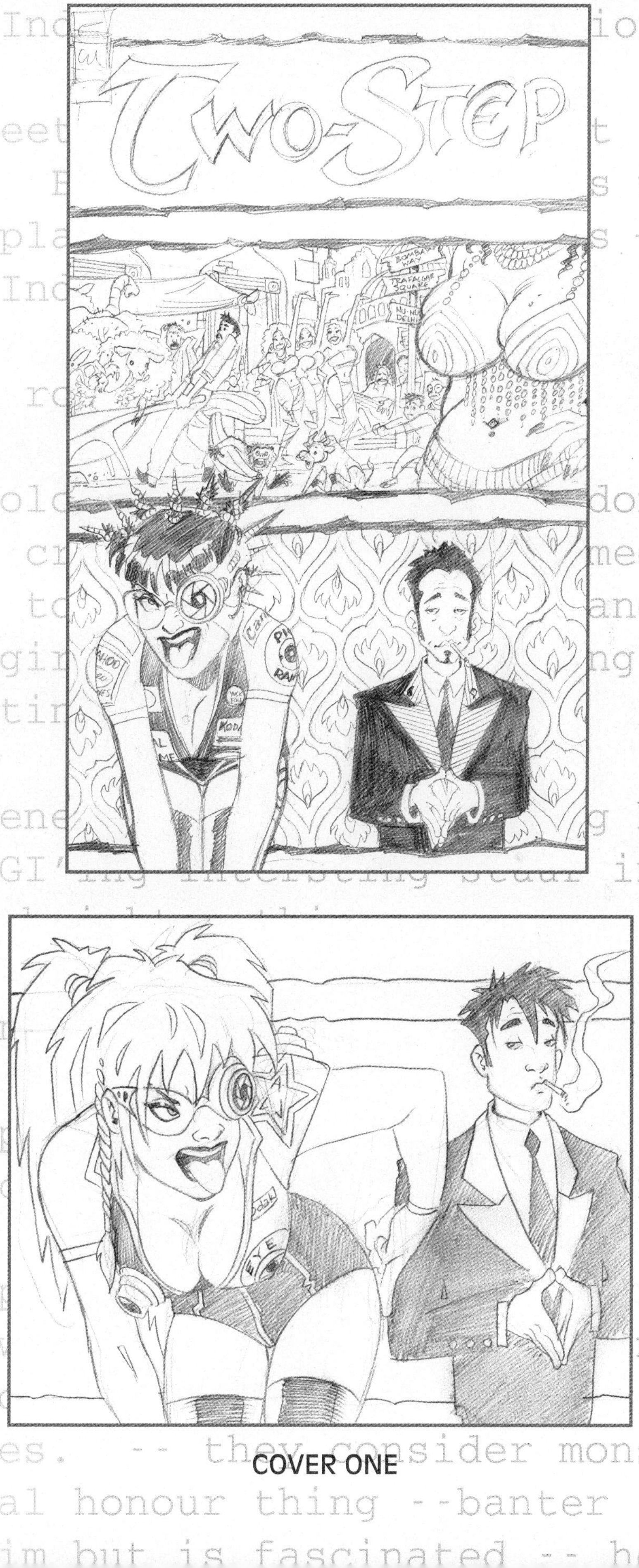
TWO-STEP
TRAFALGAR SQUARE

COVER ONE

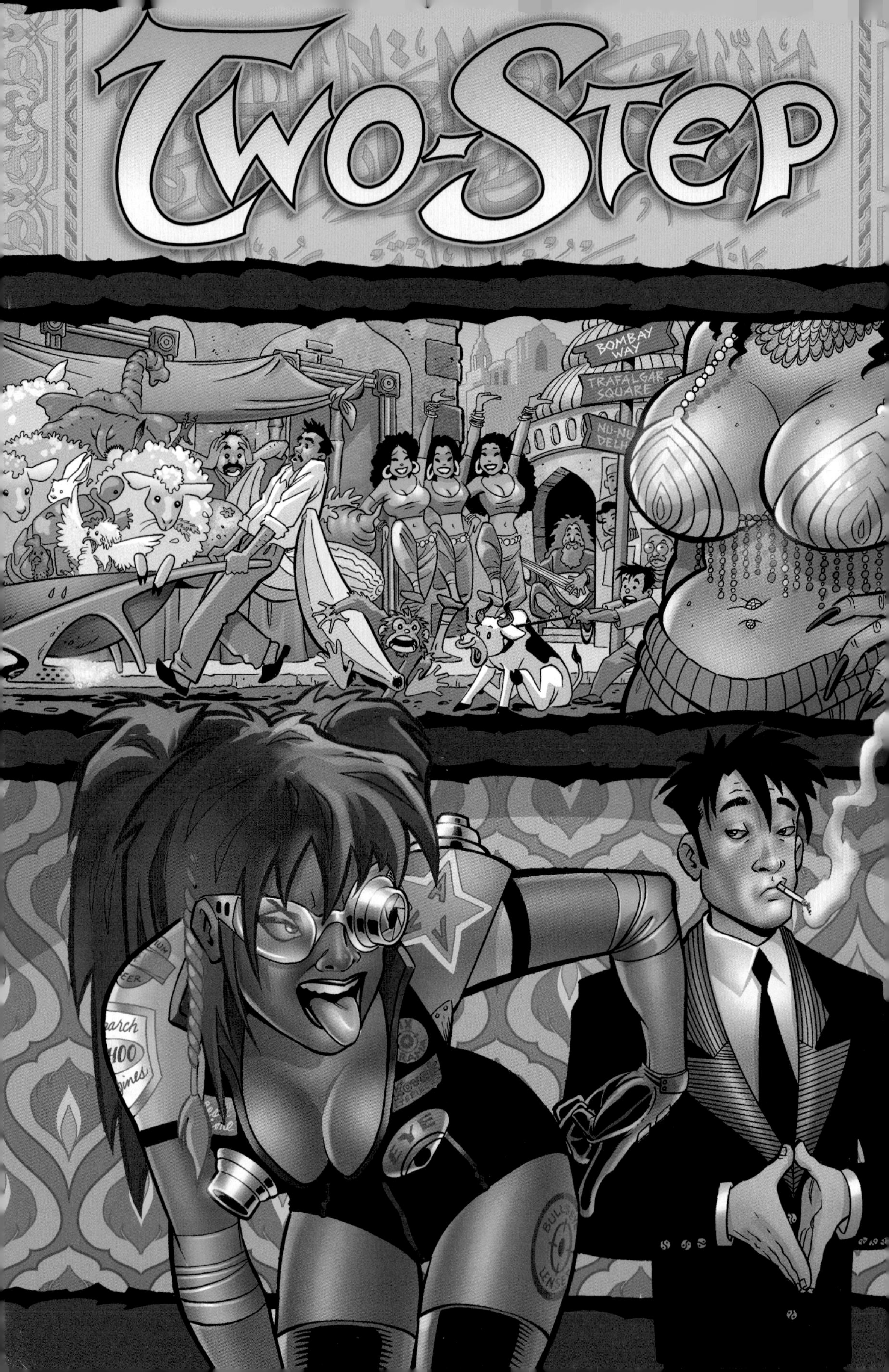
TWO-STEP
BOMBAY WAY
TRAFALGAR SQUARE

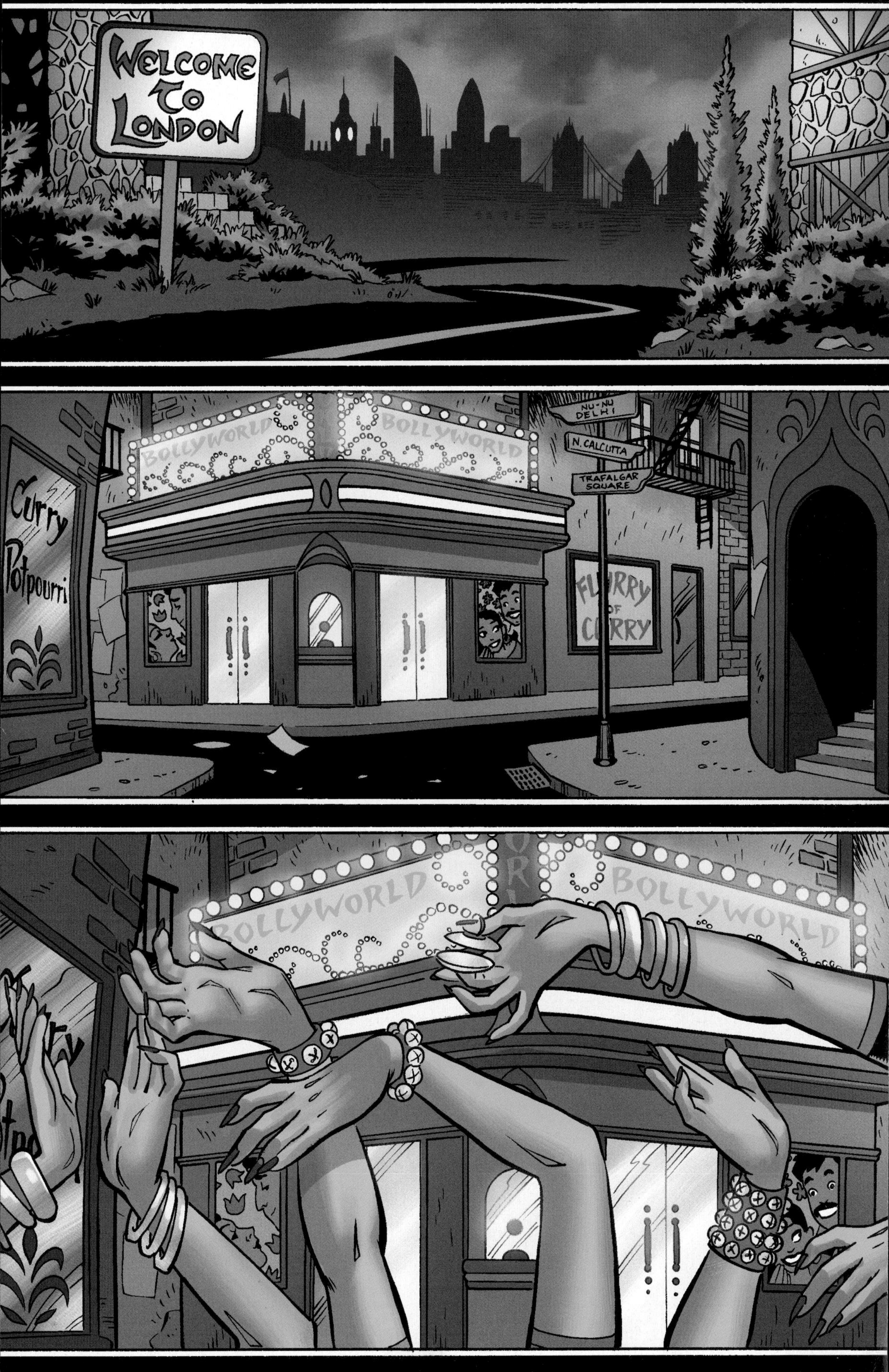
WELCOME TO LONDON
BOLLYWORLD
BOLLYWORLD
NU-NU DELHI
N. CALCUTTA
TRAFALGAR SQUARE
Curry Potpourri
FLURRY OF CURRY
BOLLYWORLD
BOLLYWORLD

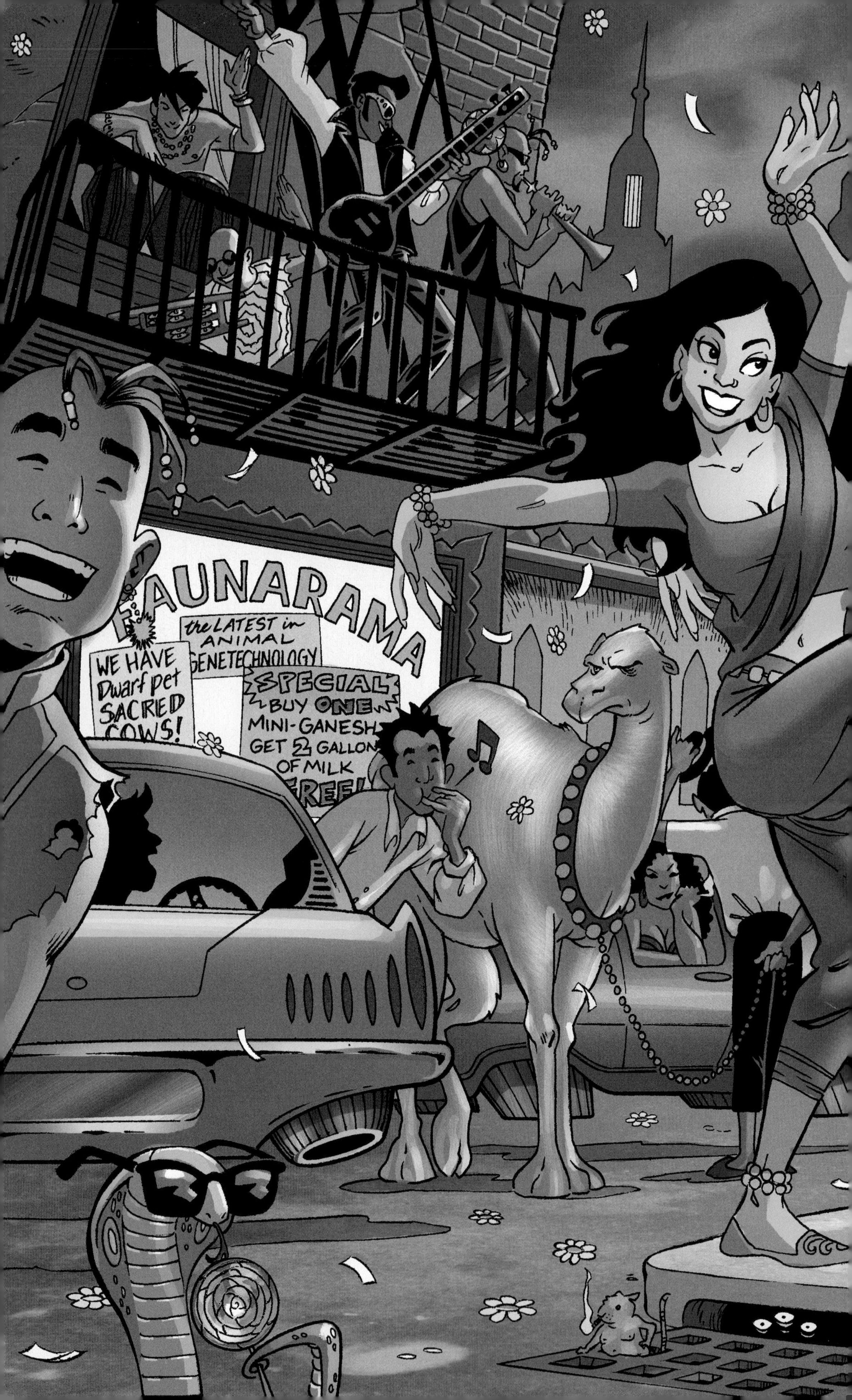
FAUNARAMA
the LATEST in ANIMAL GENETECHNOLOGY
WE HAVE Dwarf pet SACRED COWS!
SPECIAL BUY ONE MINI-GANESH GET 2 GALLON OF MILK FREE!

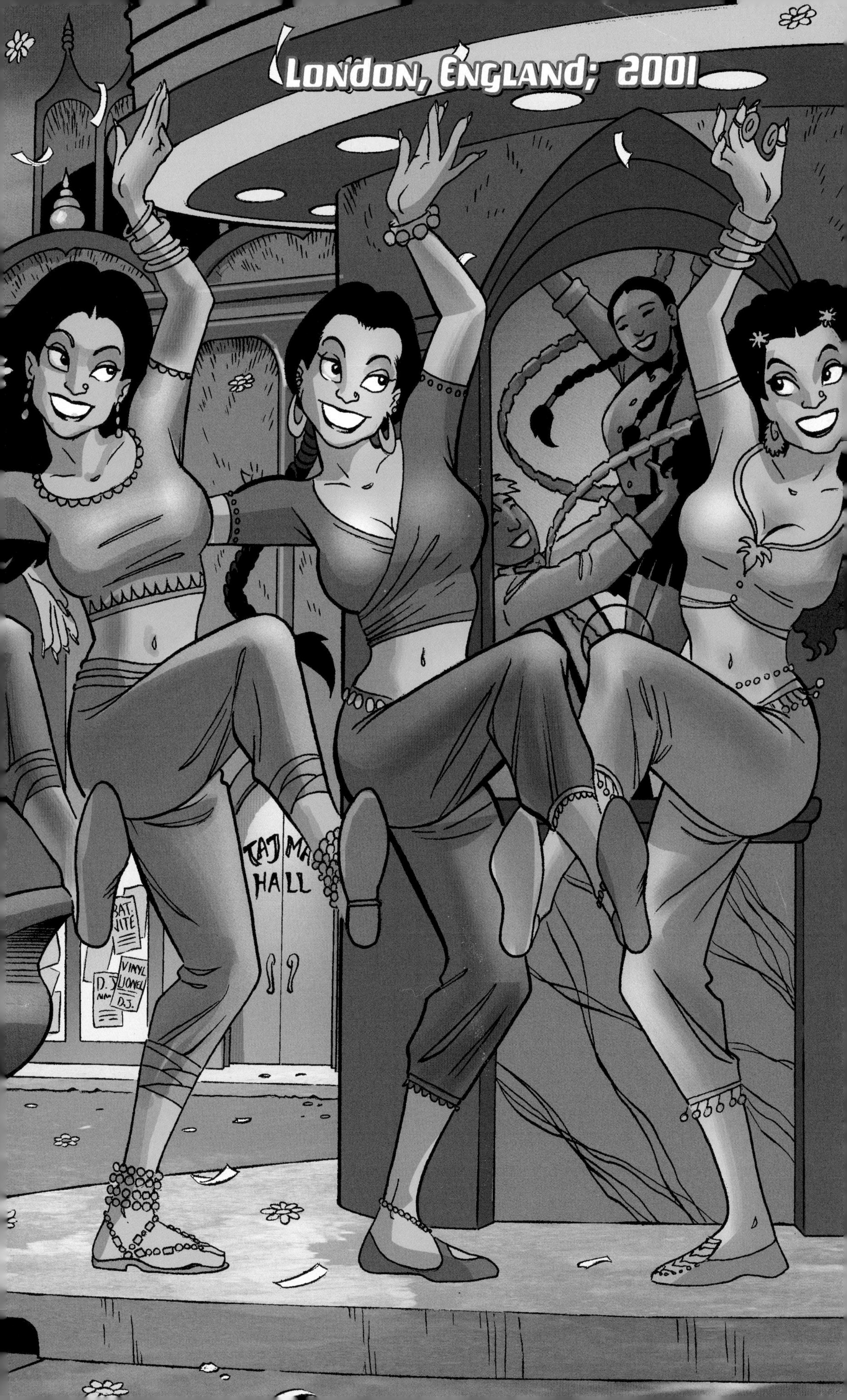
LONDON, ENGLAND; 2001
TAJ MA
HALL
BAT. NITE
VINYL LIONEL D.J.

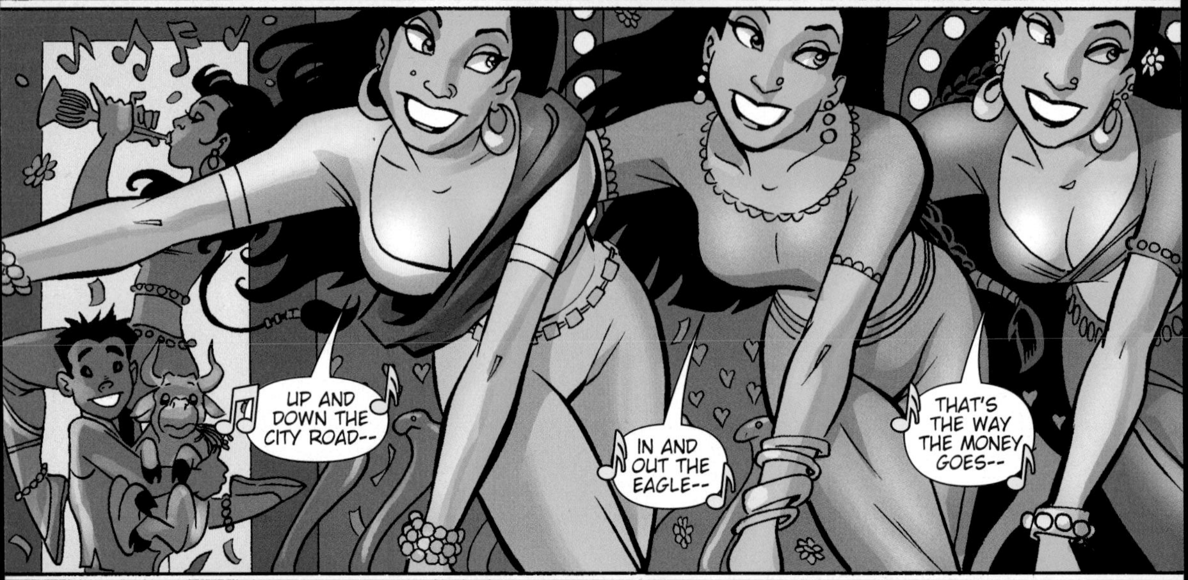
UP AND DOWN THE CITY ROAD--
IN AND OUT THE EAGLE--
THAT'S THE WAY THE MONEY GOES--

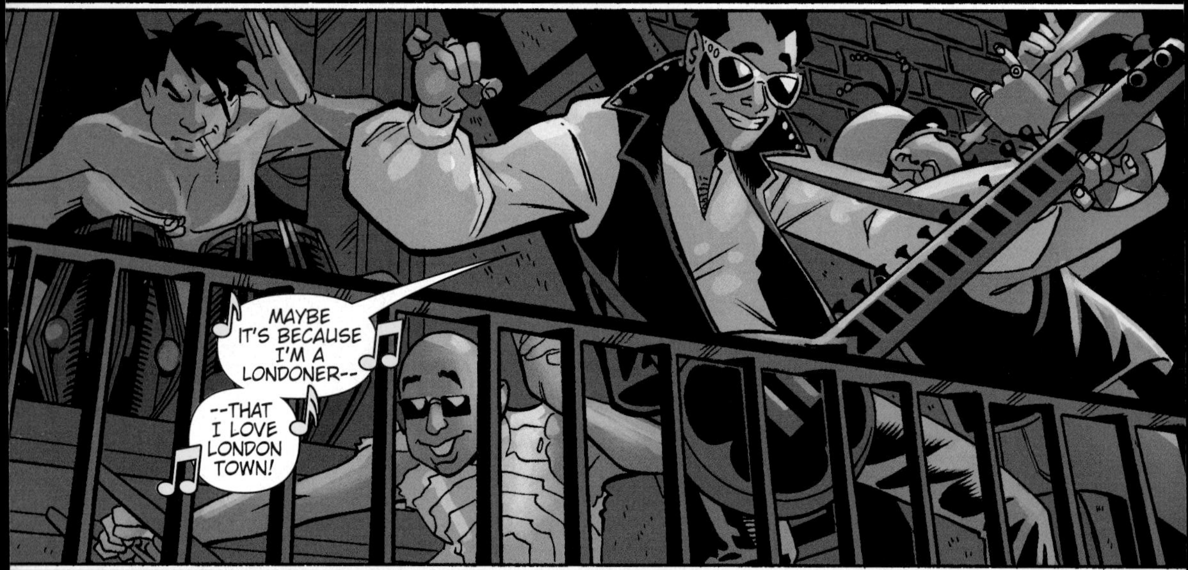
MAYBE IT'S BECAUSE I'M A LONDONER--
--THAT I LOVE LONDON TOWN!

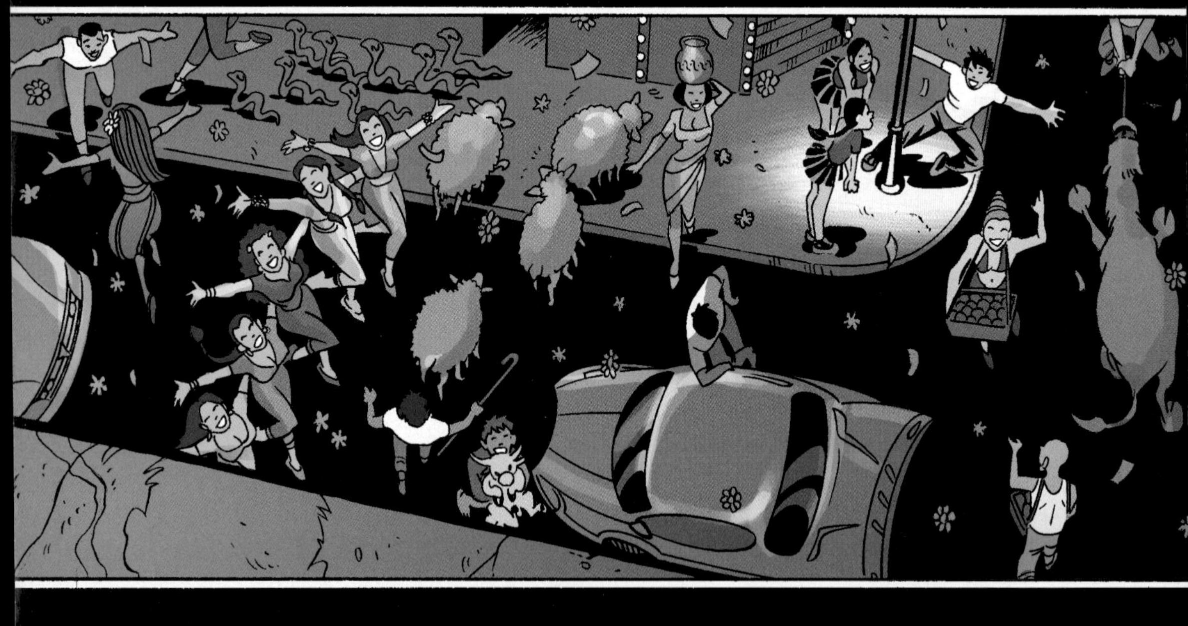

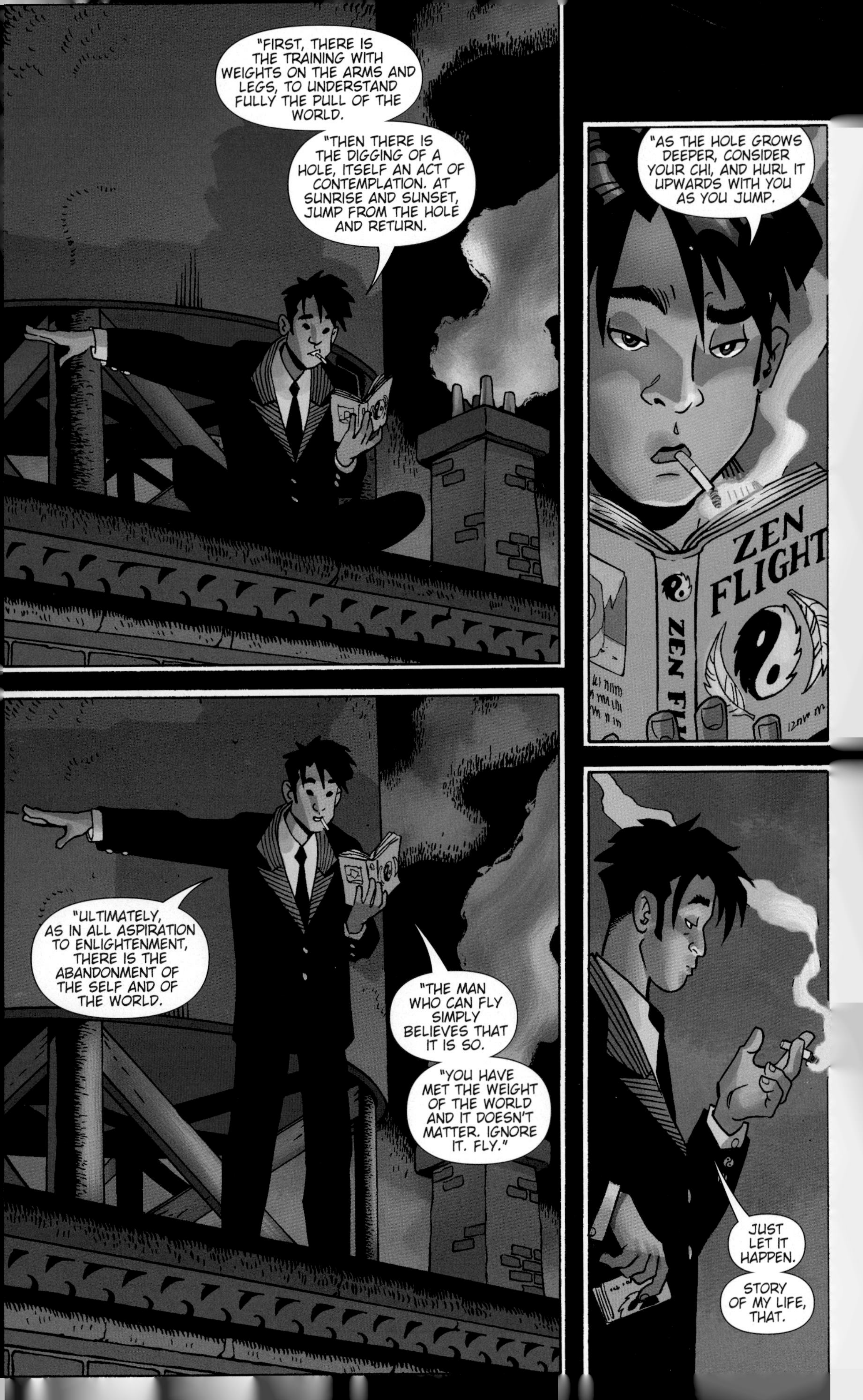
"FIRST, THERE IS THE TRAINING WITH WEIGHTS ON THE ARMS AND LEGS, TO UNDERSTAND FULLY THE PULL OF THE WORLD.
"THEN THERE IS THE DIGGING OF A HOLE, ITSELF AN ACT OF CONTEMPLATION. AT SUNRISE AND SUNSET, JUMP FROM THE HOLE AND RETURN.
"AS THE HOLE GROWS DEEPER, CONSIDER YOUR CHI, AND HURL IT UPWARDS WITH YOU AS YOU JUMP.
ZEN FLIGHT
ZEN FL
"ULTIMATELY, AS IN ALL ASPIRATION TO ENLIGHTENMENT, THERE IS THE ABANDONMENT OF THE SELF AND OF THE WORLD.
"THE MAN WHO CAN FLY SIMPLY BELIEVES THAT IT IS SO.
"YOU HAVE MET THE WEIGHT OF THE WORLD AND IT DOESN'T MATTER. IGNORE IT. FLY."
JUST LET IT HAPPEN.
STORY OF MY LIFE, THAT.

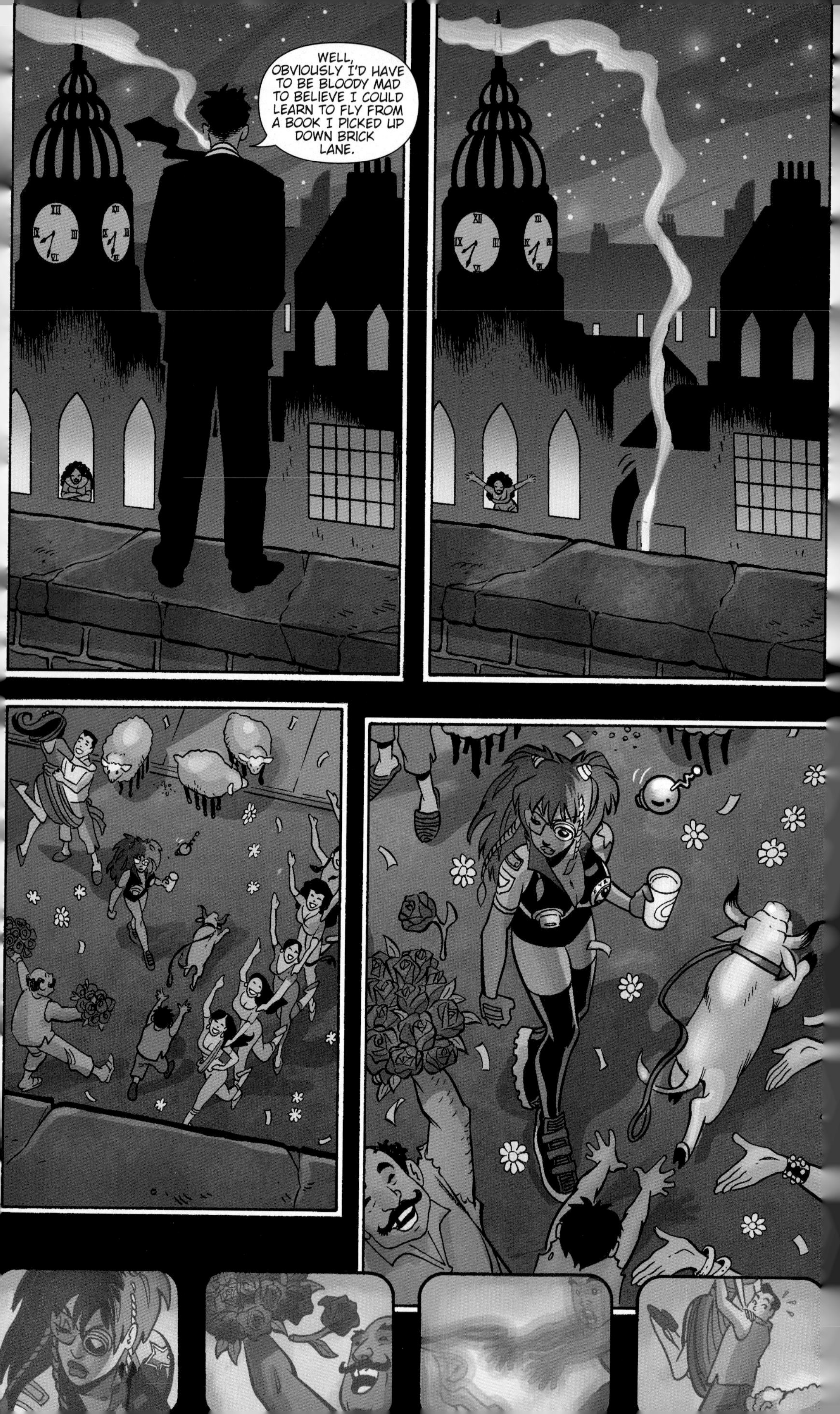
WELL, OBVIOUSLY I'D HAVE TO BE BLOODY MAD TO BELIEVE I COULD LEARN TO FLY FROM A BOOK I PICKED UP DOWN BRICK LANE.

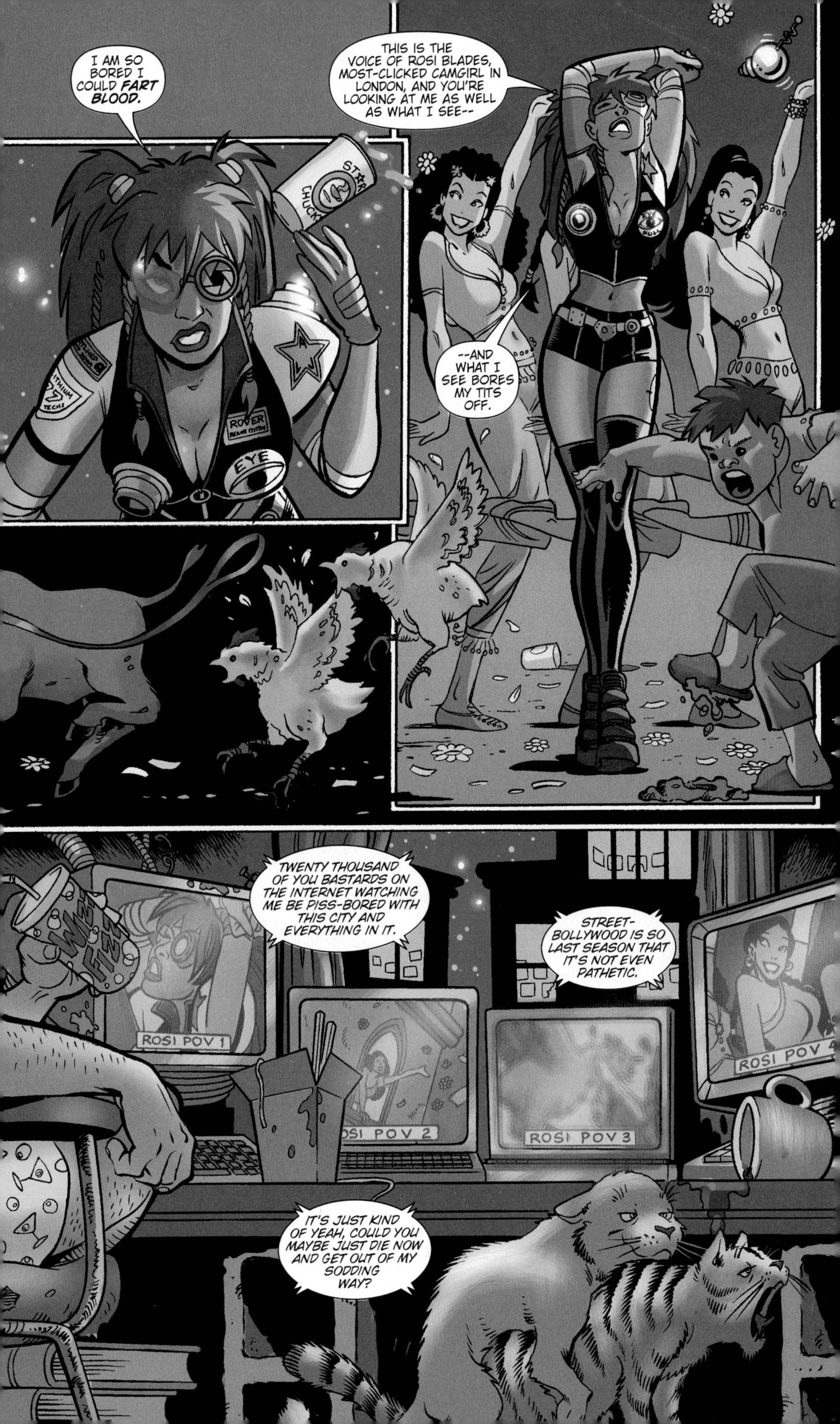
I AM SO BORED I COULD FART BLOOD.
THIS IS THE VOICE OF ROSI BLADES, MOST-CLICKED CAMGIRL IN LONDON, AND YOU'RE LOOKING AT ME AS WELL AS WHAT I SEE--
--AND WHAT I SEE BORES MY TITS OFF.
TWENTY THOUSAND OF YOU BASTARDS ON THE INTERNET WATCHING ME BE PISS-BORED WITH THIS CITY AND EVERYTHING IN IT.
STREET-BOLLYWOOD IS SO LAST SEASON THAT IT'S NOT EVEN PATHETIC.
IT'S JUST KIND OF YEAH, COULD YOU MAYBE JUST DIE NOW AND GET OUT OF MY SODDING WAY?
ROSI POV 1
ROSI POV 2
ROSI POV 3
ROSI POV 4
ROVER
EYE

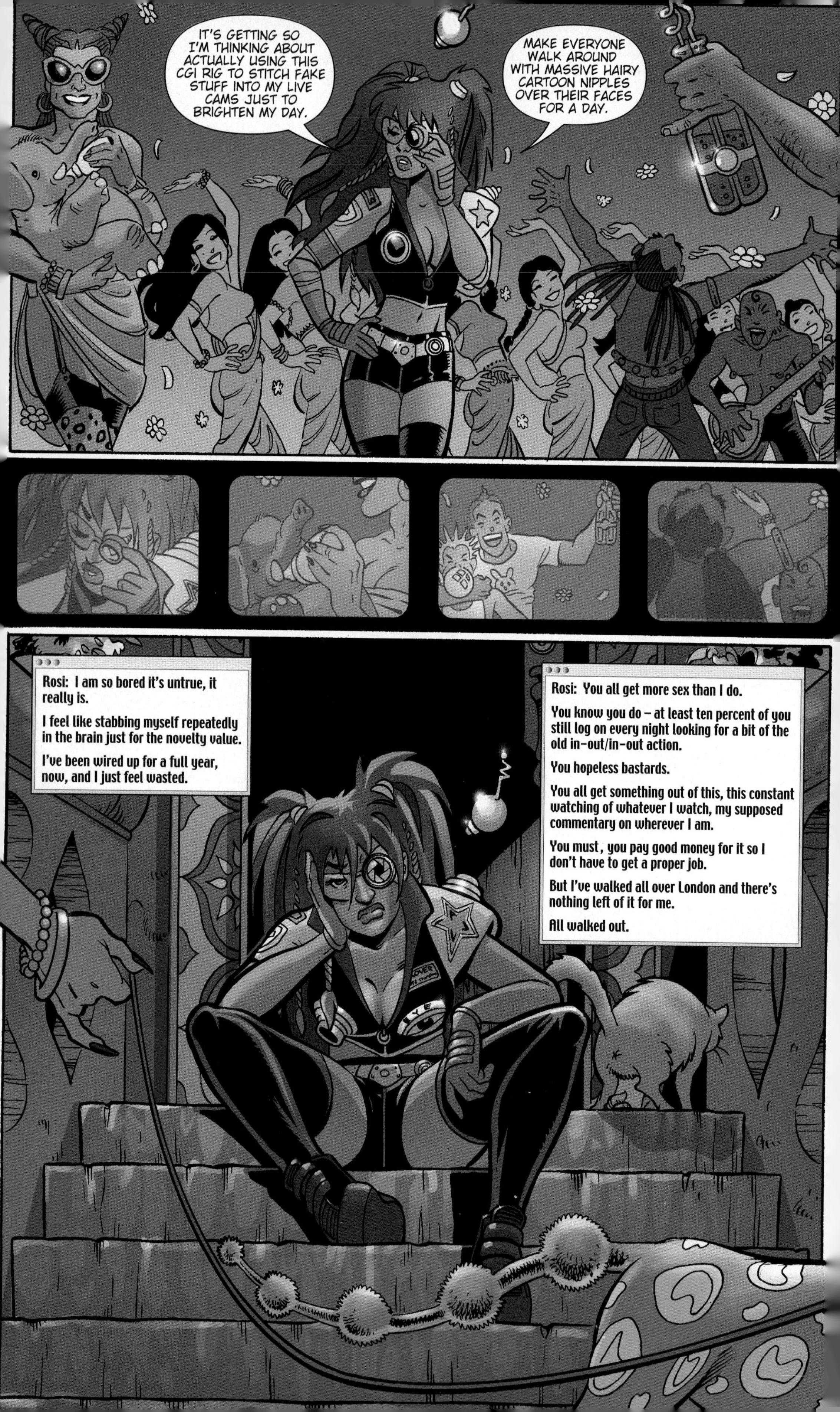
IT'S GETTING SO I'M THINKING ABOUT ACTUALLY USING THIS CGI RIG TO STITCH FAKE STUFF INTO MY LIVE CAMS JUST TO BRIGHTEN MY DAY.
MAKE EVERYONE WALK AROUND WITH MASSIVE HAIRY CARTOON NIPPLES OVER THEIR FACES FOR A DAY.
Rosi: I am so bored it's untrue, it really is.
I feel like stabbing myself repeatedly in the brain just for the novelty value.
I've been wired up for a full year, now, and I just feel wasted.
Rosi: You all get more sex than I do.
You know you do – at least ten percent of you still log on every night looking for a bit of the old in-out/in-out action.
You hopeless bastards.
You all get something out of this, this constant watching of whatever I watch, my supposed commentary on wherever I am.
You must, you pay good money for it so I don't have to get a proper job.
But I've walked all over London and there's nothing left of it for me.
All walked out.

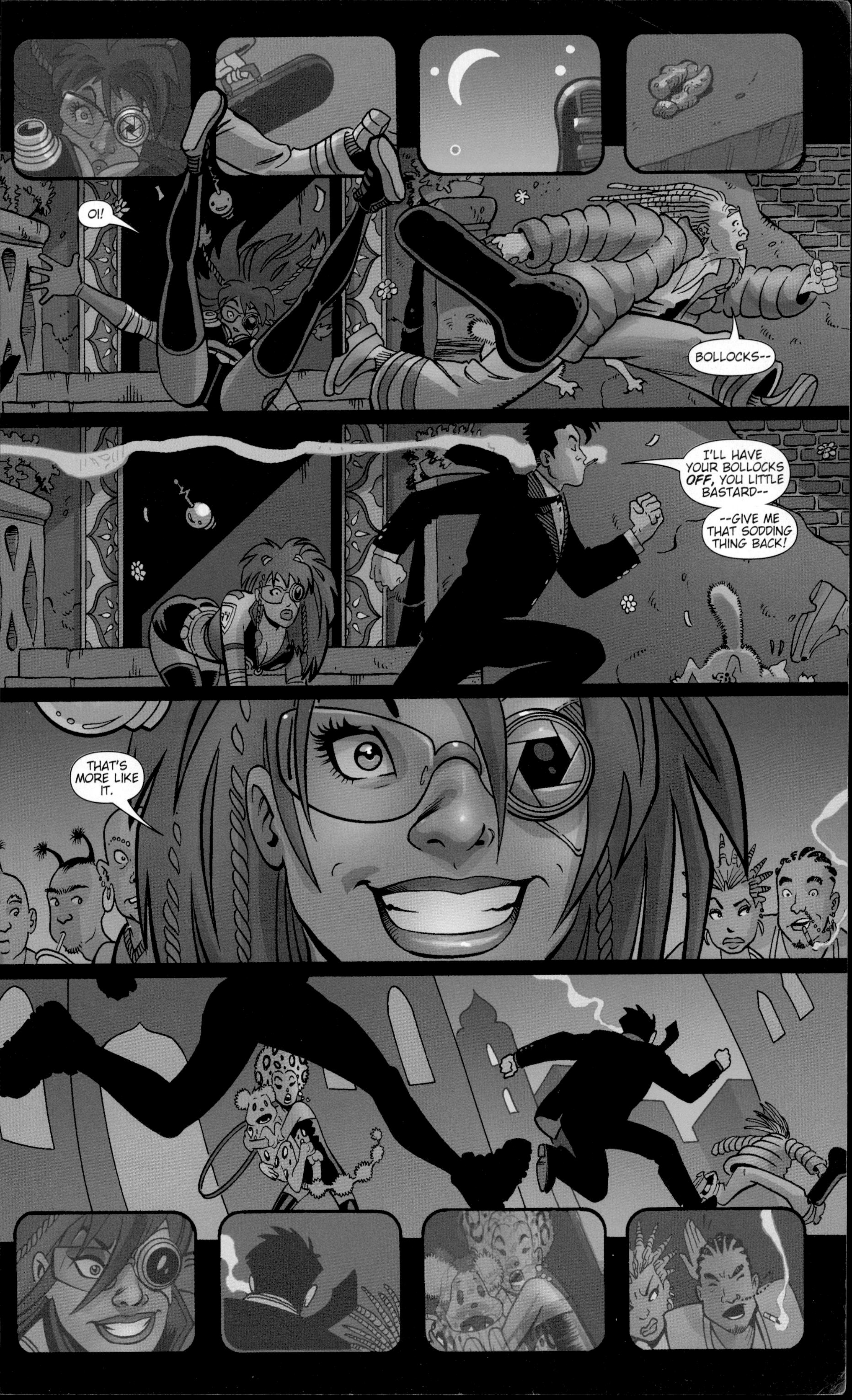
OI!
BOLLOCKS--
I'LL HAVE YOUR BOLLOCKS OFF, YOU LITTLE BASTARD--
--GIVE ME THAT SODDING THING BACK!
THAT'S MORE LIKE IT.

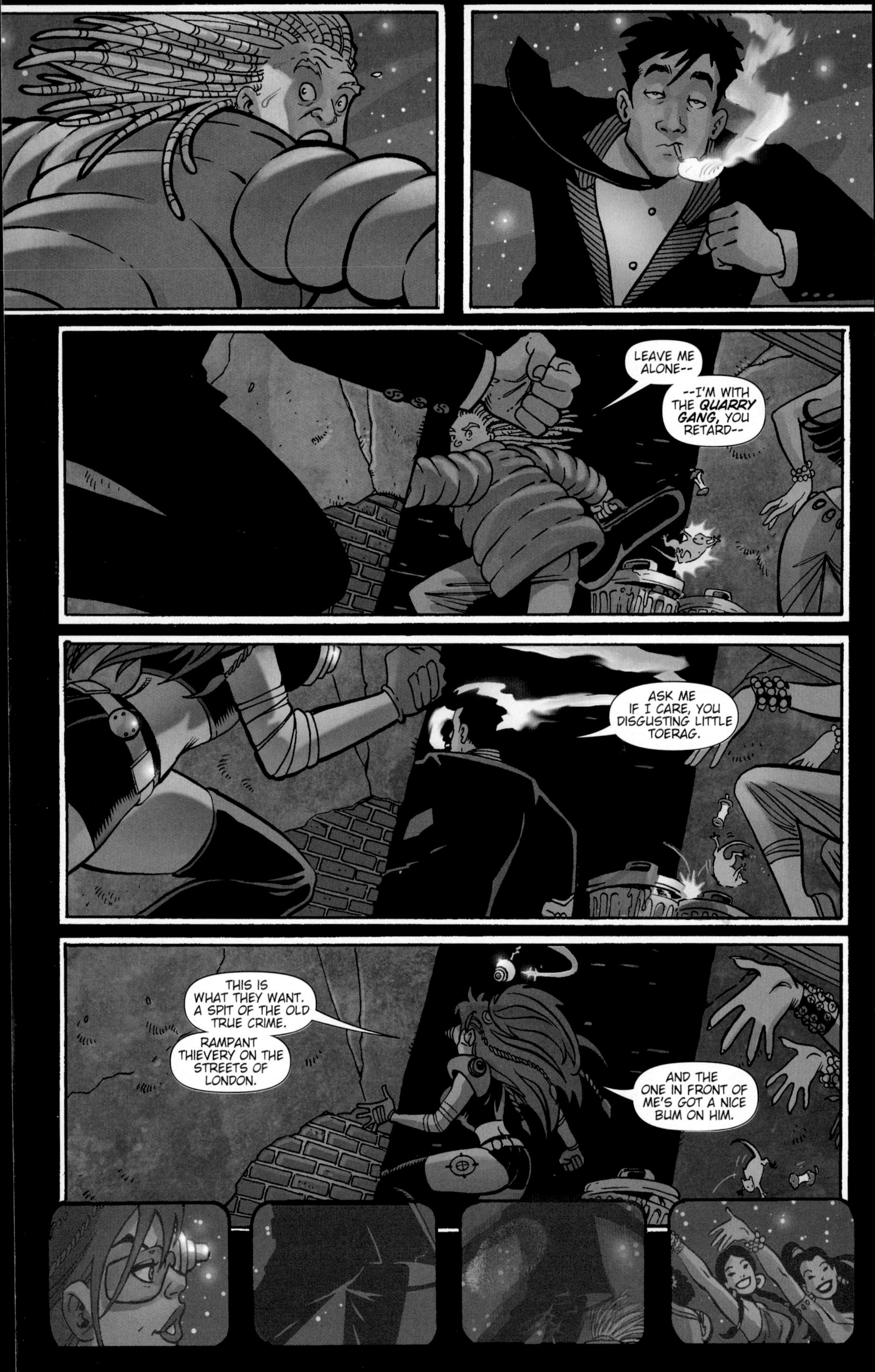
LEAVE ME ALONE--
--I'M WITH THE **QUARRY GANG,** YOU RETARD--
ASK ME IF I CARE, YOU DISGUSTING LITTLE TOERAG.
THIS IS WHAT THEY WANT. A SPIT OF THE OLD TRUE CRIME.
RAMPANT THIEVERY ON THE STREETS OF LONDON.
AND THE ONE IN FRONT OF ME'S GOT A NICE BUM ON HIM.

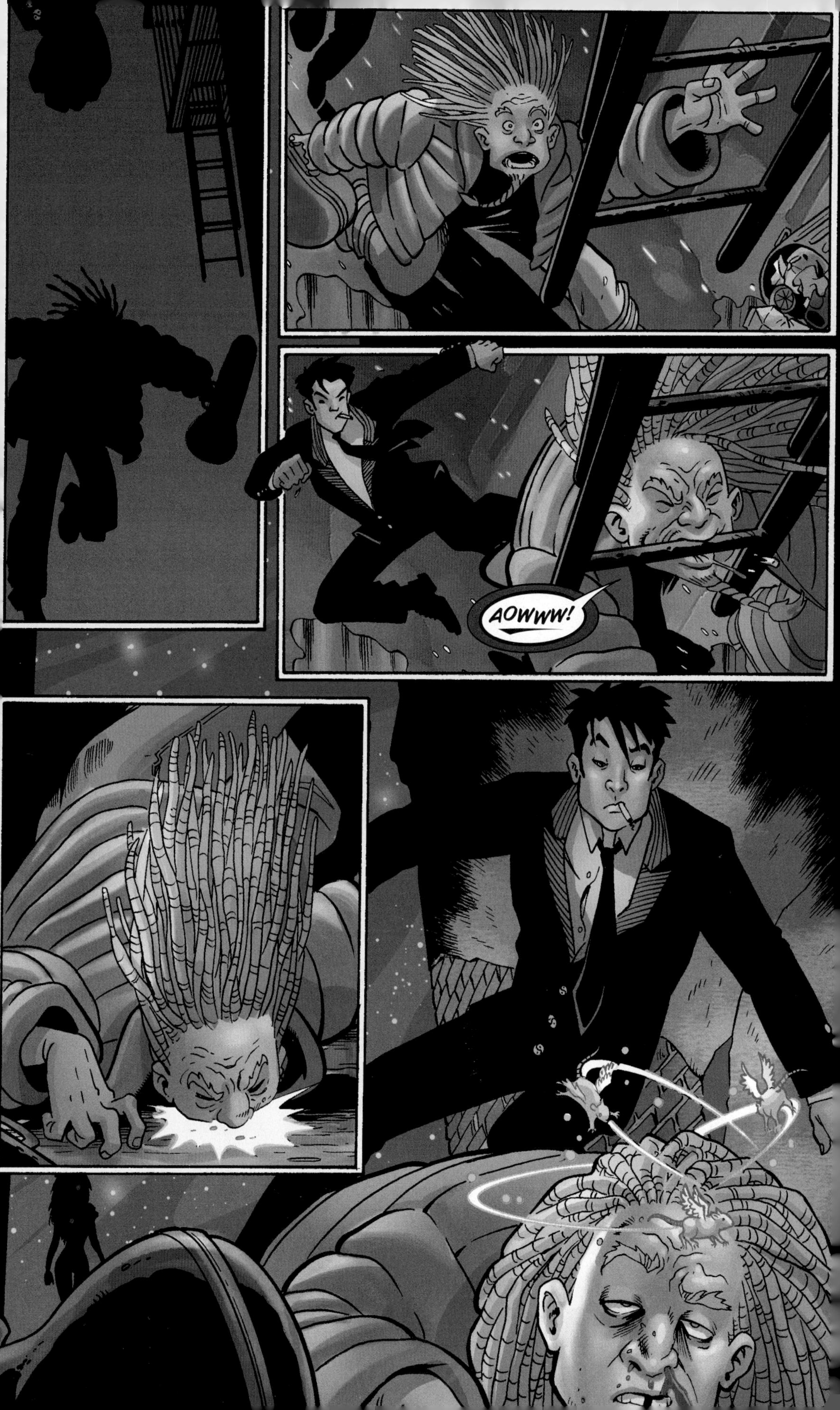
AOWWW!

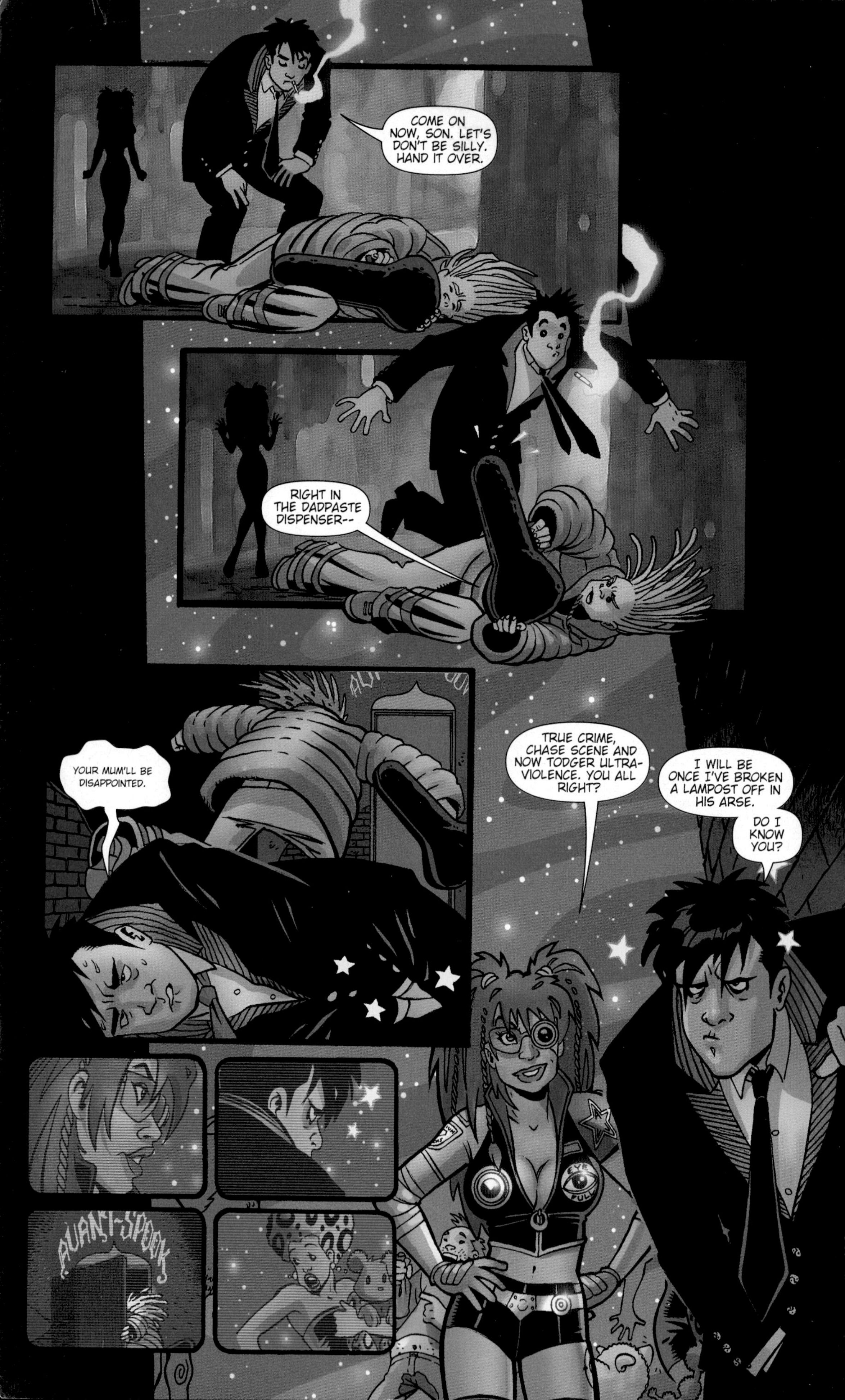
COME ON NOW, SON. LET'S DON'T BE SILLY. HAND IT OVER.
RIGHT IN THE DADPASTE DISPENSER--
YOUR MUM'LL BE DISAPPOINTED.
TRUE CRIME, CHASE SCENE AND NOW TODGER ULTRA-VIOLENCE. YOU ALL RIGHT?
I WILL BE ONCE I'VE BROKEN A LAMPOST OFF IN HIS ARSE.
DO I KNOW YOU?
AVANT-SPOOK

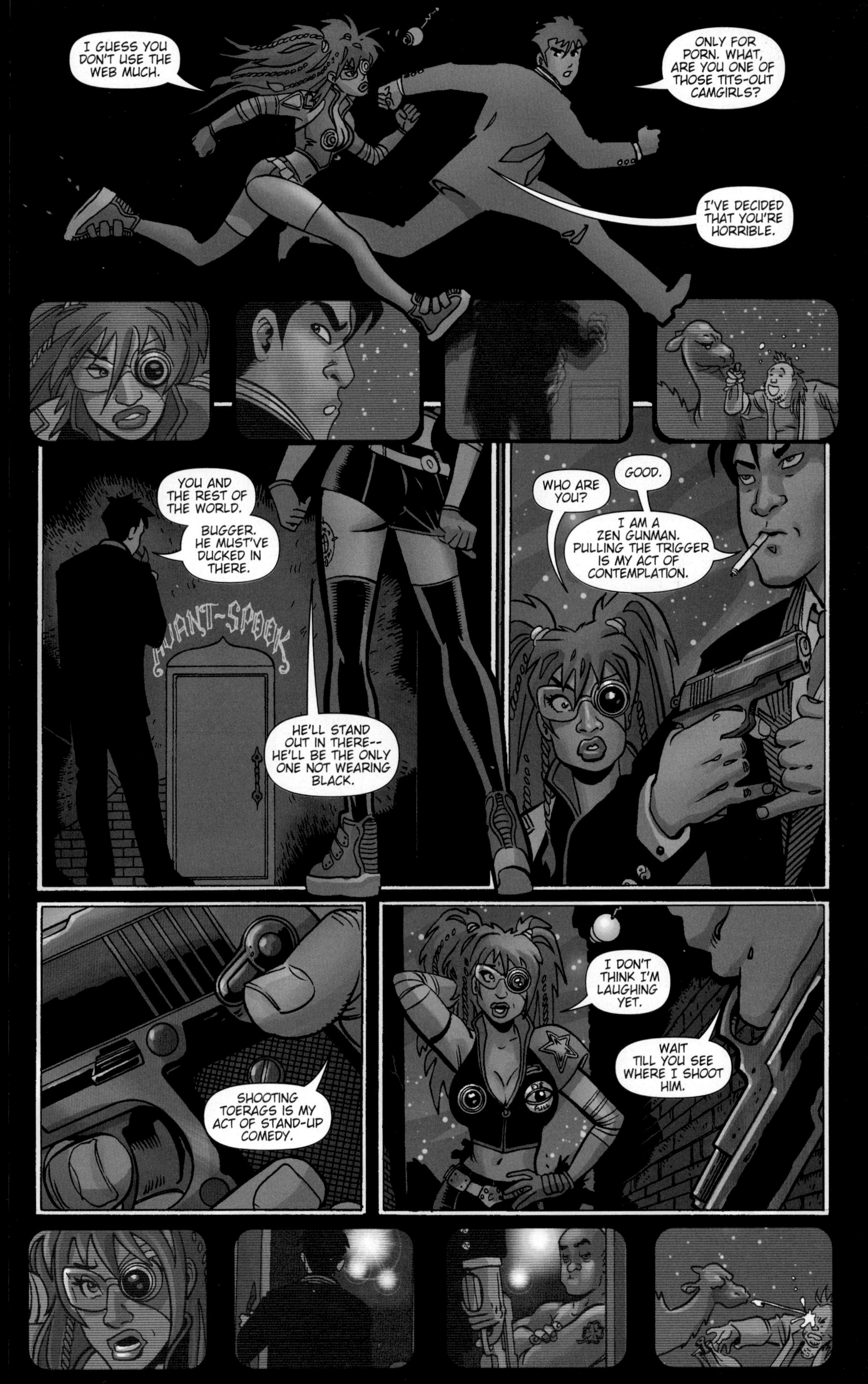
I GUESS YOU DON'T USE THE WEB MUCH.
ONLY FOR PORN. WHAT, ARE YOU ONE OF THOSE TITS-OUT CAMGIRLS?
I'VE DECIDED THAT YOU'RE HORRIBLE.
YOU AND THE REST OF THE WORLD.
BUGGER. HE MUST'VE DUCKED IN THERE.
HAUNT-SPOOK
HE'LL STAND OUT IN THERE-- HE'LL BE THE ONLY ONE NOT WEARING BLACK.
GOOD.
WHO ARE YOU?
I AM A ZEN GUNMAN. PULLING THE TRIGGER IS MY ACT OF CONTEMPLATION.
SHOOTING TOERAGS IS MY ACT OF STAND-UP COMEDY.
I DON'T THINK I'M LAUGHING YET.
WAIT TILL YOU SEE WHERE I SHOOT HIM.

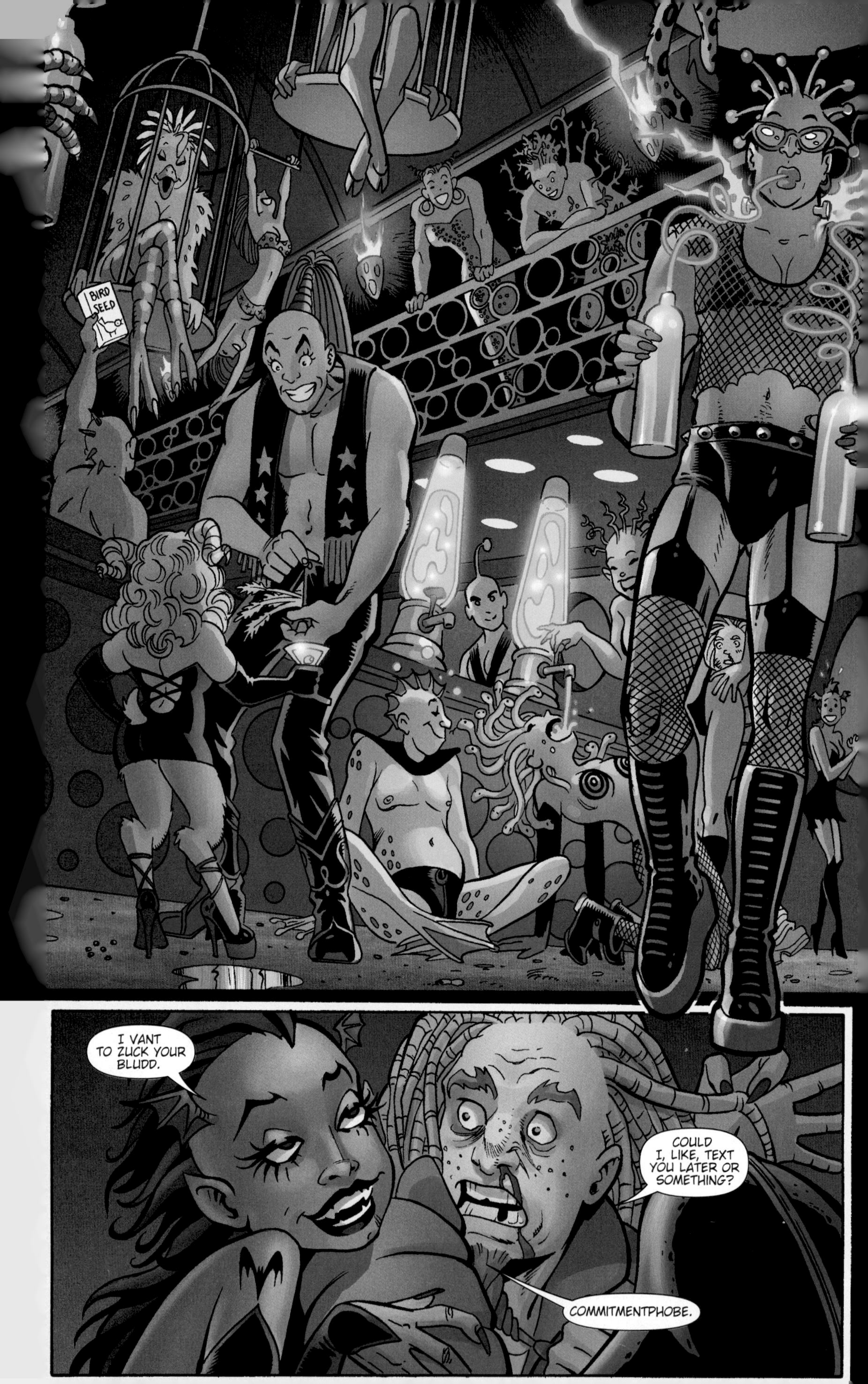
BIRD SEED
I VANT TO ZUCK YOUR BLUDD.
COULD I, LIKE, TEXT YOU LATER OR SOMETHING?
COMMITMENTPHOBE.

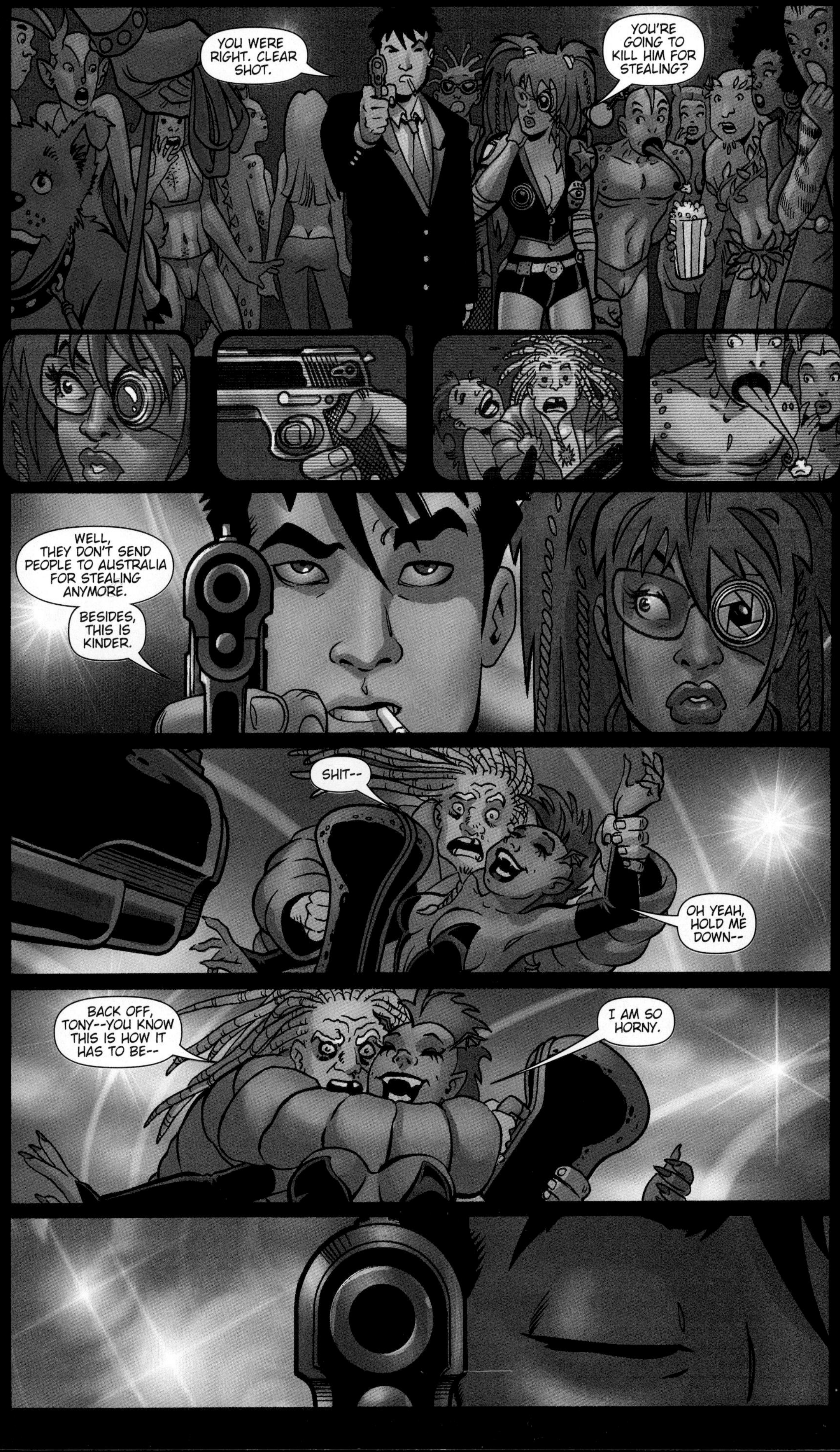
YOU WERE RIGHT. CLEAR SHOT.
YOU'RE GOING TO KILL HIM FOR STEALING?
WELL, THEY DON'T SEND PEOPLE TO AUSTRALIA FOR STEALING ANYMORE.
BESIDES, THIS IS KINDER.
SHIT--
OH YEAH, HOLD ME DOWN--
BACK OFF, TONY--YOU KNOW THIS IS HOW IT HAS TO BE--
I AM SO HORNY.

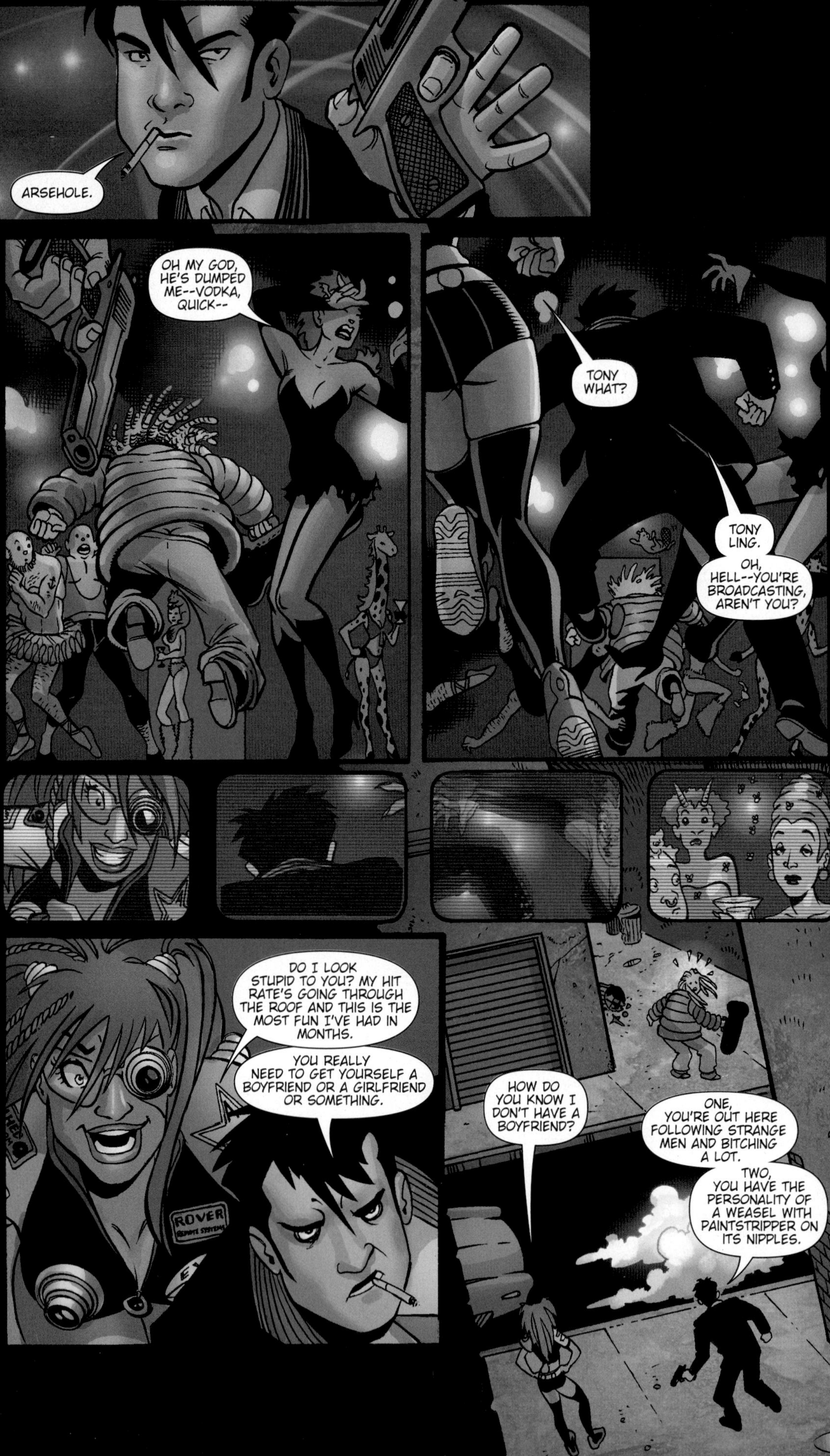
ARSEHOLE.
OH MY GOD, HE'S DUMPED ME--VODKA, QUICK--
TONY WHAT?
TONY LING.
OH, HELL--YOU'RE BROADCASTING, AREN'T YOU?
DO I LOOK STUPID TO YOU? MY HIT RATE'S GOING THROUGH THE ROOF AND THIS IS THE MOST FUN I'VE HAD IN MONTHS.
YOU REALLY NEED TO GET YOURSELF A BOYFRIEND OR A GIRLFRIEND OR SOMETHING.
ROVER
HOW DO YOU KNOW I DON'T HAVE A BOYFRIEND?
ONE, YOU'RE OUT HERE FOLLOWING STRANGE MEN AND BITCHING A LOT.
TWO, YOU HAVE THE PERSONALITY OF A WEASEL WITH PAINTSTRIPPER ON ITS NIPPLES.

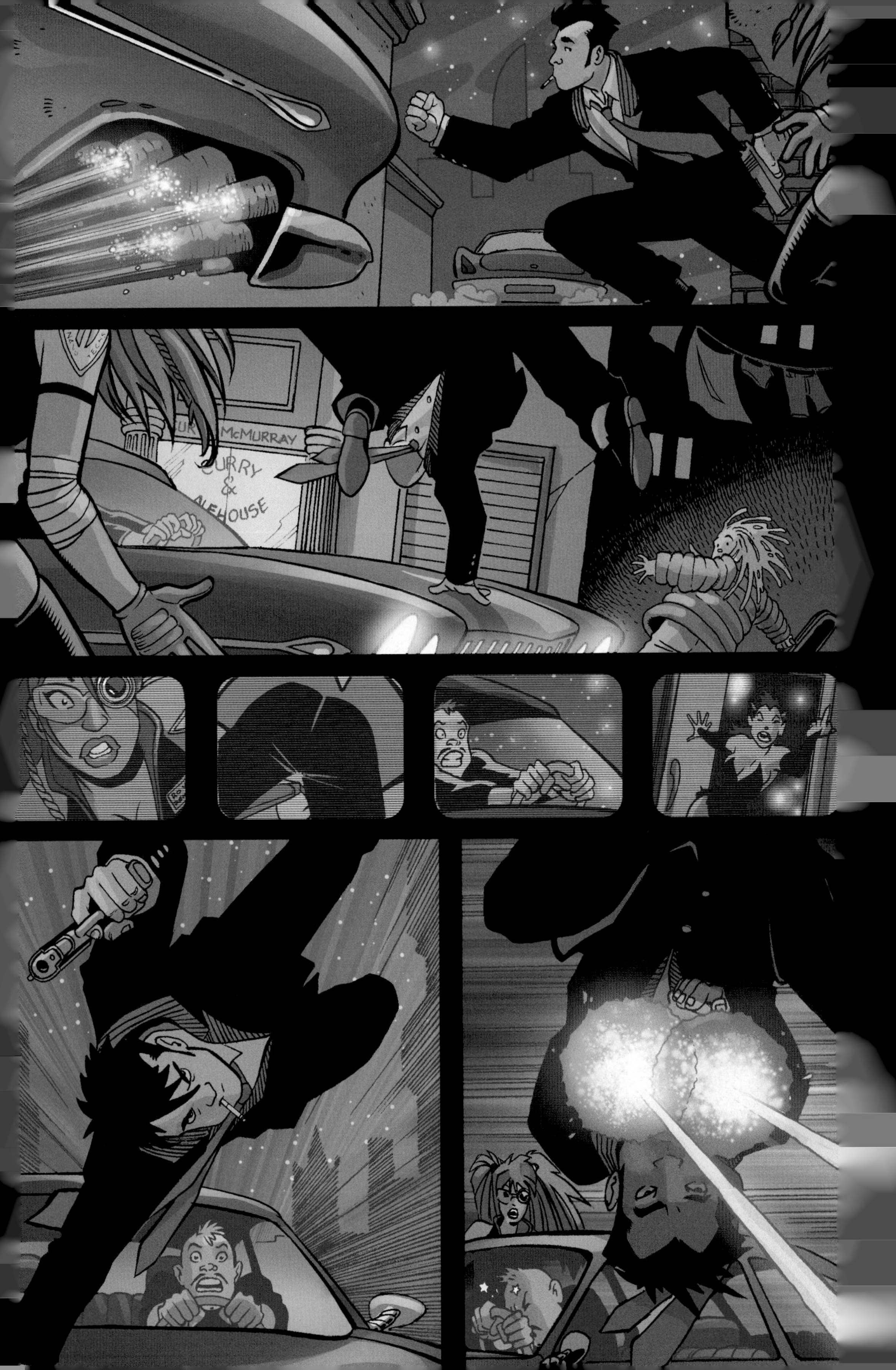
McMURRAY
CURRY
&
ALEHOUSE

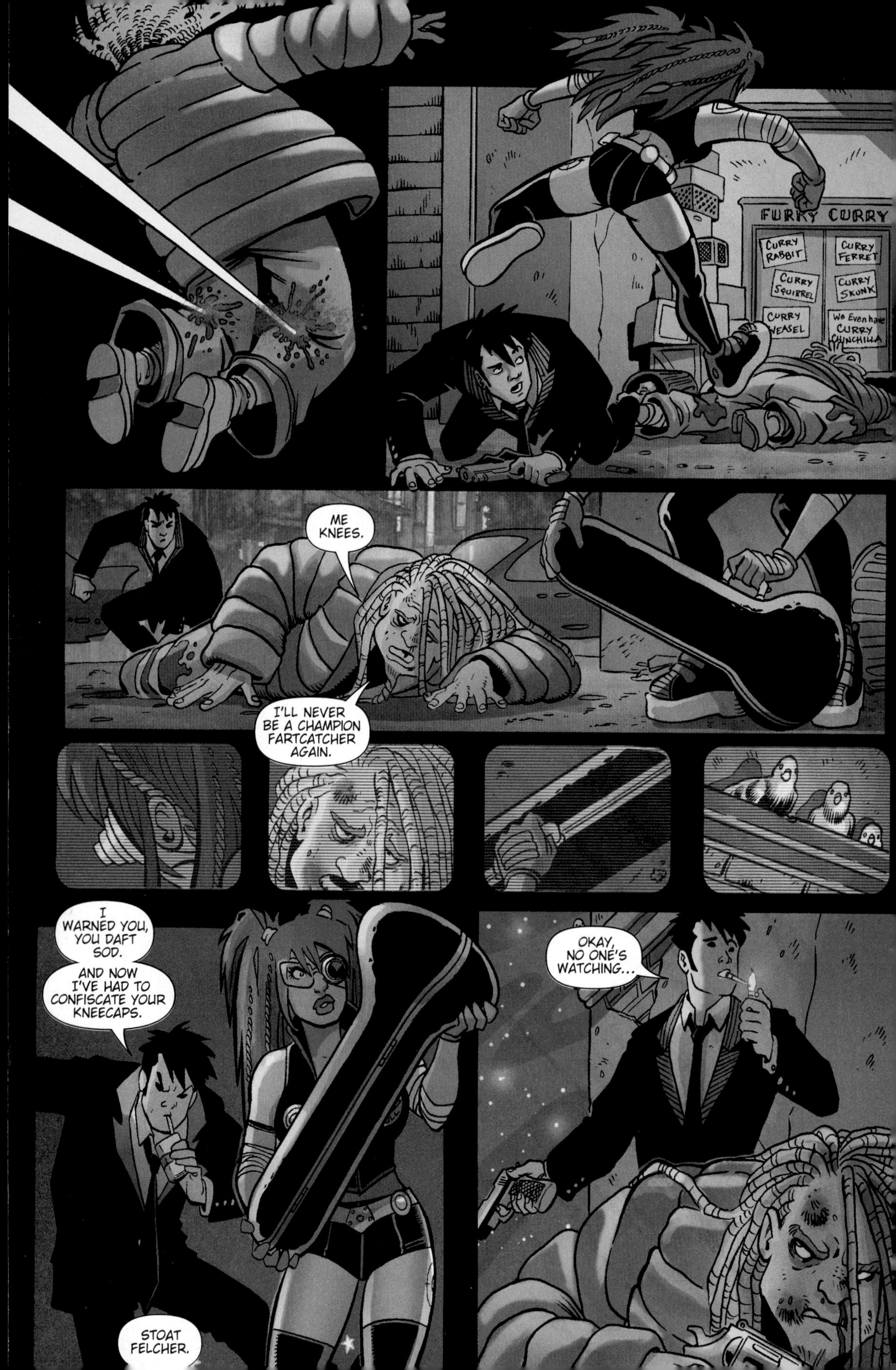

FURRY CURRY
CURRY RABBIT
CURRY FERRET
CURRY SQUIRREL
CURRY SKUNK
CURRY WEASEL
We Even have CURRY CHINCHILLA
ME KNEES.
I'LL NEVER BE A CHAMPION FARTCATCHER AGAIN.
I WARNED YOU, YOU DAFT SOD.
AND NOW I'VE HAD TO CONFISCATE YOUR KNEECAPS.
STOAT FELCHER.
OKAY, NO ONE'S WATCHING...

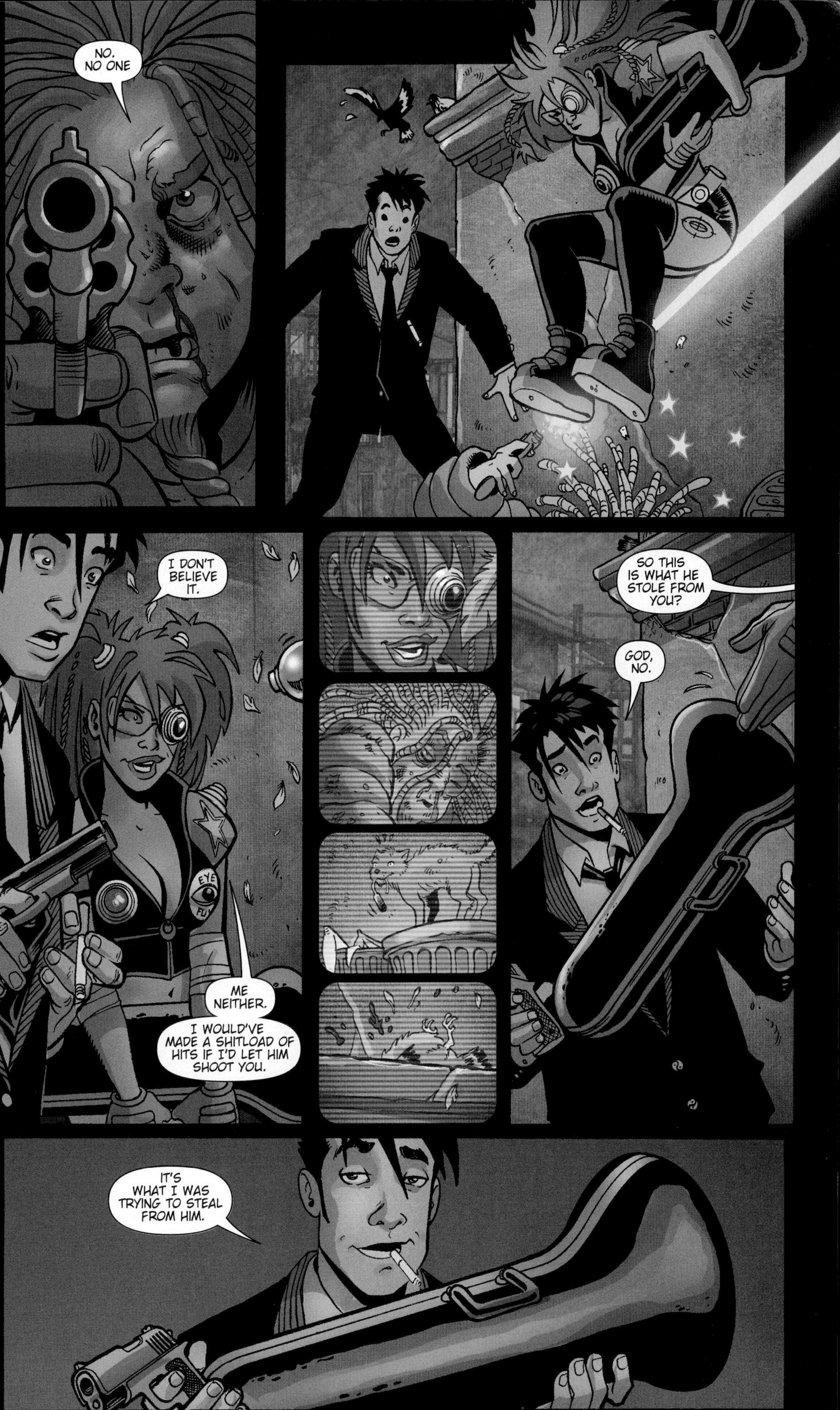

NO. NO ONE
I DON'T BELIEVE IT.
ME NEITHER.
I WOULD'VE MADE A SHITLOAD OF HITS IF I'D LET HIM SHOOT YOU.
SO THIS IS WHAT HE STOLE FROM YOU?
GOD, NO.
IT'S WHAT I WAS TRYING TO STEAL FROM HIM.

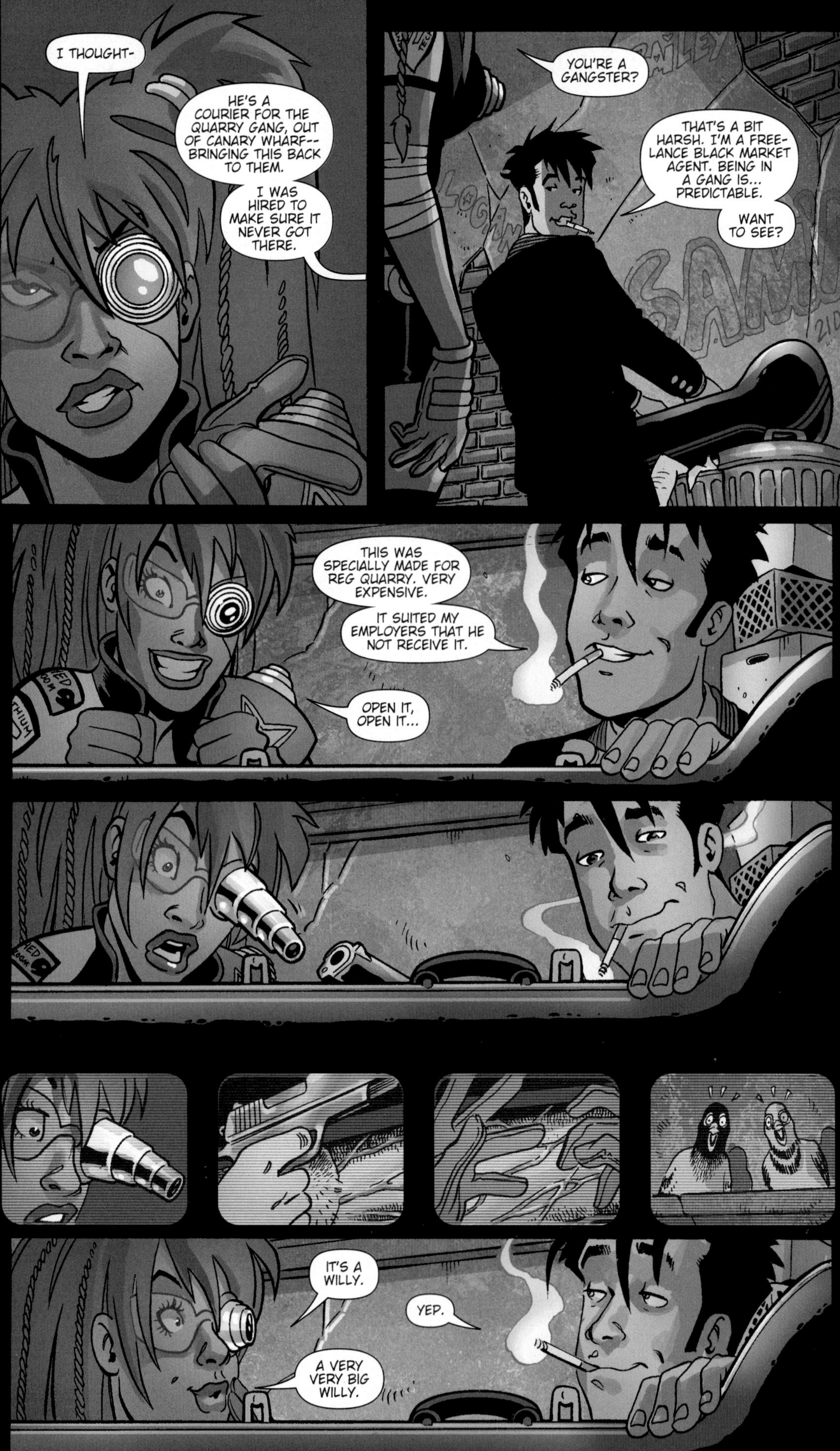
I THOUGHT-
HE'S A COURIER FOR THE QUARRY GANG, OUT OF CANARY WHARF--BRINGING THIS BACK TO THEM.
I WAS HIRED TO MAKE SURE IT NEVER GOT THERE.
YOU'RE A GANGSTER?
THAT'S A BIT HARSH. I'M A FREE-LANCE BLACK MARKET AGENT. BEING IN A GANG IS... PREDICTABLE.
WANT TO SEE?
THIS WAS SPECIALLY MADE FOR REG QUARRY. VERY EXPENSIVE.
IT SUITED MY EMPLOYERS THAT HE NOT RECEIVE IT.
OPEN IT, OPEN IT...
IT'S A WILLY.
YEP.
A VERY VERY BIG WILLY.

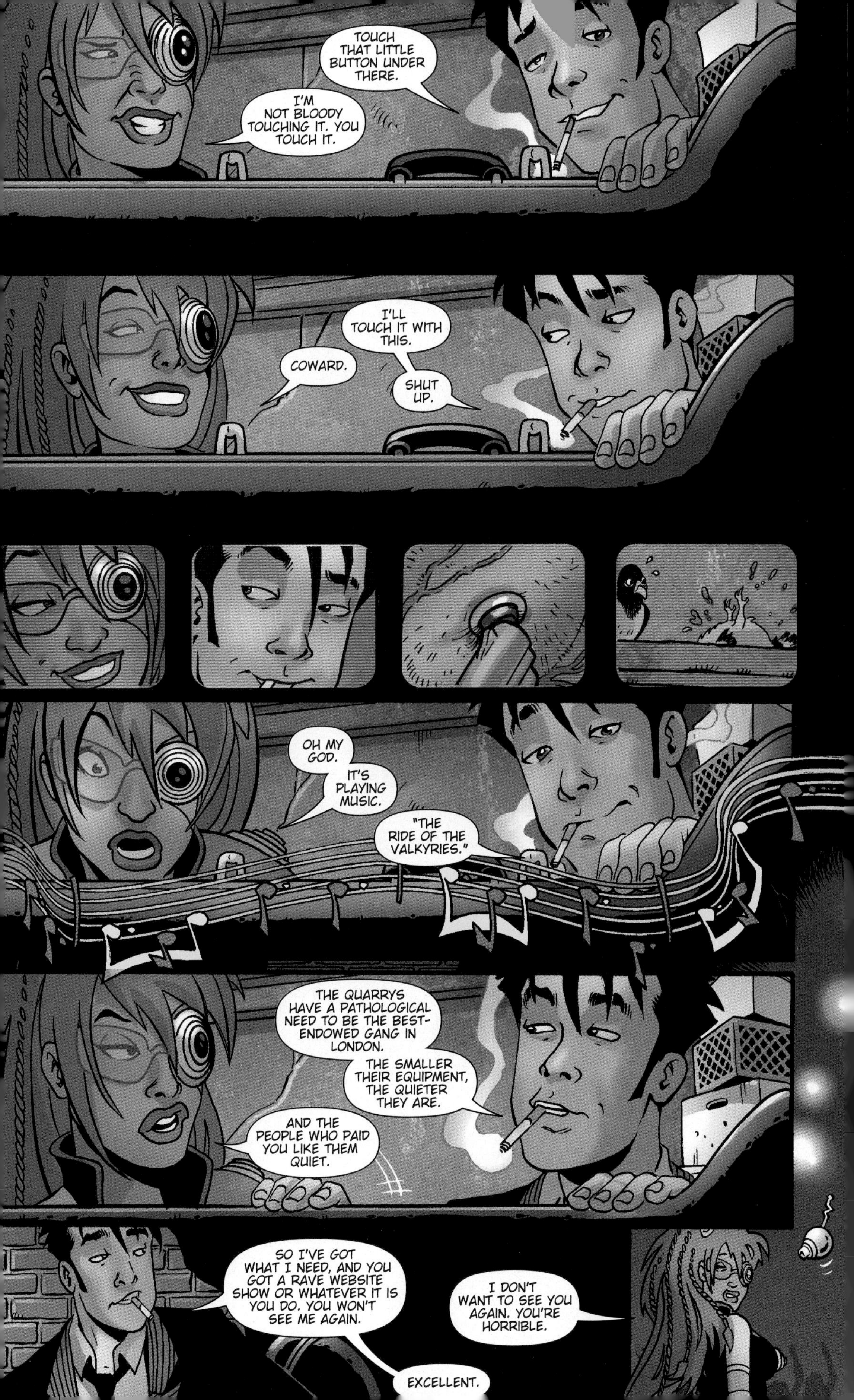
TOUCH THAT LITTLE BUTTON UNDER THERE.
I'M NOT BLOODY TOUCHING IT. YOU TOUCH IT.
I'LL TOUCH IT WITH THIS.
COWARD.
SHUT UP.
OH MY GOD.
IT'S PLAYING MUSIC.
"THE RIDE OF THE VALKYRIES."
THE QUARRYS HAVE A PATHOLOGICAL NEED TO BE THE BEST-ENDOWED GANG IN LONDON.
THE SMALLER THEIR EQUIPMENT, THE QUIETER THEY ARE.
AND THE PEOPLE WHO PAID YOU LIKE THEM QUIET.
SO I'VE GOT WHAT I NEED, AND YOU GOT A RAVE WEBSITE SHOW OR WHATEVER IT IS YOU DO. YOU WON'T SEE ME AGAIN.
I DON'T WANT TO SEE YOU AGAIN. YOU'RE HORRIBLE.
EXCELLENT.

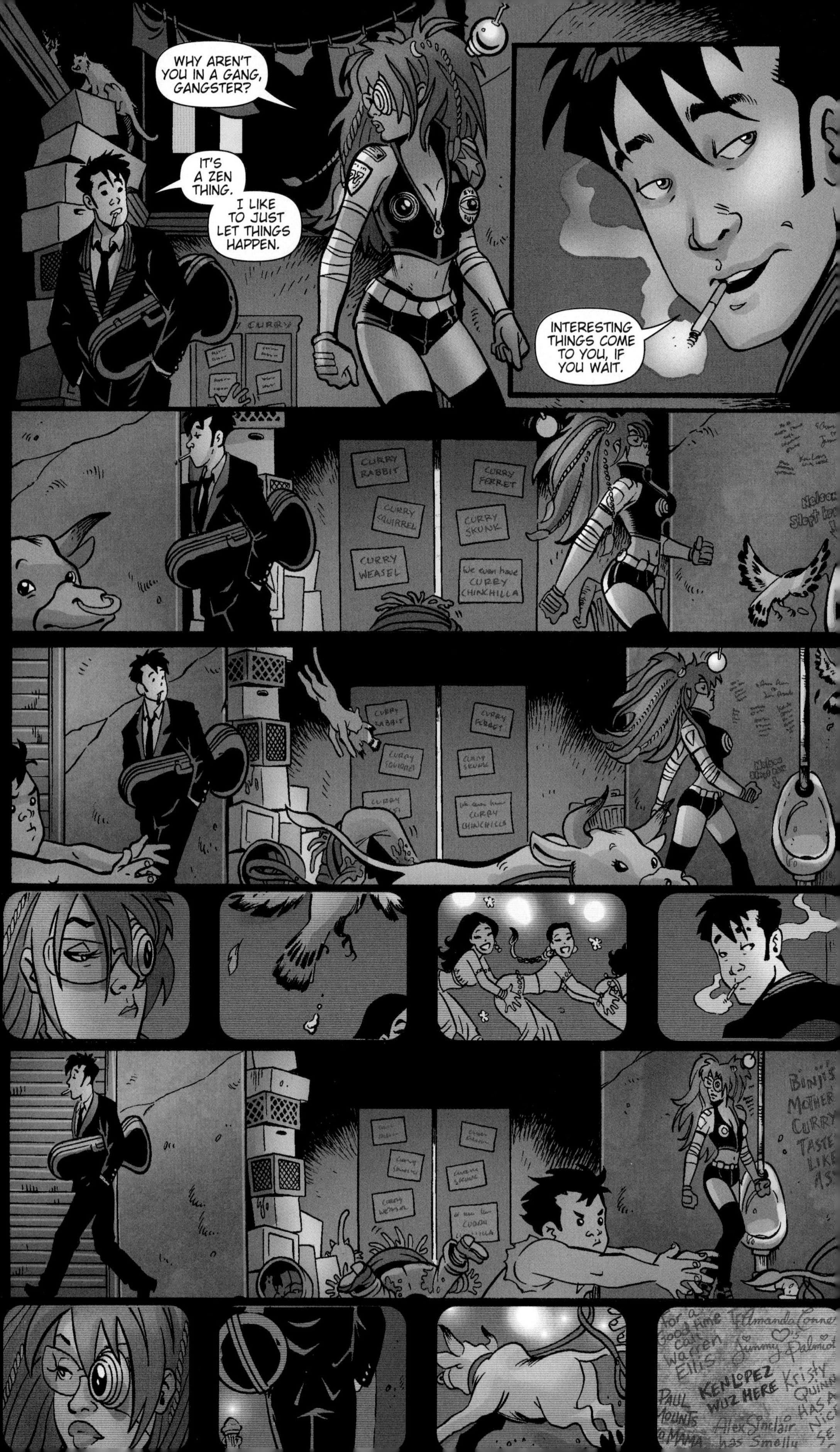

WHY AREN'T YOU IN A GANG, GANGSTER?
IT'S A ZEN THING.
I LIKE TO JUST LET THINGS HAPPEN.
INTERESTING THINGS COME TO YOU, IF YOU WAIT.
CURRY RABBIT
CURRY SQUIRREL
CURRY WEASEL
CURRY FERRET
CURRY SKUNK
We even have CURRY CHINCHILLA
For a good time call Warren Ellis
KEN LOPEZ WUZ HERE
Kristy Quinn
Alex Sinclair has Smelly

-- giant robots wrestling & shagging on
ames as zenboy walks past, reading

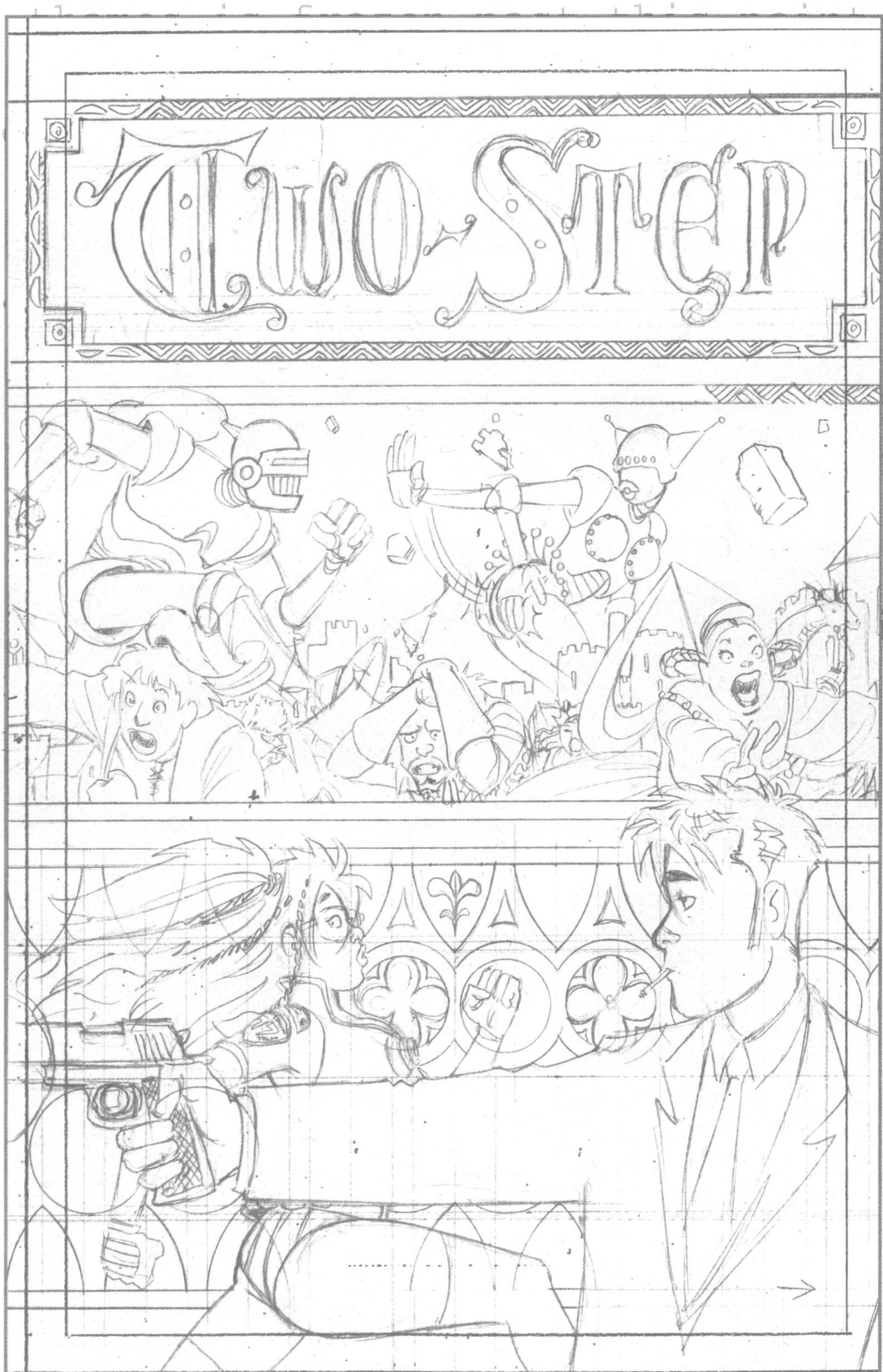
Two Step

COVER TWO

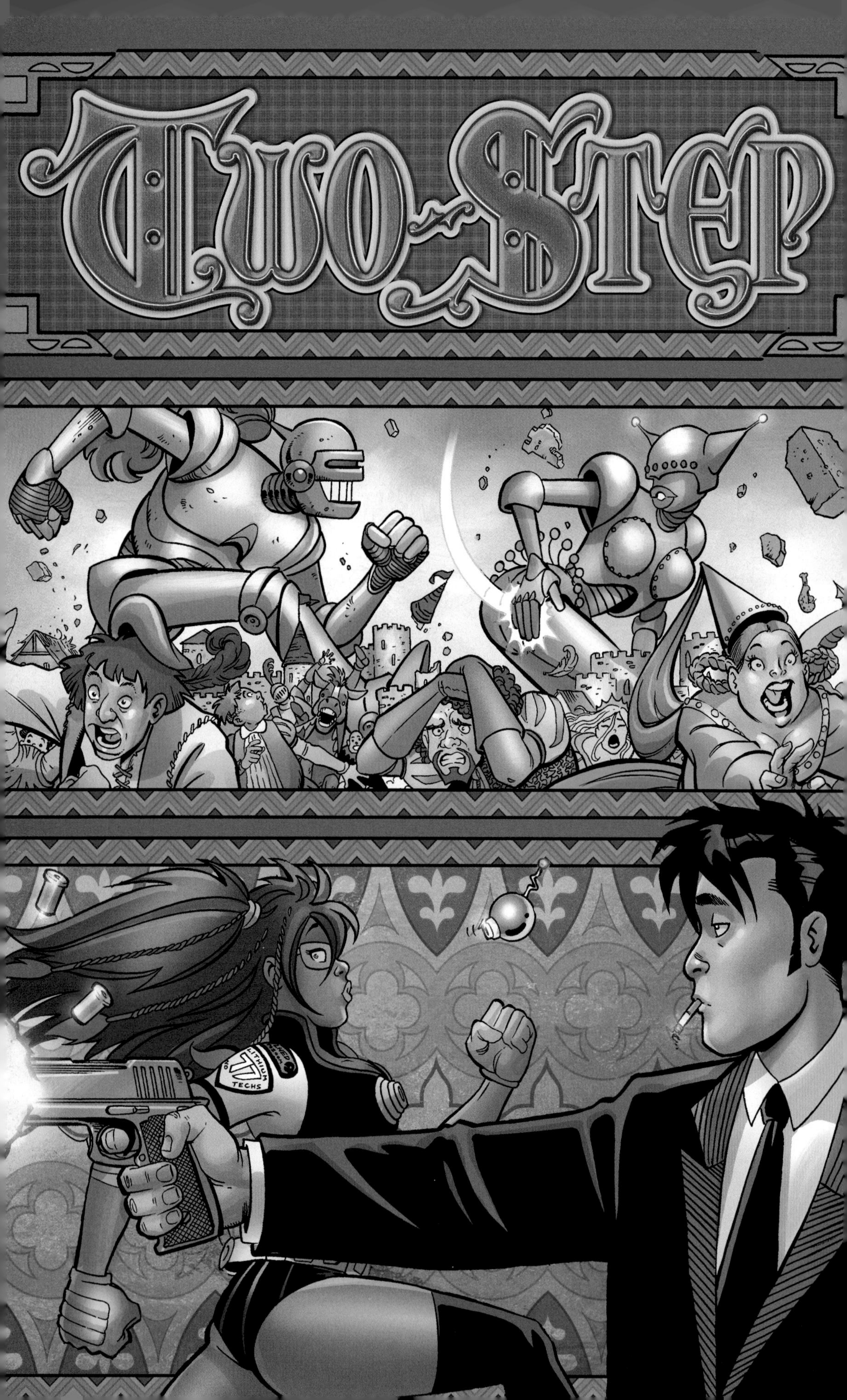
Two-Step

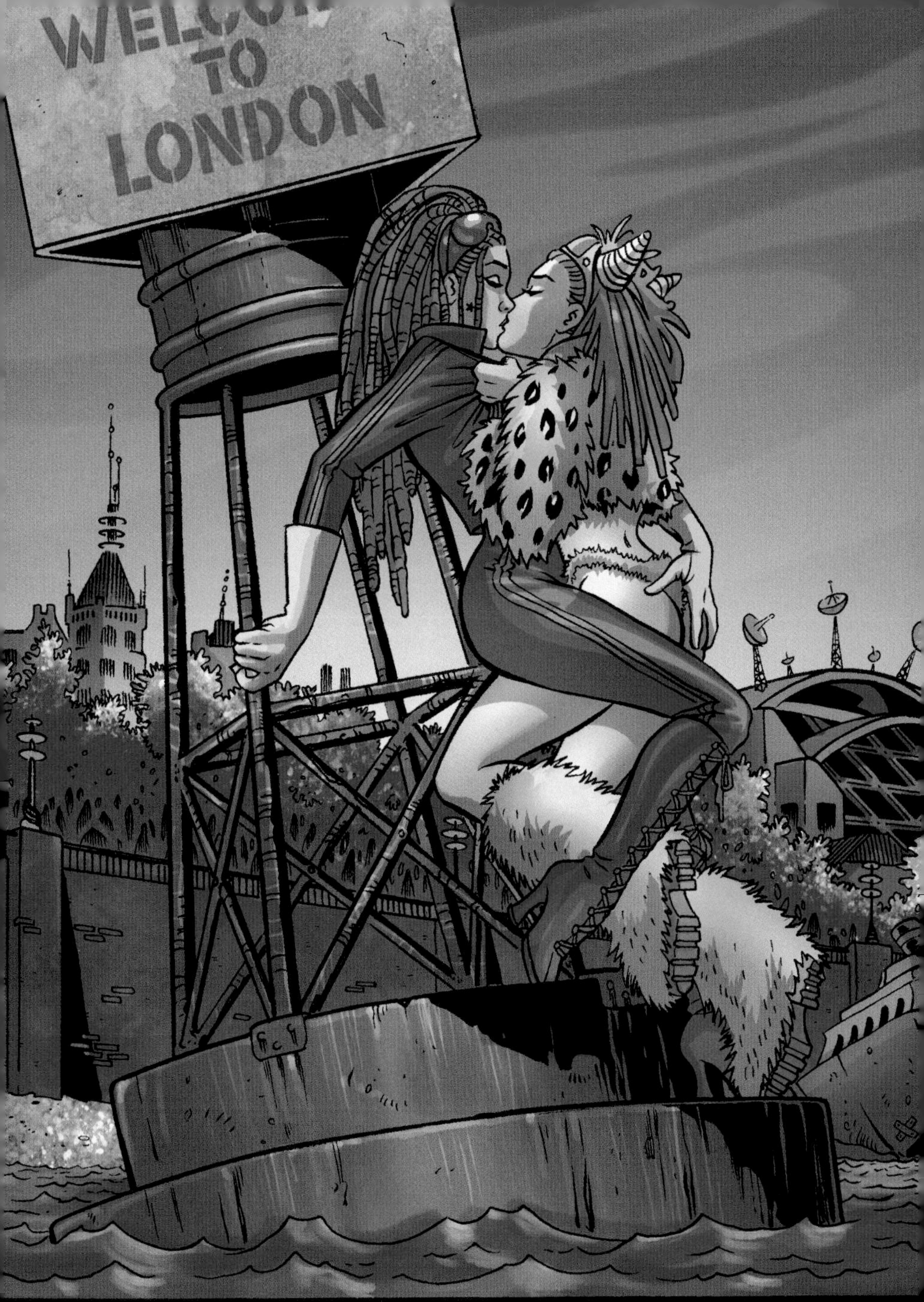
WELCO
TO
LONDON

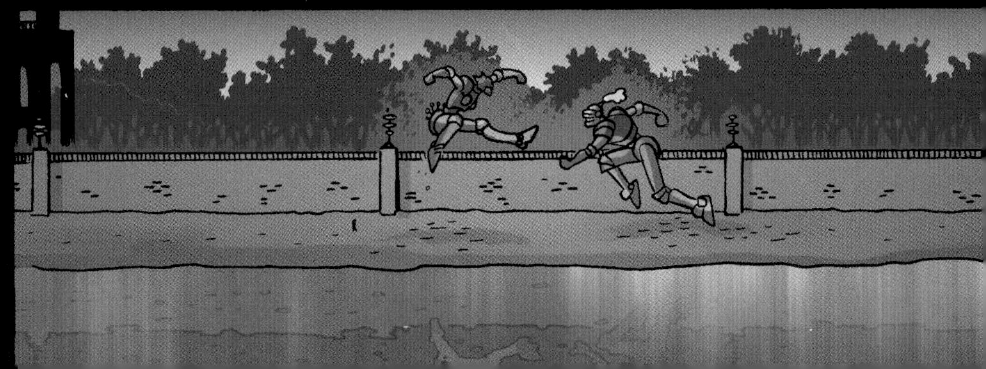

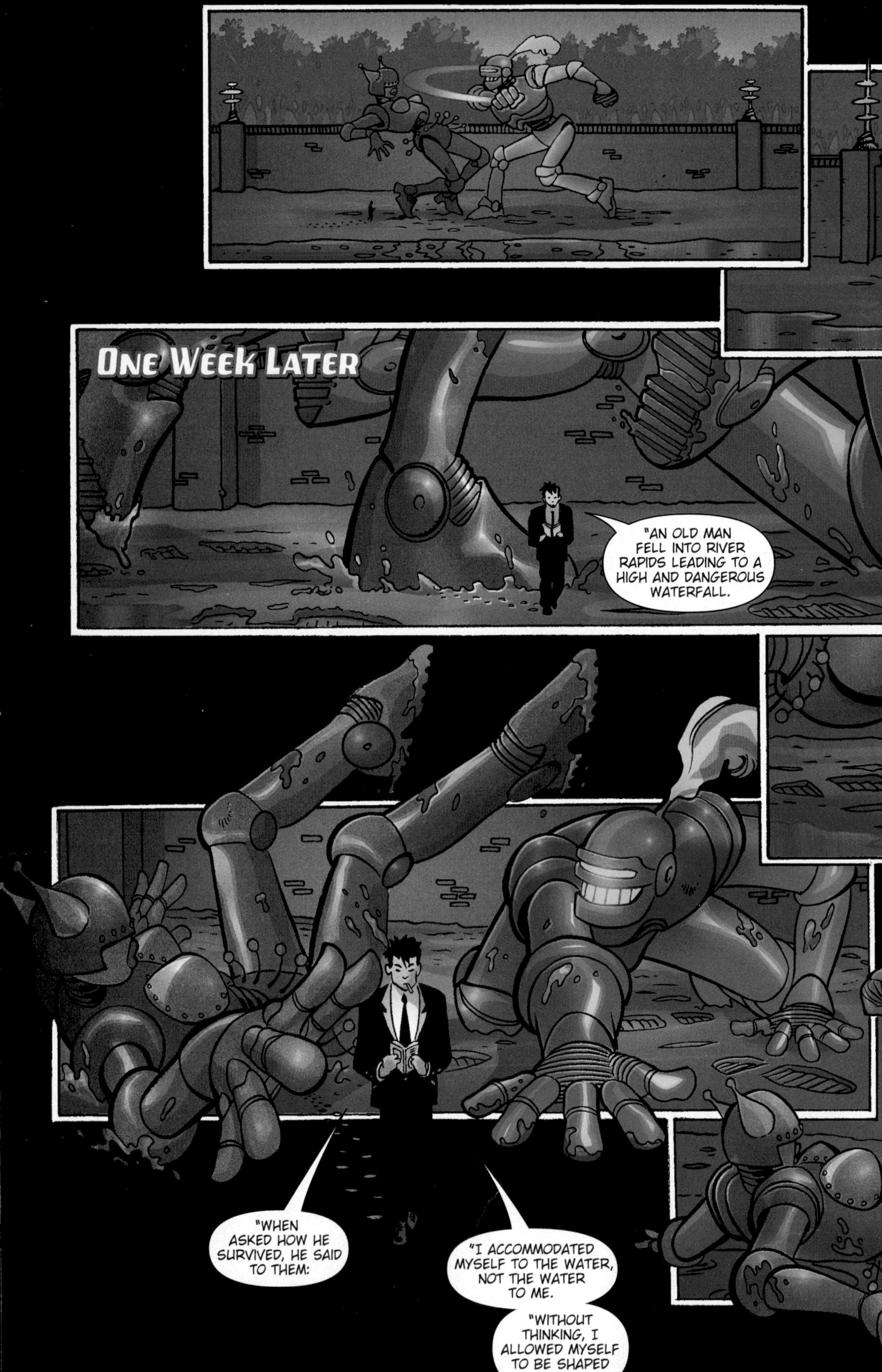
ONE WEEK LATER
"AN OLD MAN FELL INTO RIVER RAPIDS LEADING TO A HIGH AND DANGEROUS WATERFALL.
"WHEN ASKED HOW HE SURVIVED, HE SAID TO THEM:
"I ACCOMMODATED MYSELF TO THE WATER, NOT THE WATER TO ME.
"WITHOUT THINKING, I ALLOWED MYSELF TO BE SHAPED BY IT.

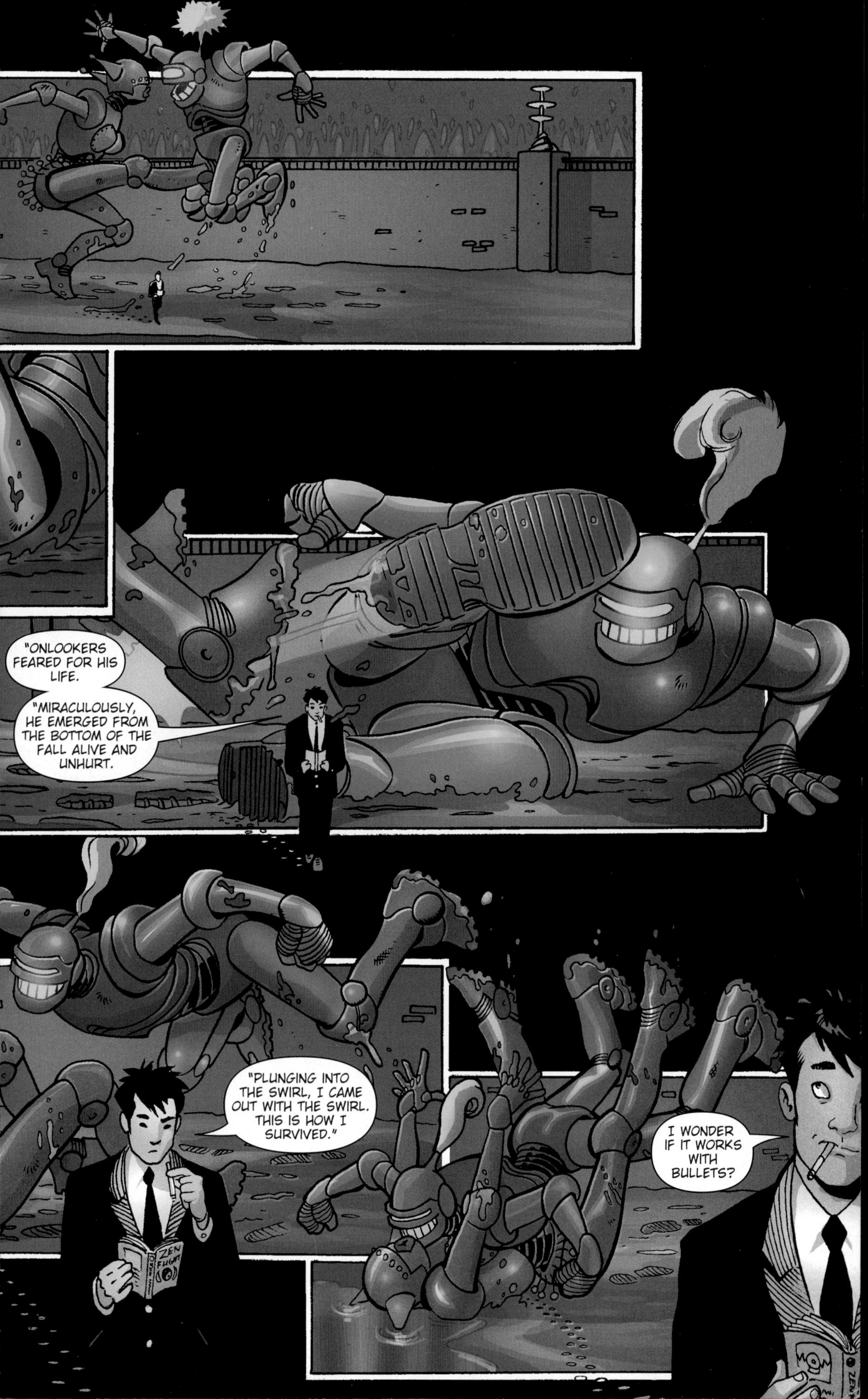
"ONLOOKERS FEARED FOR HIS LIFE.
"MIRACULOUSLY, HE EMERGED FROM THE BOTTOM OF THE FALL ALIVE AND UNHURT.
"PLUNGING INTO THE SWIRL, I CAME OUT WITH THE SWIRL. THIS IS HOW I SURVIVED."
I WONDER IF IT WORKS WITH BULLETS?
ZEN

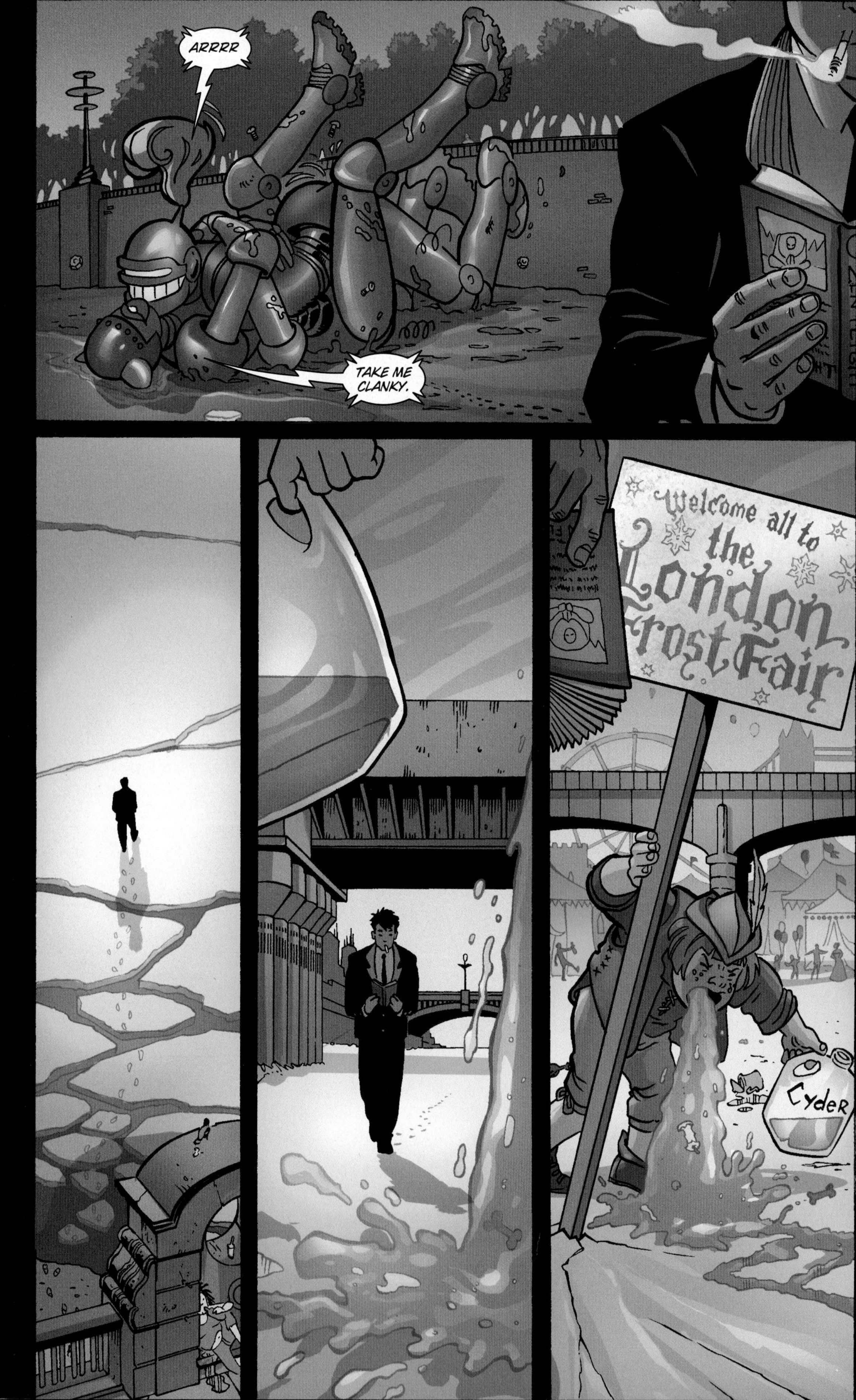
ARRRR
TAKE ME CLANKY.
Welcome all to the London Frost Fair
Cyder

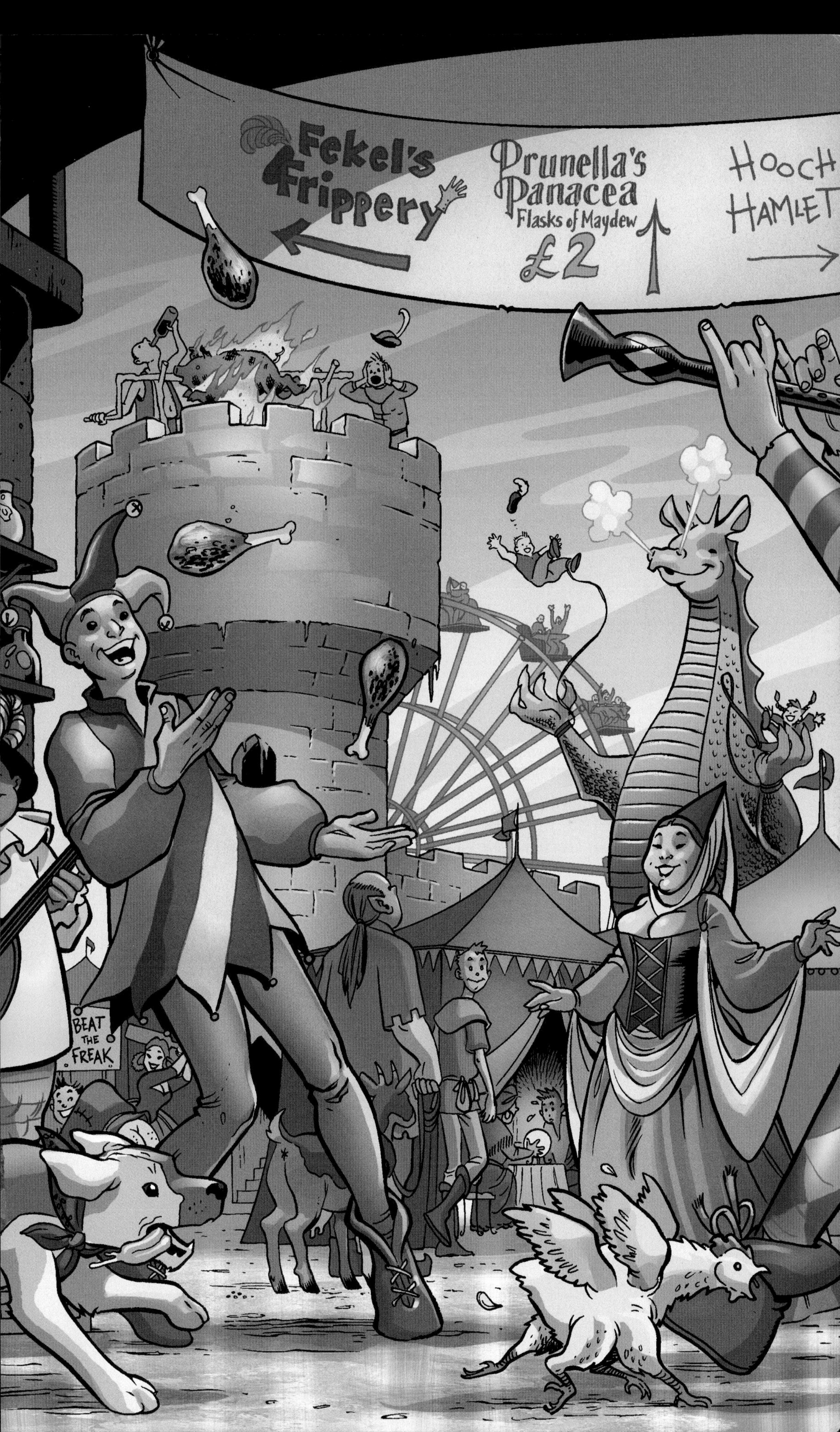
Fekel's Frippery
Prunella's Panacea
Flasks of Maydew
£2
Hooch Hamlet
BEAT THE FREAK

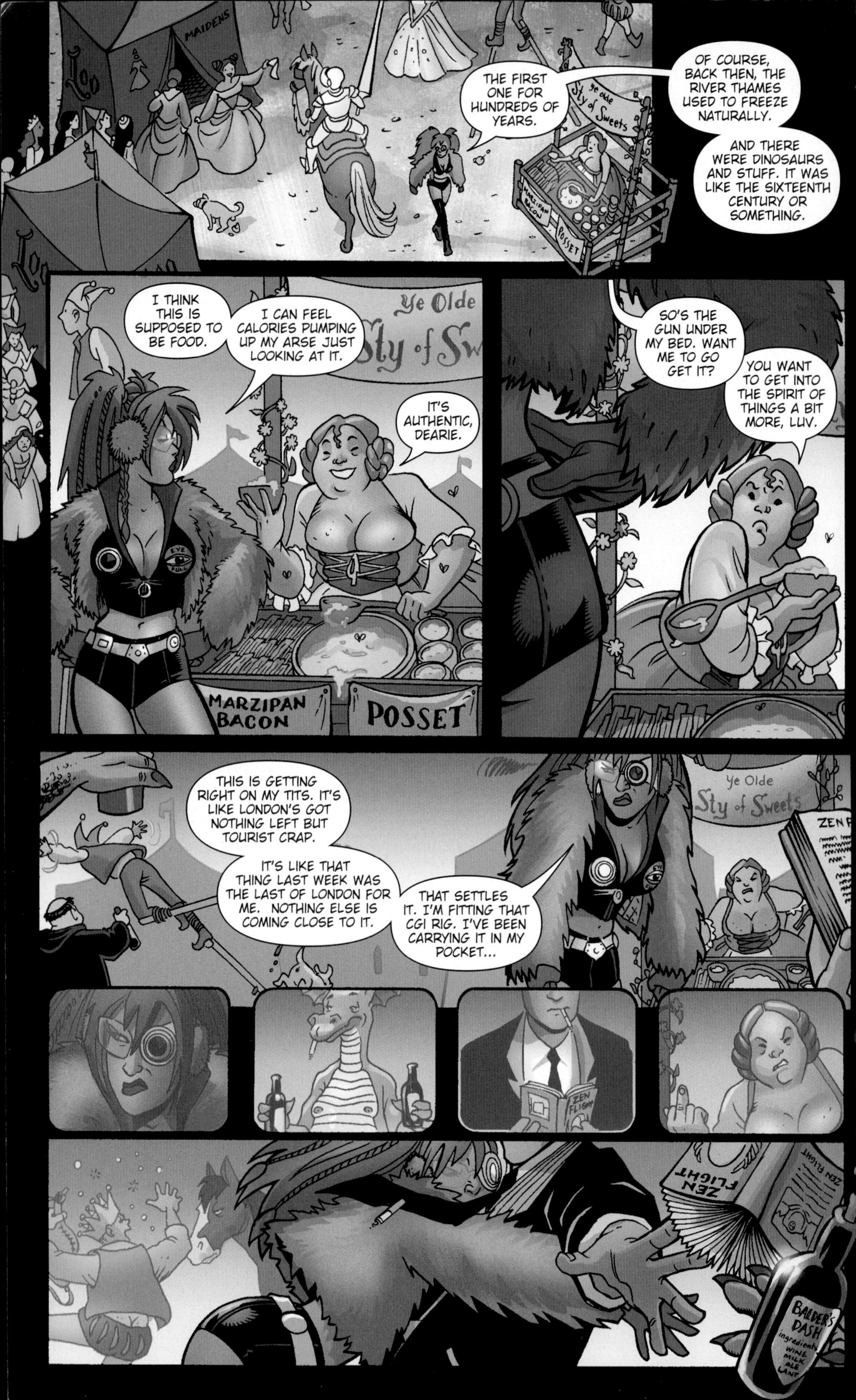
MAIDENS
Loo
Ye Olde Sty of Sweets
THE FIRST ONE FOR HUNDREDS OF YEARS.
OF COURSE, BACK THEN, THE RIVER THAMES USED TO FREEZE NATURALLY.
AND THERE WERE DINOSAURS AND STUFF. IT WAS LIKE THE SIXTEENTH CENTURY OR SOMETHING.
I THINK THIS IS SUPPOSED TO BE FOOD.
I CAN FEEL CALORIES PUMPING UP MY ARSE JUST LOOKING AT IT.
Ye Olde Sty of Sw
IT'S AUTHENTIC, DEARIE.
EYE FULL
MARZIPAN BACON
POSSET
SO'S THE GUN UNDER MY BED. WANT ME TO GO GET IT?
YOU WANT TO GET INTO THE SPIRIT OF THINGS A BIT MORE, LUV.
THIS IS GETTING RIGHT ON MY TITS. IT'S LIKE LONDON'S GOT NOTHING LEFT BUT TOURIST CRAP.
IT'S LIKE THAT THING LAST WEEK WAS THE LAST OF LONDON FOR ME. NOTHING ELSE IS COMING CLOSE TO IT.
THAT SETTLES IT. I'M FITTING THAT CGI RIG. I'VE BEEN CARRYING IT IN MY POCKET...
Ye Olde Sty of Sweets
ZEN FLIGHT
ZEN FLIGHT
BALDER'S DASH
ingredients
WINE
MILK
ALE
LANT

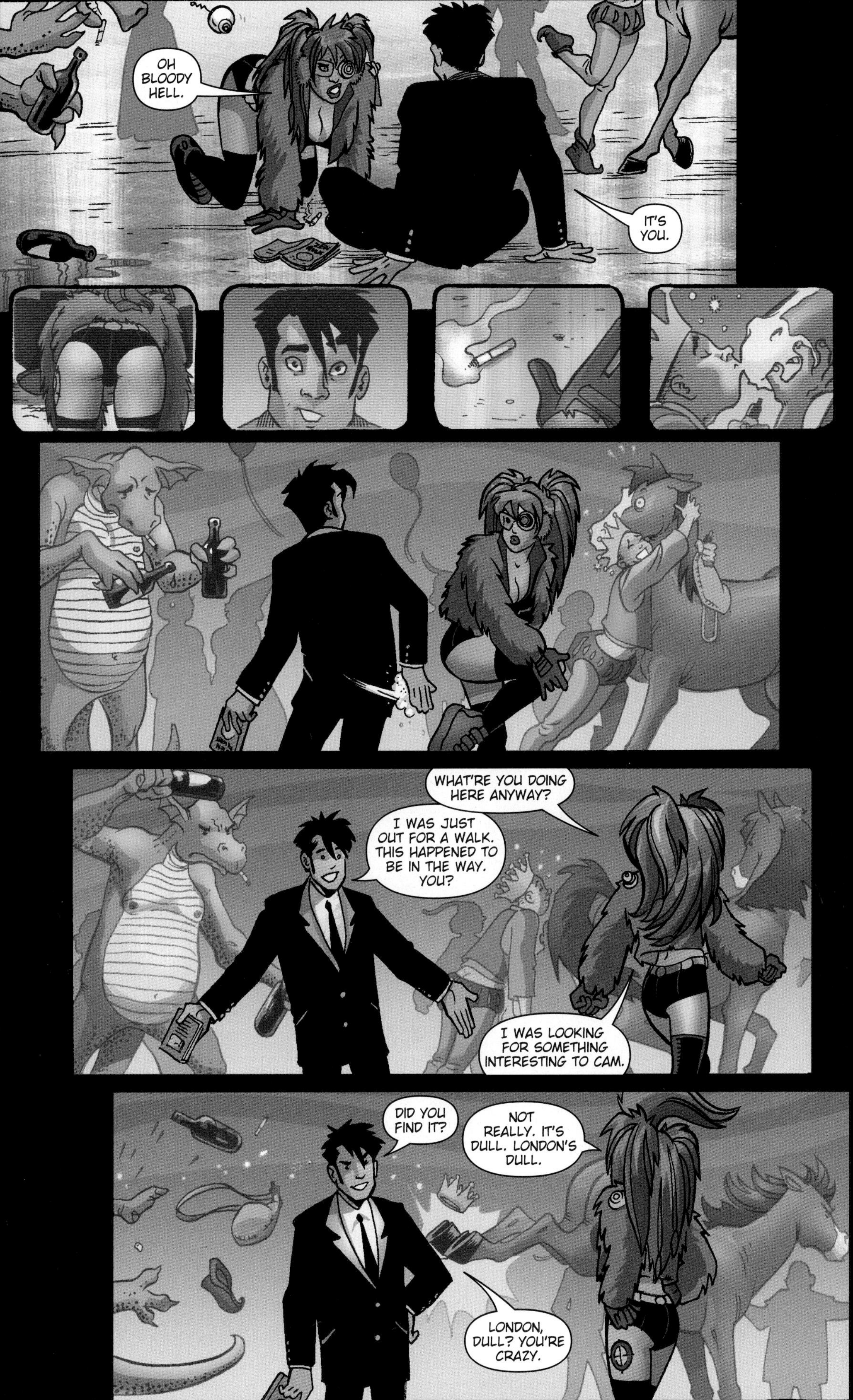

OH BLOODY HELL.
IT'S YOU.
WHAT'RE YOU DOING HERE ANYWAY?
I WAS JUST OUT FOR A WALK. THIS HAPPENED TO BE IN THE WAY. YOU?
I WAS LOOKING FOR SOMETHING INTERESTING TO CAM.
DID YOU FIND IT?
NOT REALLY. IT'S DULL. LONDON'S DULL.
LONDON, DULL? YOU'RE CRAZY.

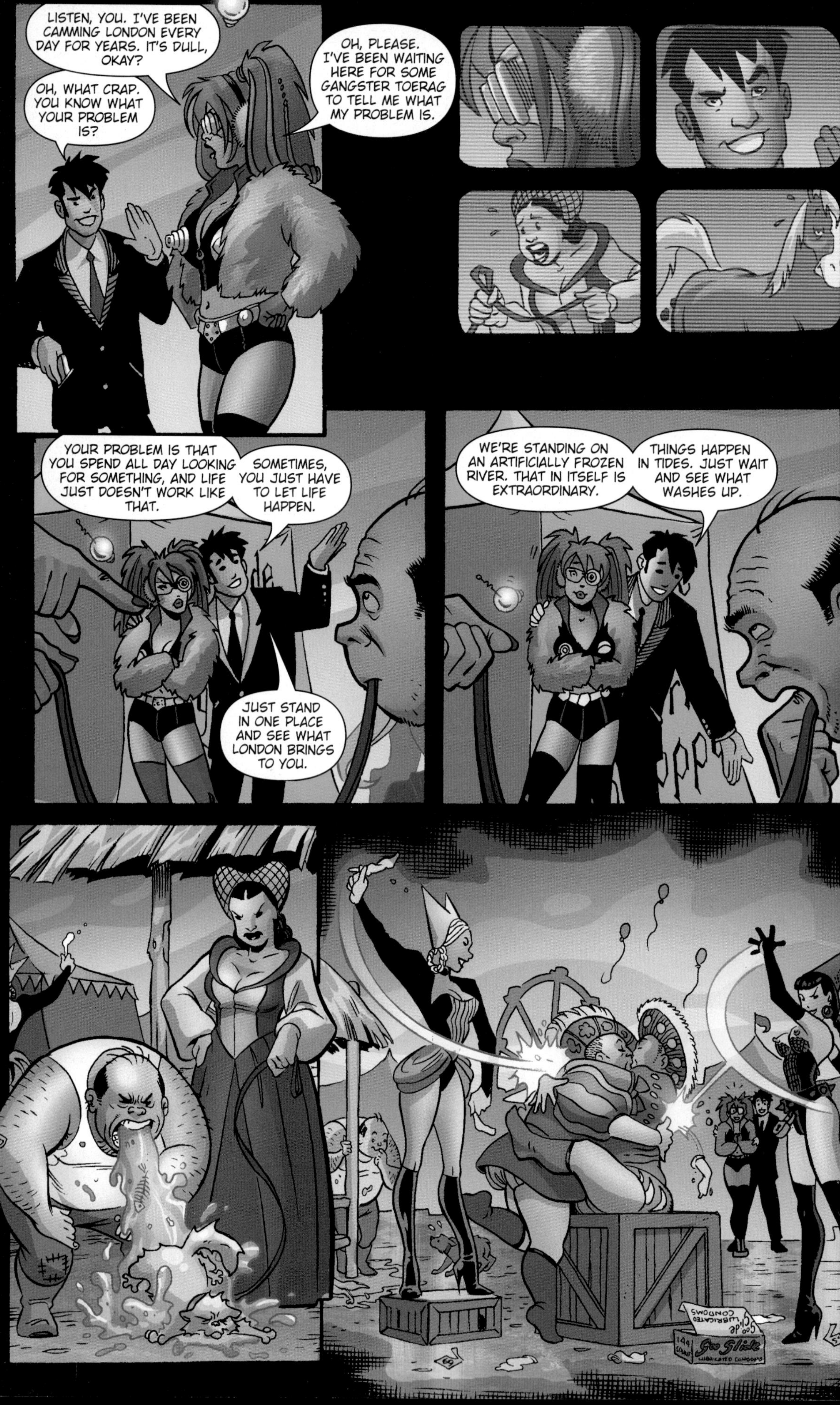
LISTEN, YOU. I'VE BEEN CAMMING LONDON EVERY DAY FOR YEARS. IT'S DULL, OKAY?
OH, WHAT CRAP. YOU KNOW WHAT YOUR PROBLEM IS?
OH, PLEASE. I'VE BEEN WAITING HERE FOR SOME GANGSTER TOERAG TO TELL ME WHAT MY PROBLEM IS.
YOUR PROBLEM IS THAT YOU SPEND ALL DAY LOOKING FOR SOMETHING, AND LIFE JUST DOESN'T WORK LIKE THAT.
SOMETIMES, YOU JUST HAVE TO LET LIFE HAPPEN.
JUST STAND IN ONE PLACE AND SEE WHAT LONDON BRINGS TO YOU.
WE'RE STANDING ON AN ARTIFICIALLY FROZEN RIVER. THAT IN ITSELF IS EXTRAORDINARY.
THINGS HAPPEN IN TIDES. JUST WAIT AND SEE WHAT WASHES UP.
Goo Glide LUBRICATED CONDOMS
144 COUNT
Goo Slick LUBRICATED CONDOMS

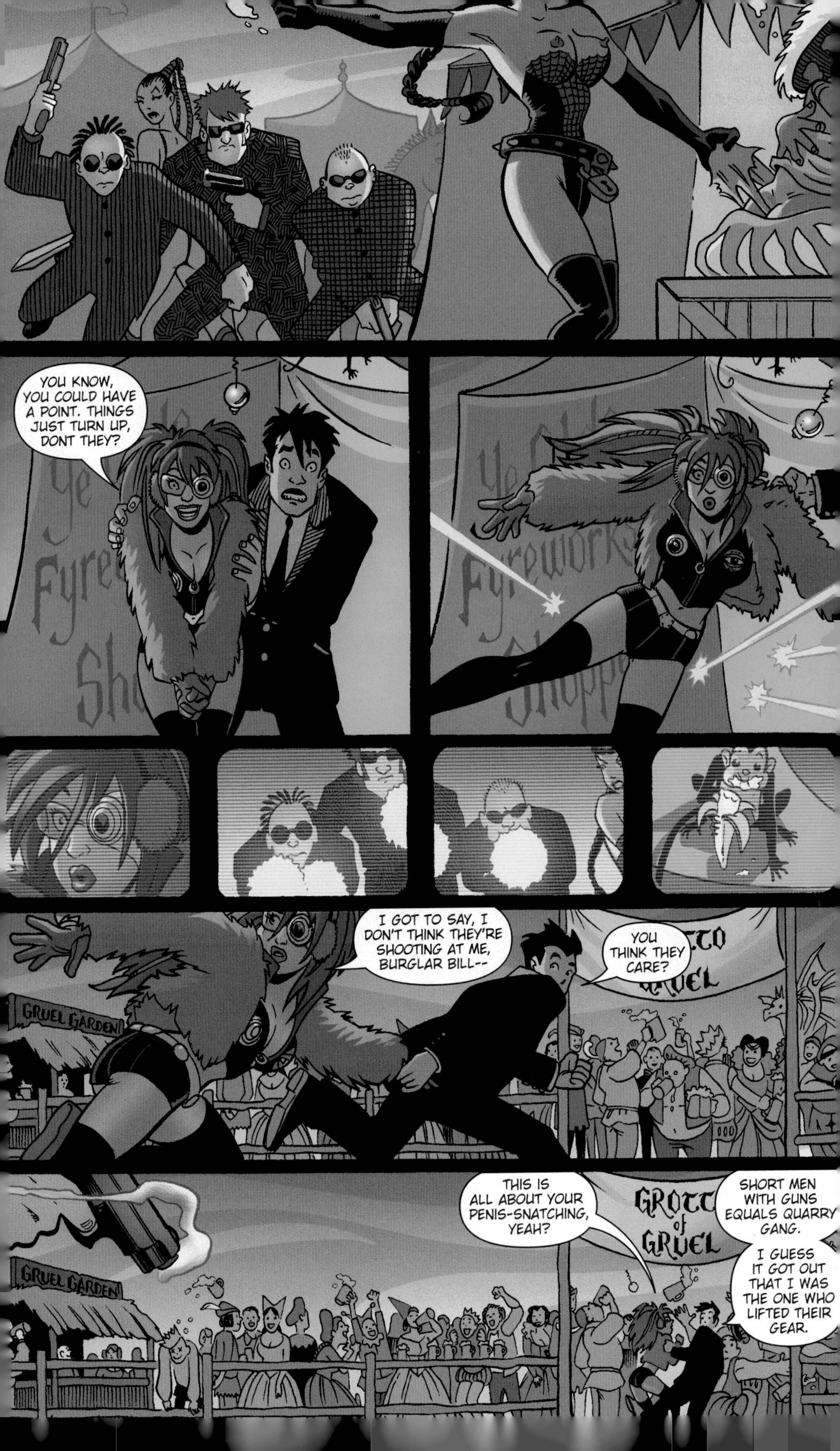
YOU KNOW, YOU COULD HAVE A POINT. THINGS JUST TURN UP, DONT THEY?
I GOT TO SAY, I DON'T THINK THEY'RE SHOOTING AT ME, BURGLAR BILL--
YOU THINK THEY CARE?
GRUEL GARDEN
GRUEL GARDEN
THIS IS ALL ABOUT YOUR PENIS-SNATCHING, YEAH?
SHORT MEN WITH GUNS EQUALS QUARRY GANG.
I GUESS IT GOT OUT THAT I WAS THE ONE WHO LIFTED THEIR GEAR.

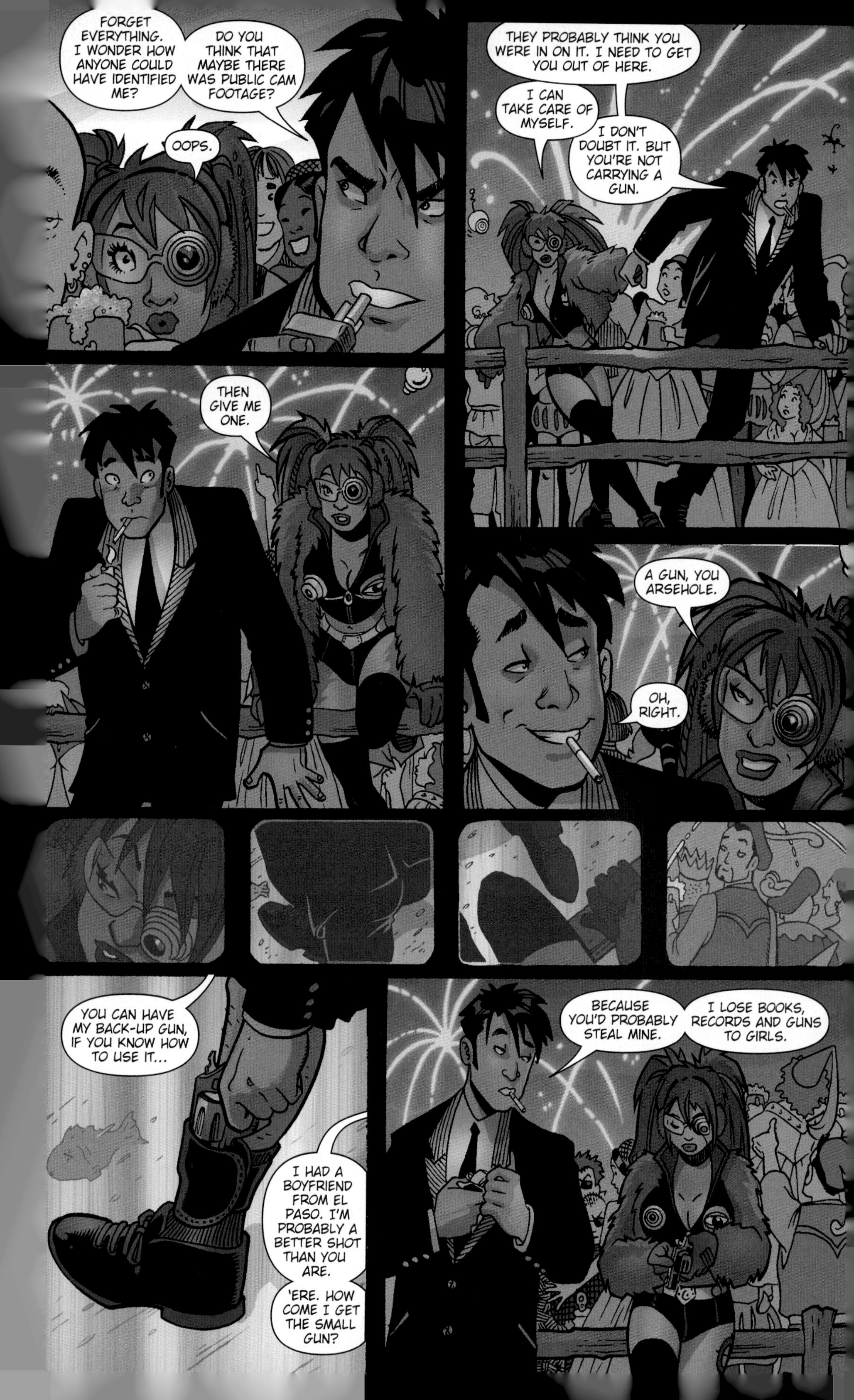

FORGET EVERYTHING. I WONDER HOW ANYONE COULD HAVE IDENTIFIED ME?
DO YOU THINK THAT MAYBE THERE WAS PUBLIC CAM FOOTAGE?
OOPS.
THEY PROBABLY THINK YOU WERE IN ON IT. I NEED TO GET YOU OUT OF HERE.
I CAN TAKE CARE OF MYSELF.
I DON'T DOUBT IT. BUT YOU'RE NOT CARRYING A GUN.
THEN GIVE ME ONE.
A GUN, YOU ARSEHOLE.
OH, RIGHT.
YOU CAN HAVE MY BACK-UP GUN, IF YOU KNOW HOW TO USE IT...
I HAD A BOYFRIEND FROM EL PASO. I'M PROBABLY A BETTER SHOT THAN YOU ARE.
'ERE. HOW COME I GET THE SMALL GUN?
BECAUSE YOU'D PROBABLY STEAL MINE.
I LOSE BOOKS, RECORDS AND GUNS TO GIRLS.

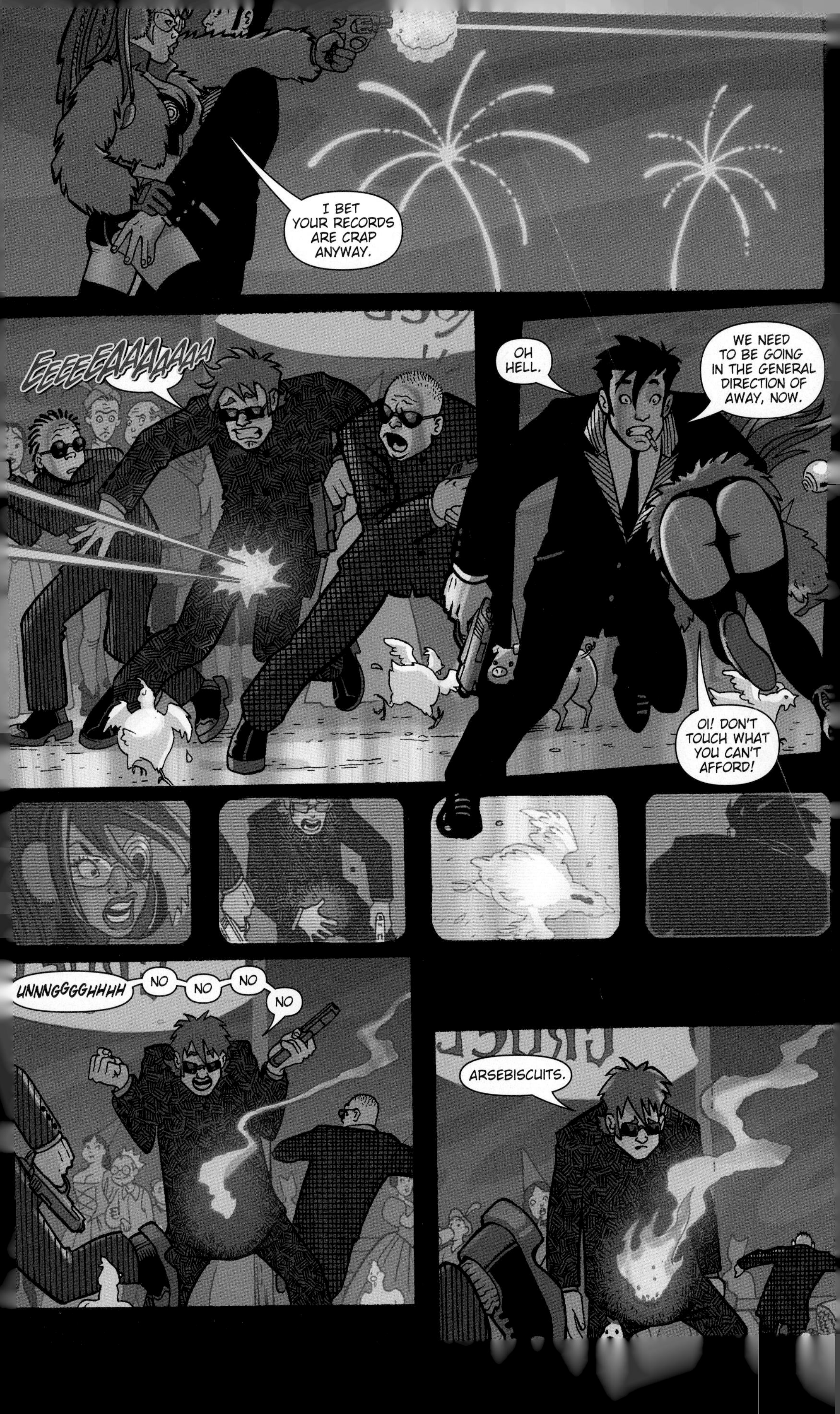
I BET YOUR RECORDS ARE CRAP ANYWAY.
EEEEEAAAAAAAA
OH HELL.
WE NEED TO BE GOING IN THE GENERAL DIRECTION OF AWAY, NOW.
OI! DON'T TOUCH WHAT YOU CAN'T AFFORD!
UNNNGGGHHHH
NO
NO
NO
NO
ARSEBISCUITS.

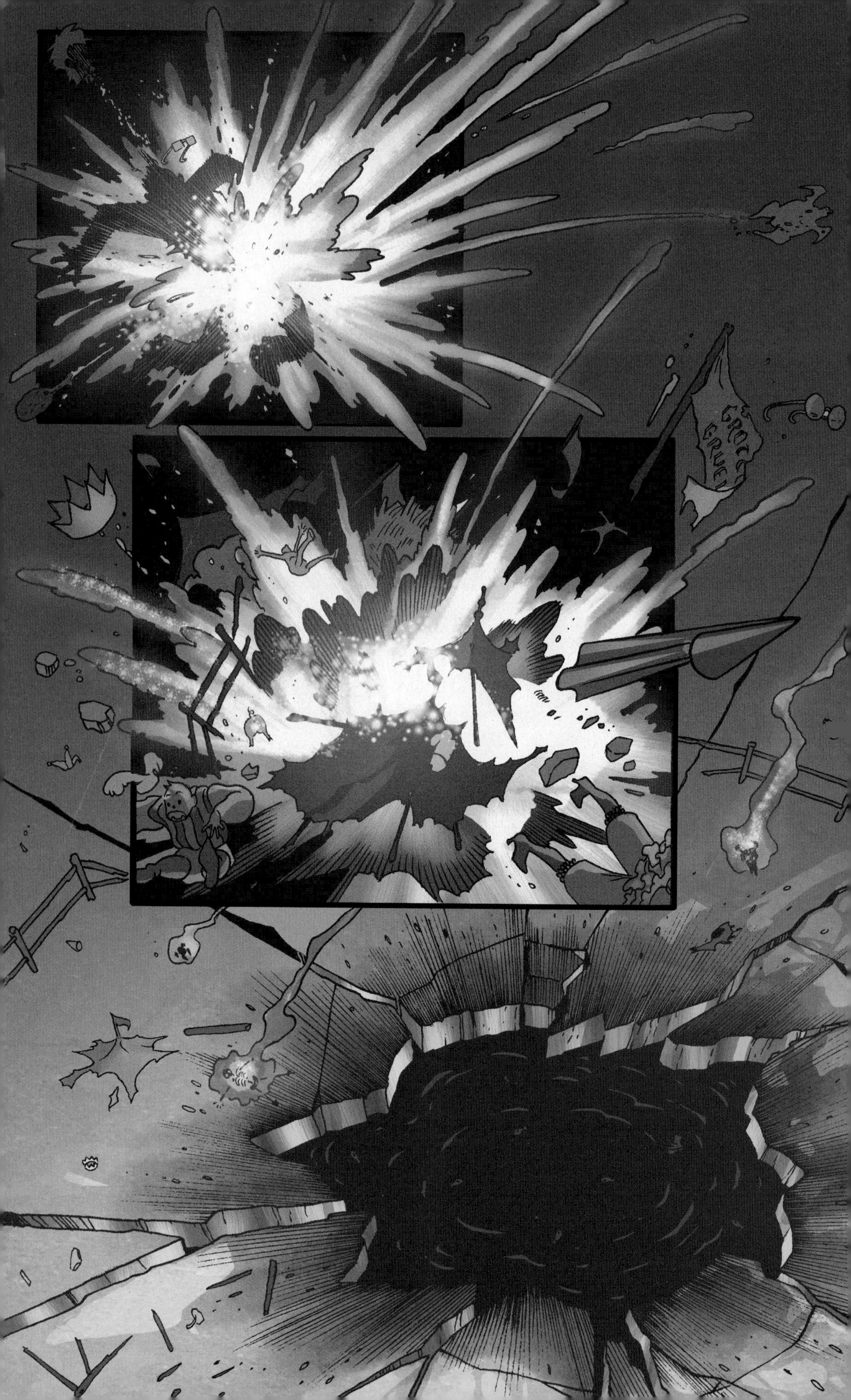
GROG
GRUE

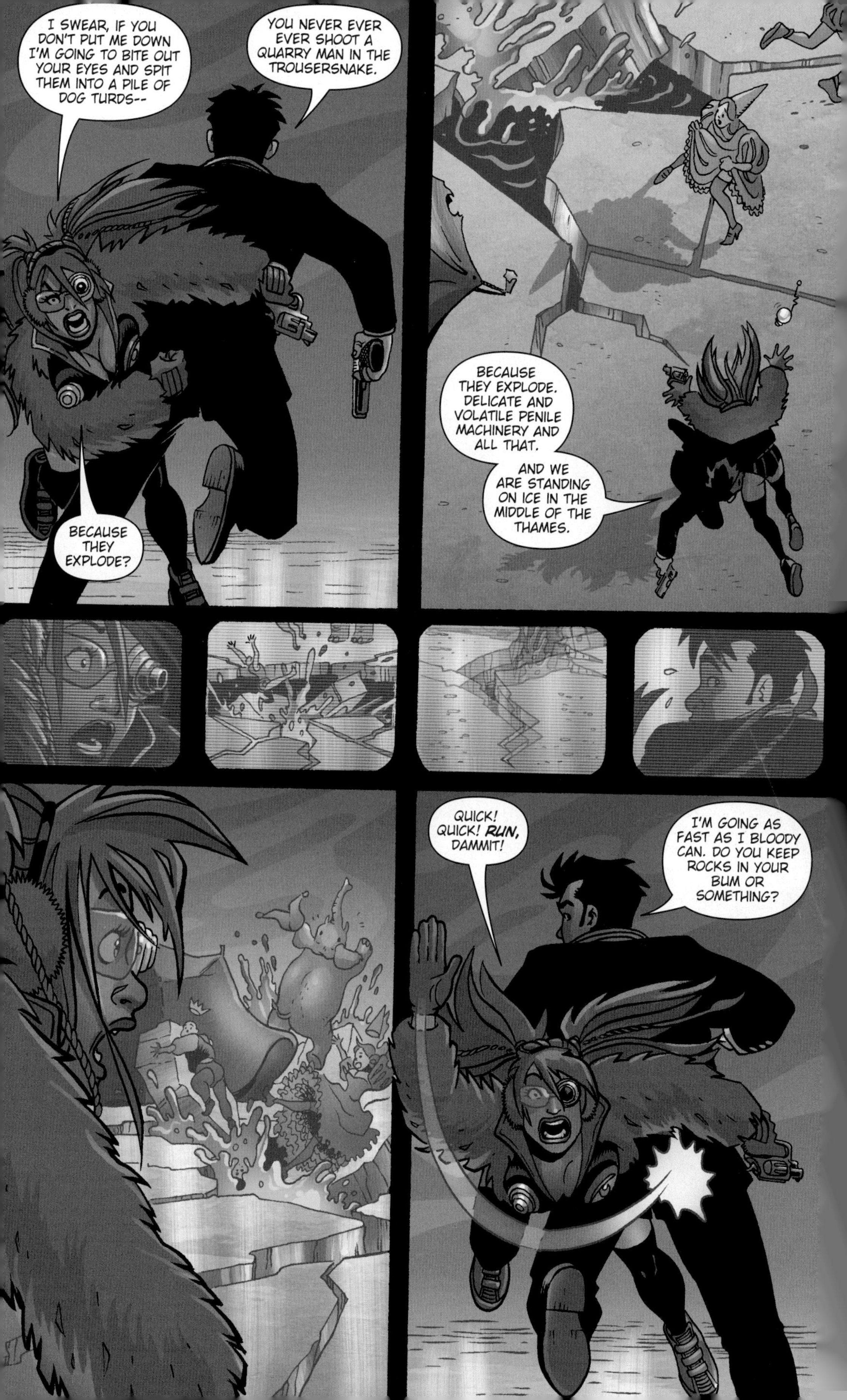
I SWEAR, IF YOU DON'T PUT ME DOWN I'M GOING TO BITE OUT YOUR EYES AND SPIT THEM INTO A PILE OF DOG TURDS--
YOU NEVER EVER SHOOT A QUARRY MAN IN THE TROUSERSNAKE.
BECAUSE THEY EXPLODE?
BECAUSE THEY EXPLODE. DELICATE AND VOLATILE PENILE MACHINERY AND ALL THAT.
AND WE ARE STANDING ON ICE IN THE MIDDLE OF THE THAMES.
QUICK! QUICK! **RUN,** DAMMIT!
I'M GOING AS FAST AS I BLOODY CAN. DO YOU KEEP ROCKS IN YOUR BUM OR SOMETHING?

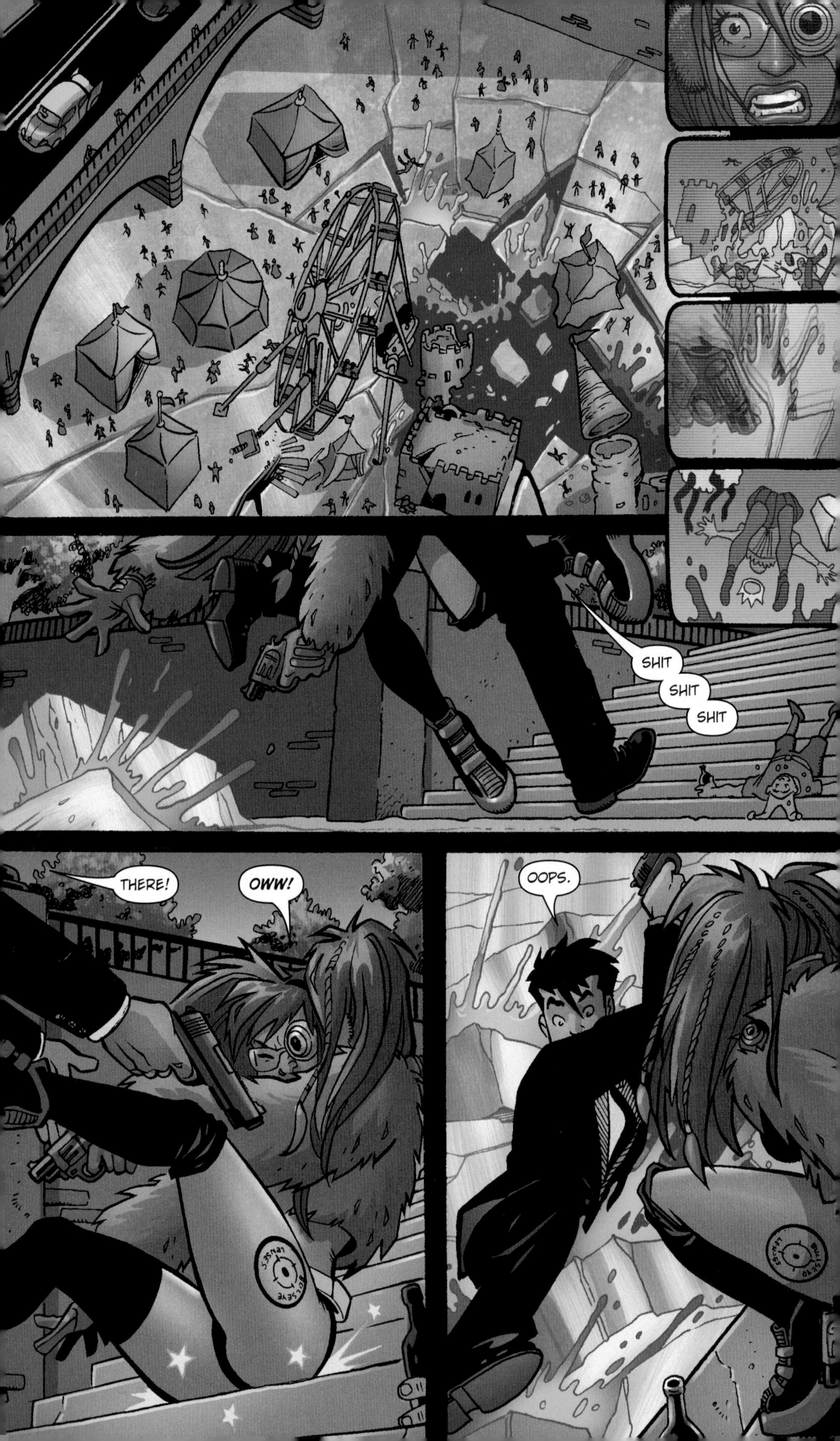
SHIT
SHIT
SHIT
THERE!
OWW!
OOPS.

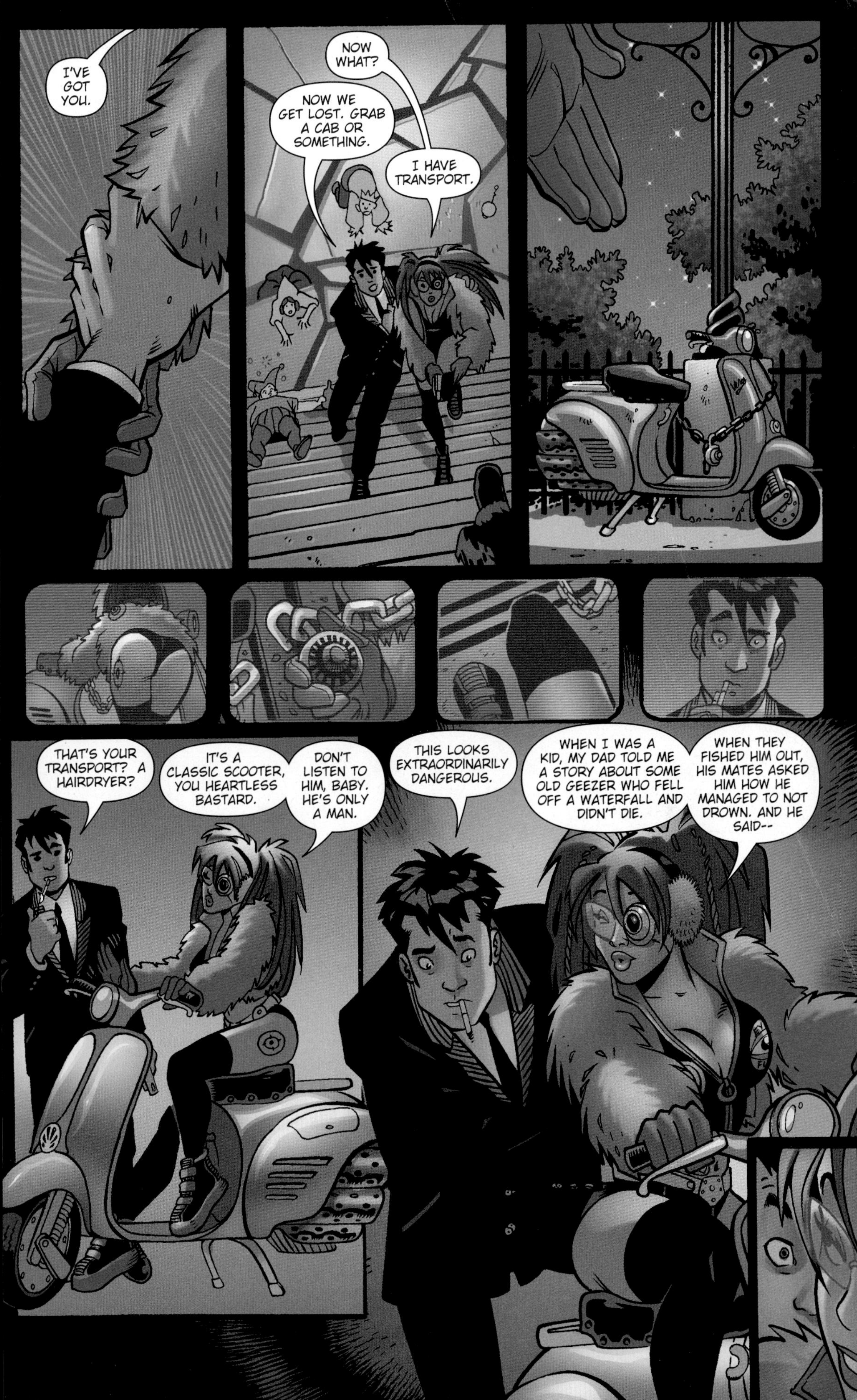
I'VE GOT YOU.
NOW WHAT?
NOW WE GET LOST. GRAB A CAB OR SOMETHING.
I HAVE TRANSPORT.
THAT'S YOUR TRANSPORT? A HAIRDRYER?
IT'S A CLASSIC SCOOTER, YOU HEARTLESS BASTARD.
DON'T LISTEN TO HIM, BABY. HE'S ONLY A MAN.
THIS LOOKS EXTRAORDINARILY DANGEROUS.
WHEN I WAS A KID, MY DAD TOLD ME A STORY ABOUT SOME OLD GEEZER WHO FELL OFF A WATERFALL AND DIDN'T DIE.
WHEN THEY FISHED HIM OUT, HIS MATES ASKED HIM HOW HE MANAGED TO NOT DROWN. AND HE SAID--

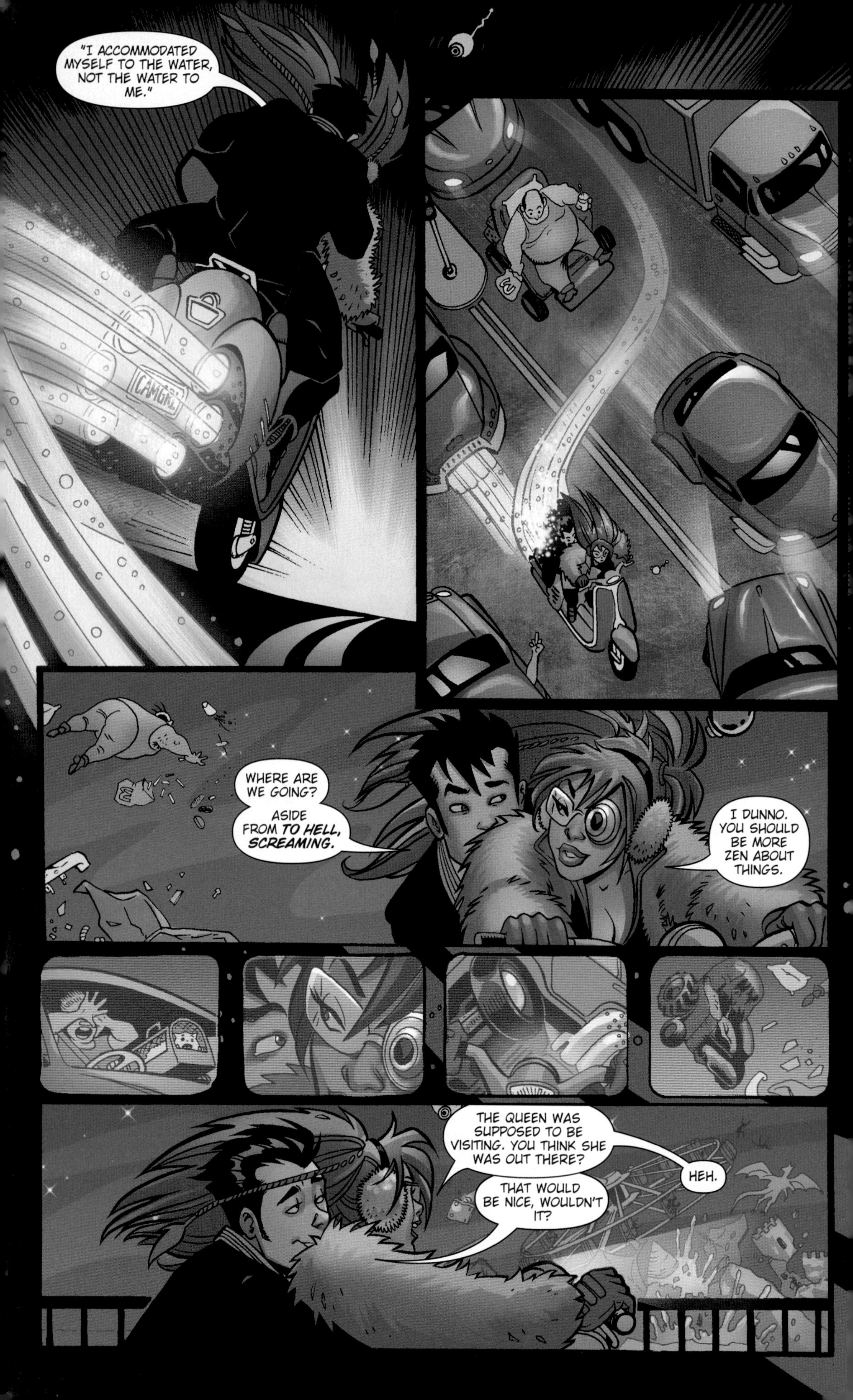
"I ACCOMMODATED MYSELF TO THE WATER, NOT THE WATER TO ME."
CAMGRL
WHERE ARE WE GOING?
ASIDE FROM ***TO HELL, SCREAMING.***
I DUNNO. YOU SHOULD BE MORE ZEN ABOUT THINGS.
THE QUEEN WAS SUPPOSED TO BE VISITING. YOU THINK SHE WAS OUT THERE?
HEH.
THAT WOULD BE NICE, WOULDN'T IT?

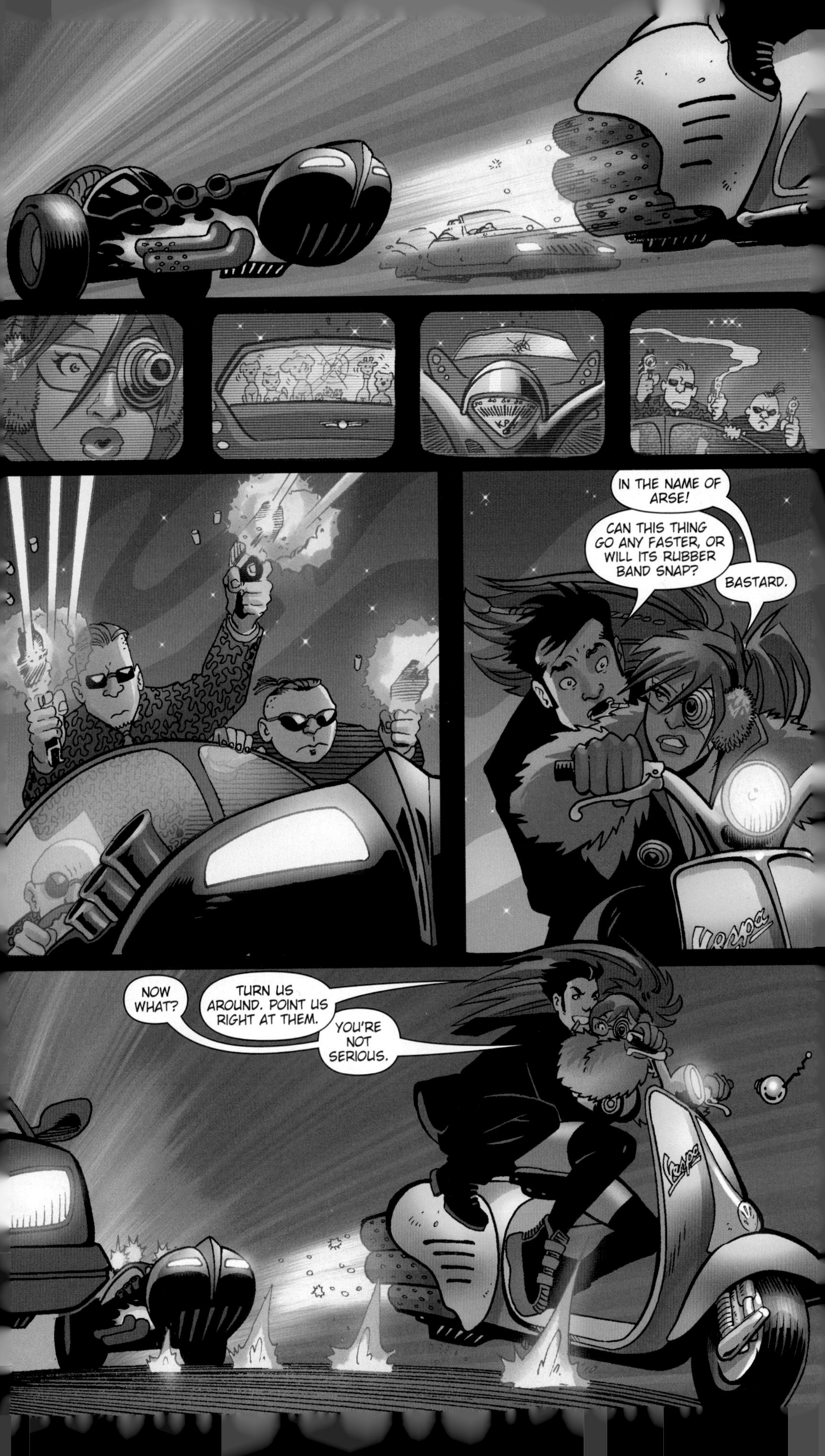
IN THE NAME OF ARSE!
CAN THIS THING GO ANY FASTER, OR WILL ITS RUBBER BAND SNAP?
BASTARD.
NOW WHAT?
TURN US AROUND. POINT US RIGHT AT THEM.
YOU'RE NOT SERIOUS.

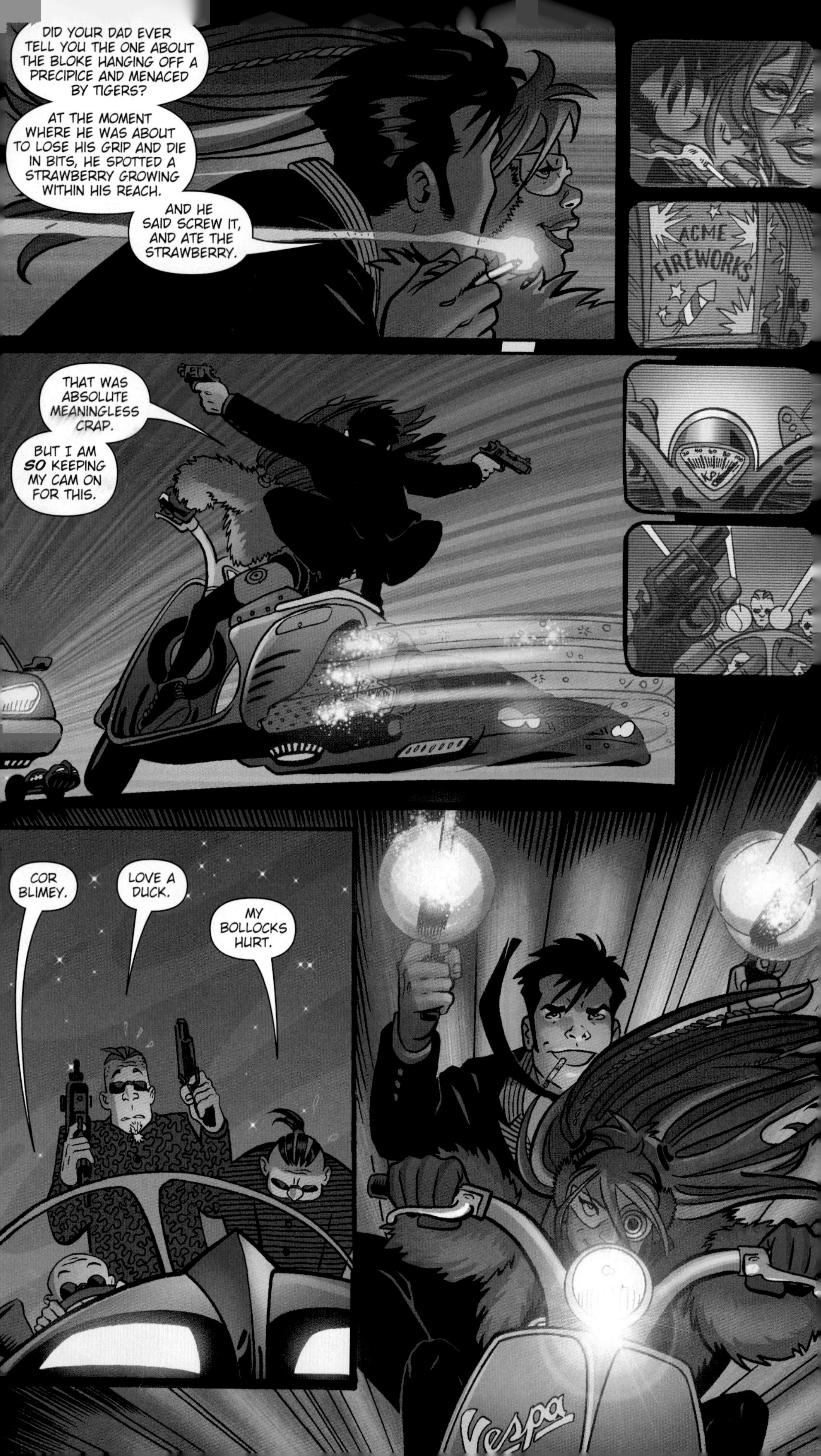
DID YOUR DAD EVER TELL YOU THE ONE ABOUT THE BLOKE HANGING OFF A PRECIPICE AND MENACED BY TIGERS?
AT THE MOMENT WHERE HE WAS ABOUT TO LOSE HIS GRIP AND DIE IN BITS, HE SPOTTED A STRAWBERRY GROWING WITHIN HIS REACH.
AND HE SAID SCREW IT, AND ATE THE STRAWBERRY.
ACME FIREWORKS
THAT WAS ABSOLUTE MEANINGLESS CRAP.
BUT I AM SO KEEPING MY CAM ON FOR THIS.
KPH
COR BLIMEY.
LOVE A DUCK.
MY BOLLOCKS HURT.
Vespa

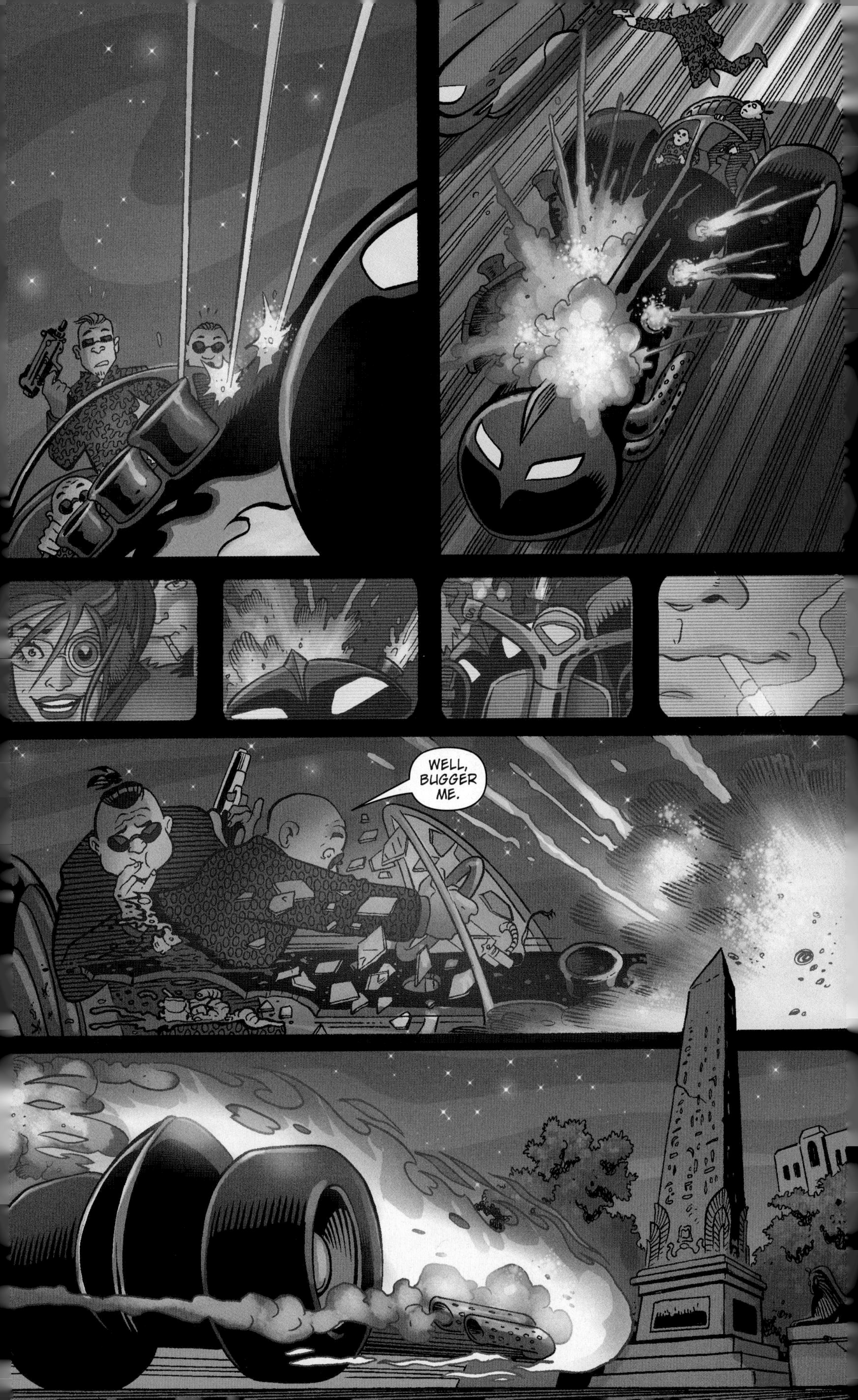
WELL, BUGGER ME.

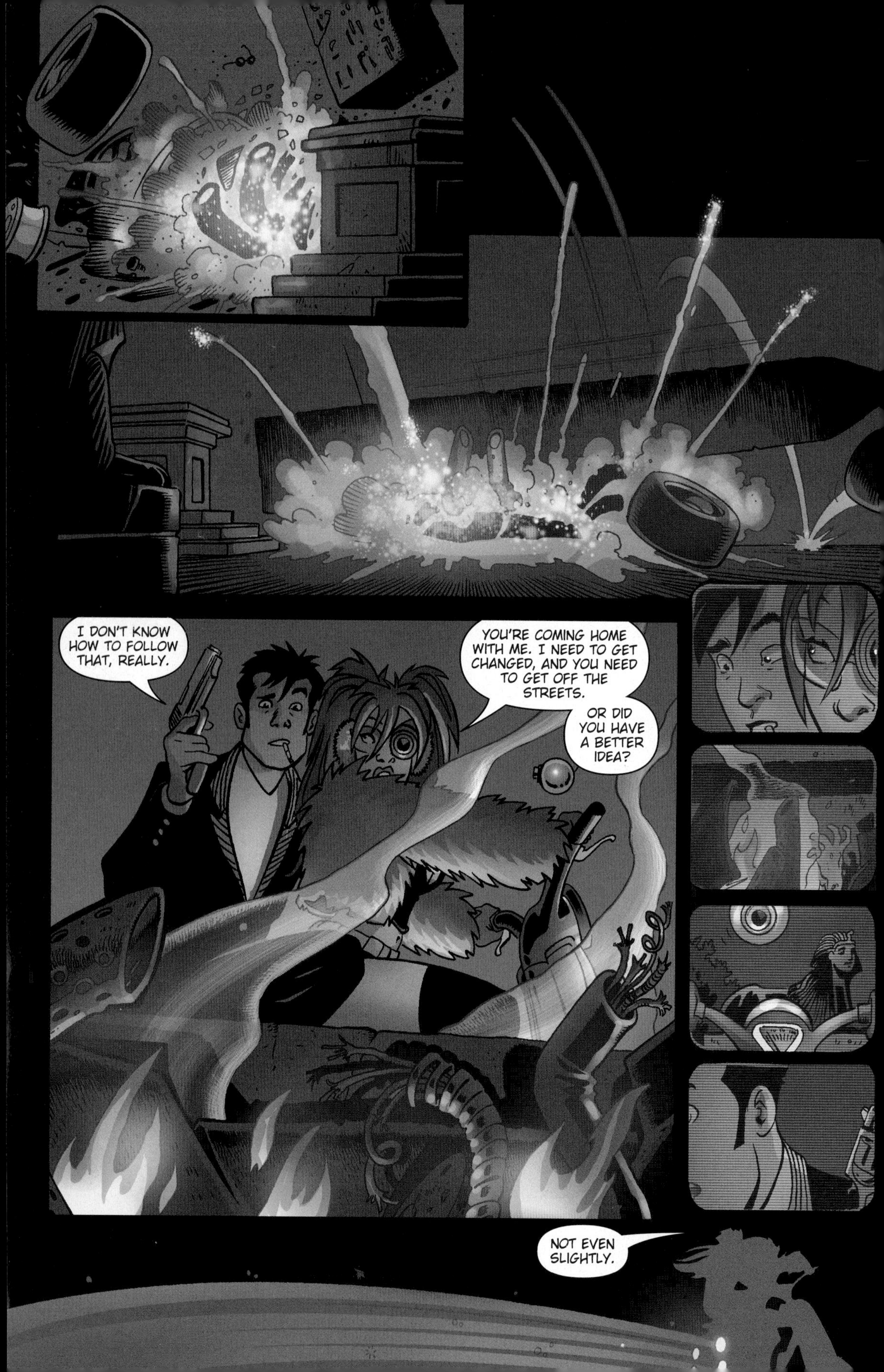
I DON'T KNOW HOW TO FOLLOW THAT, REALLY.
YOU'RE COMING HOME WITH ME. I NEED TO GET CHANGED, AND YOU NEED TO GET OFF THE STREETS.
OR DID YOU HAVE A BETTER IDEA?
NOT EVEN SLIGHTLY.

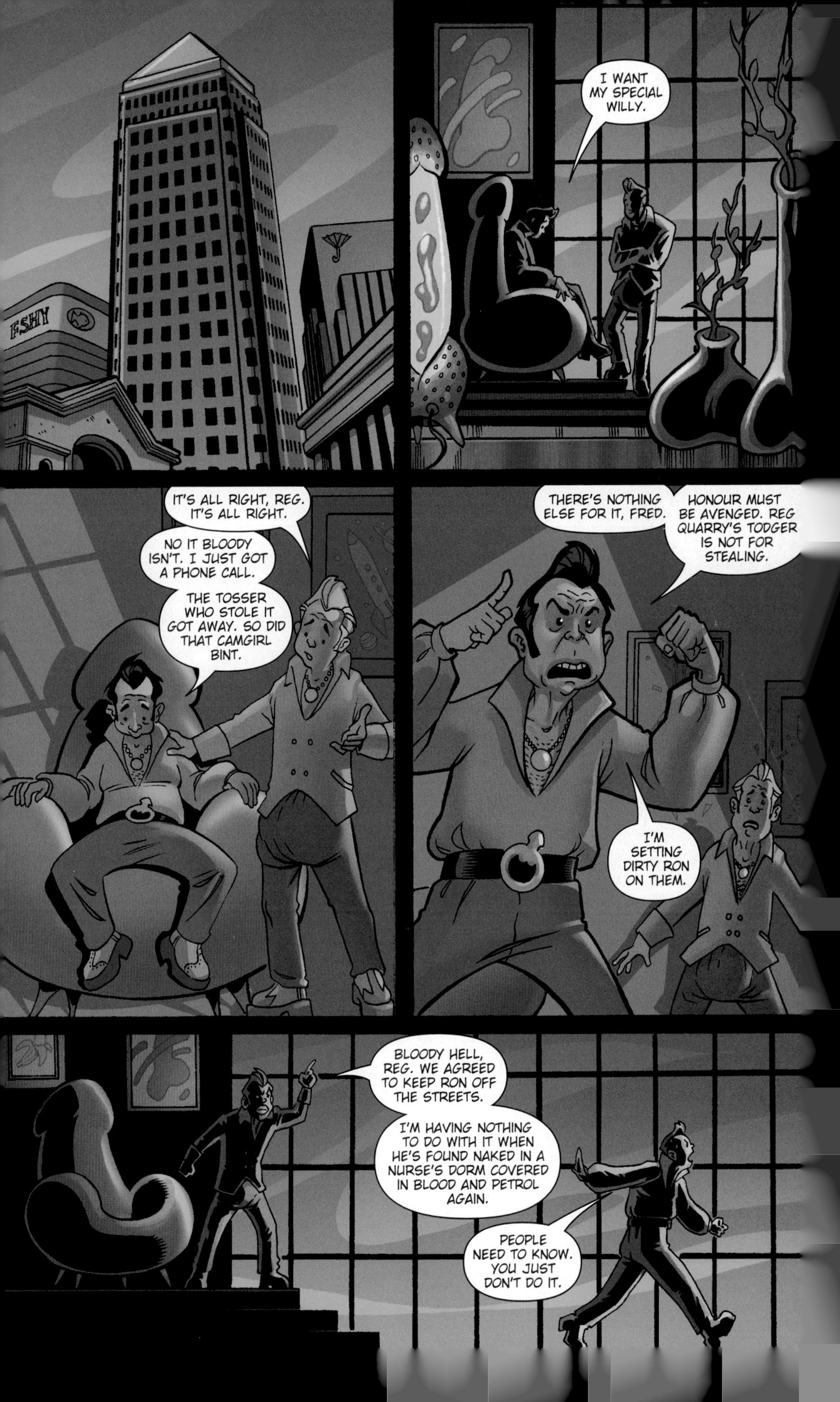
FSHY
I WANT MY SPECIAL WILLY.
IT'S ALL RIGHT, REG. IT'S ALL RIGHT.
NO IT BLOODY ISN'T. I JUST GOT A PHONE CALL.
THE TOSSER WHO STOLE IT GOT AWAY. SO DID THAT CAMGIRL BINT.
THERE'S NOTHING ELSE FOR IT, FRED.
HONOUR MUST BE AVENGED. REG QUARRY'S TODGER IS NOT FOR STEALING.
I'M SETTING DIRTY RON ON THEM.
BLOODY HELL, REG. WE AGREED TO KEEP RON OFF THE STREETS.
I'M HAVING NOTHING TO DO WITH IT WHEN HE'S FOUND NAKED IN A NURSE'S DORM COVERED IN BLOOD AND PETROL AGAIN.
PEOPLE NEED TO KNOW. YOU JUST DON'T DO IT.

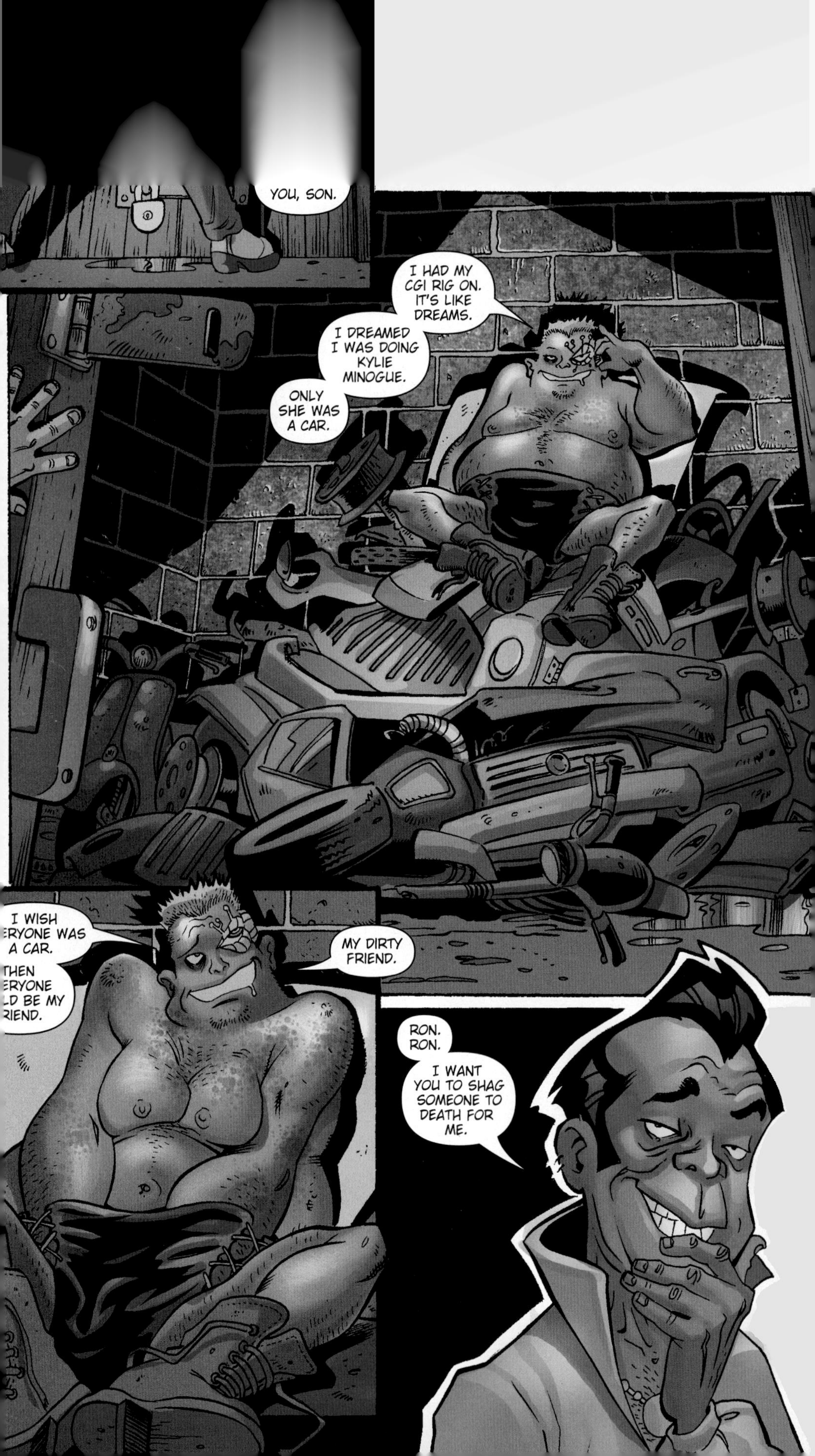
YOU, SON.
I HAD MY CGI RIG ON. IT'S LIKE DREAMS.
I DREAMED I WAS DOING KYLIE MINOGUE.
ONLY SHE WAS A CAR.
I WISH ERYONE WAS A CAR.
THEN ERYONE LD BE MY RIEND.
MY DIRTY FRIEND.
RON. RON.
I WANT YOU TO SHAG SOMEONE TO DEATH FOR ME.

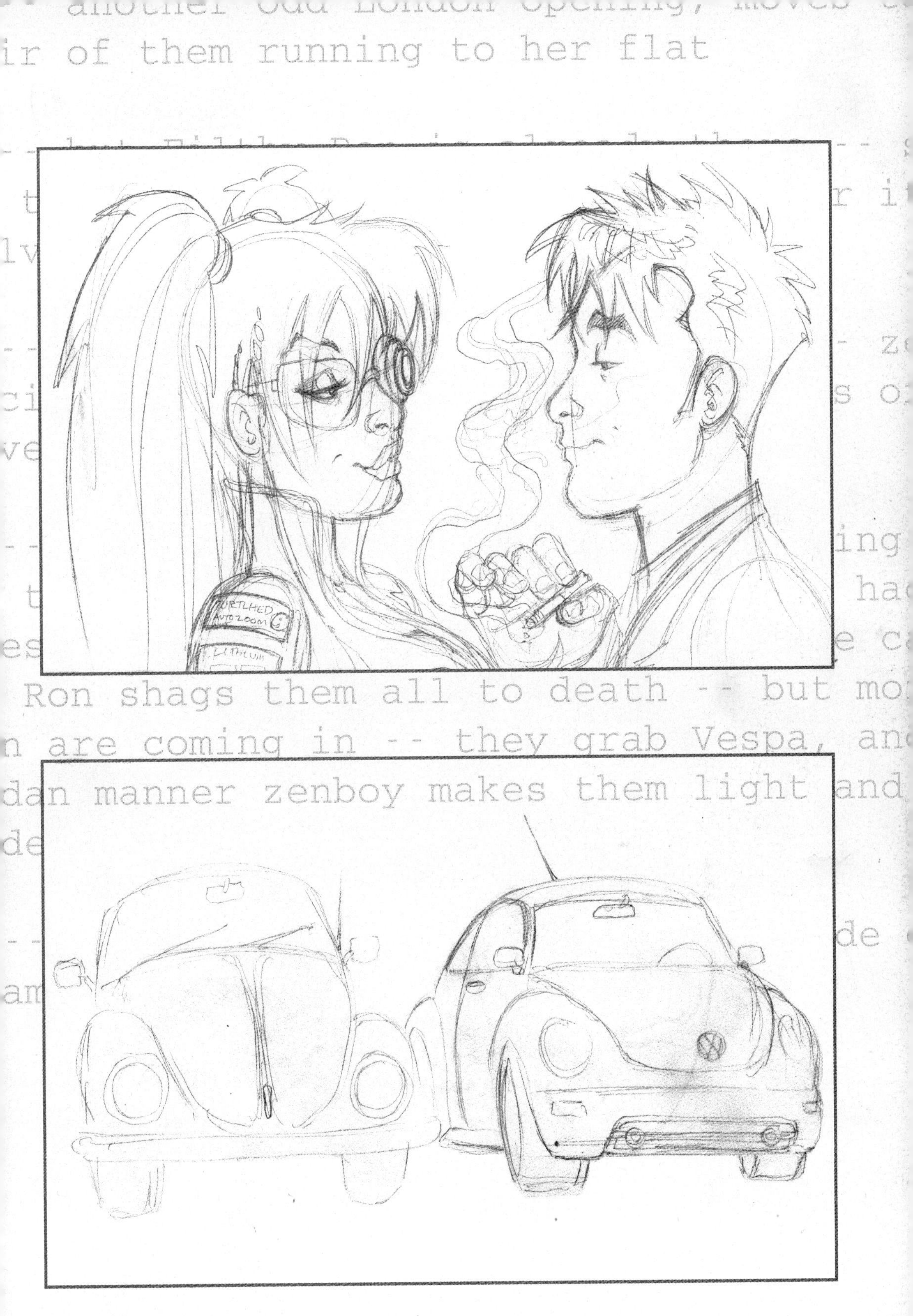
ir of them running to her flat
Ron shags them all to death -- but mo
n are coming in -- they grab Vespa, and
dan manner zenboy makes them light and
TURTLHED
AUTOZOOM

COVER THREE

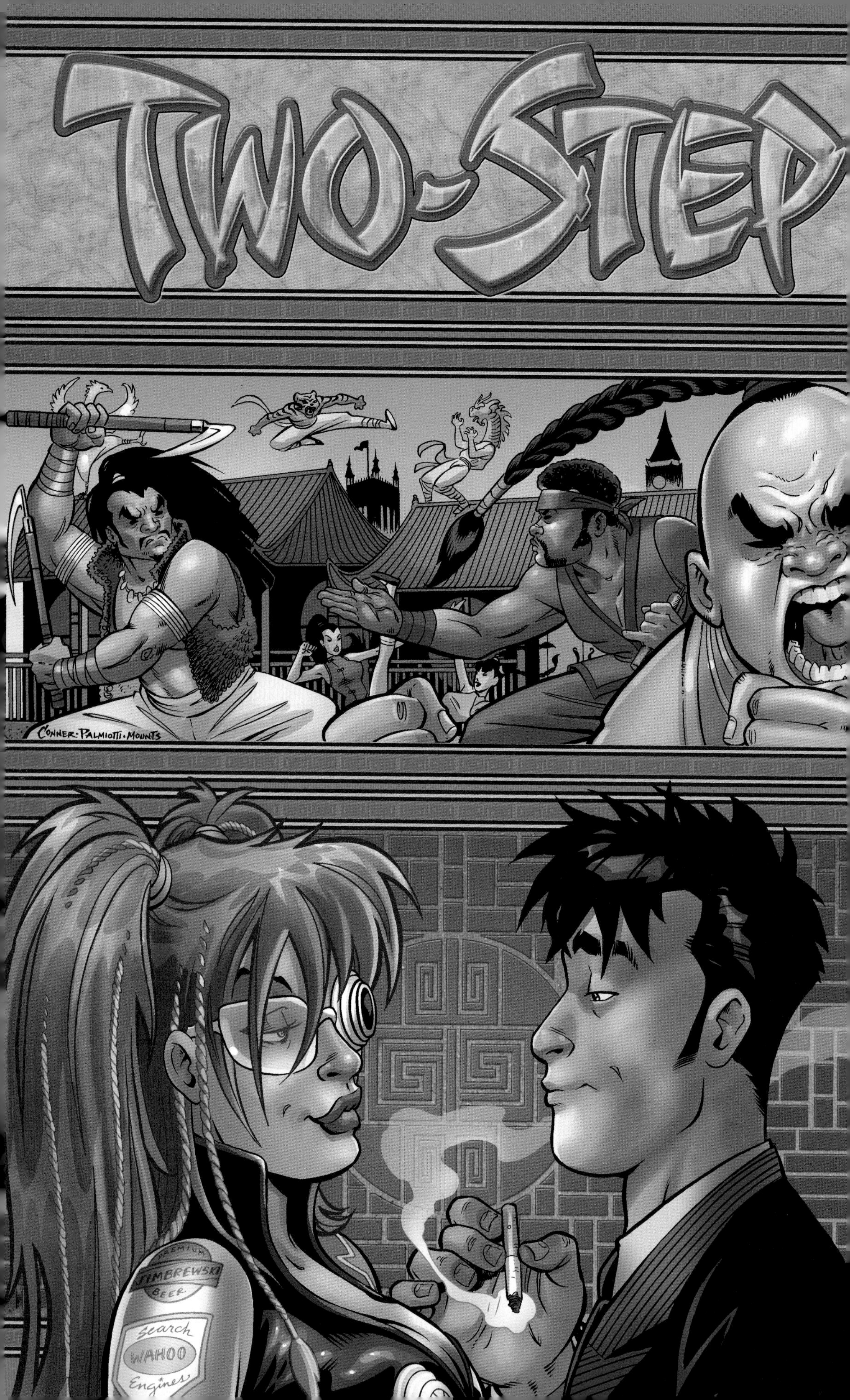
TWO-STEP
CONNER·PALMIOTTI·MOUNTS
PREMIUM
JIMBREWSKI
BEER
Search
WAHOO
Engines

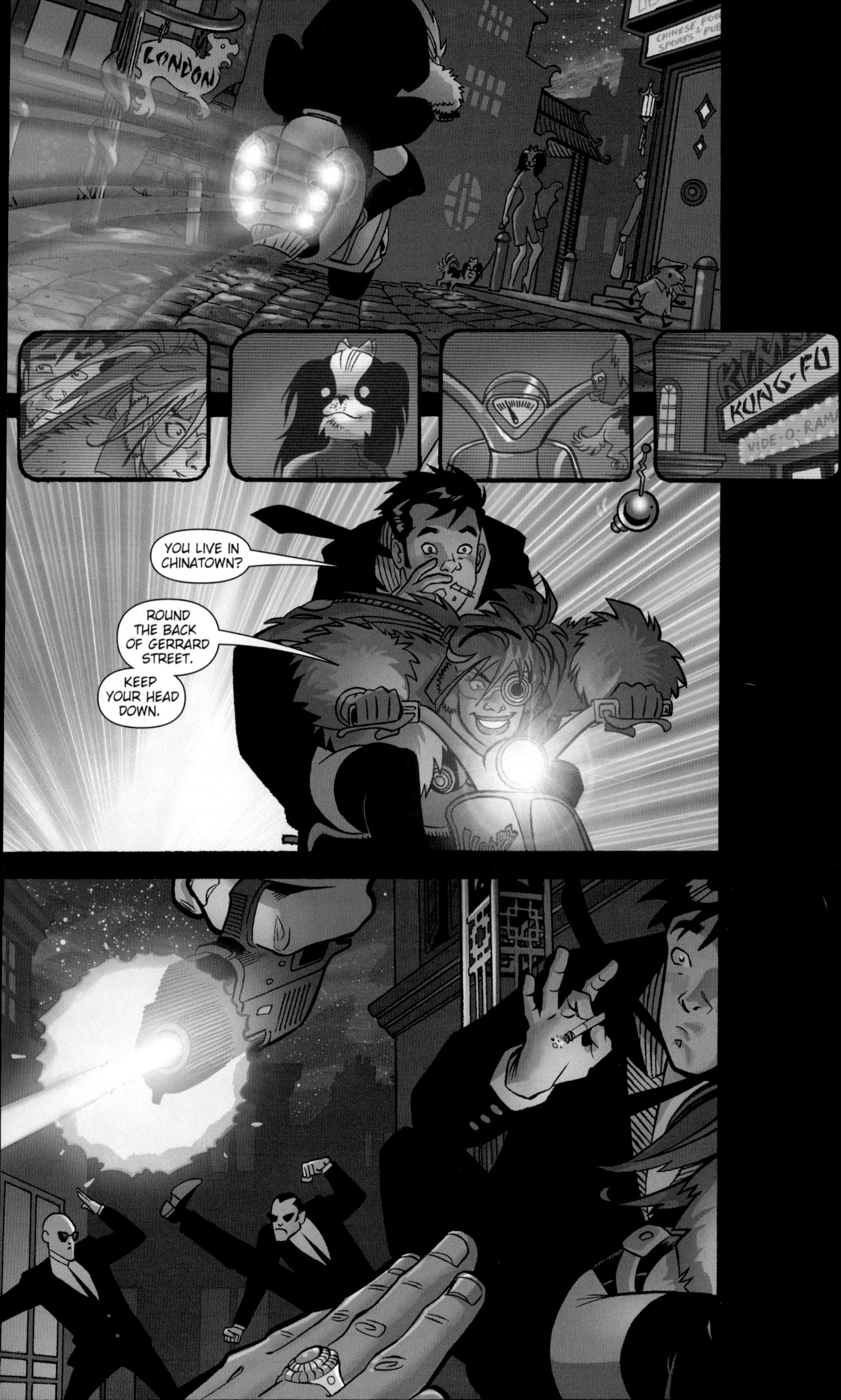
LONDON
KUNG-FU
YOU LIVE IN CHINATOWN?
ROUND THE BACK OF GERRARD STREET.
KEEP YOUR HEAD DOWN.

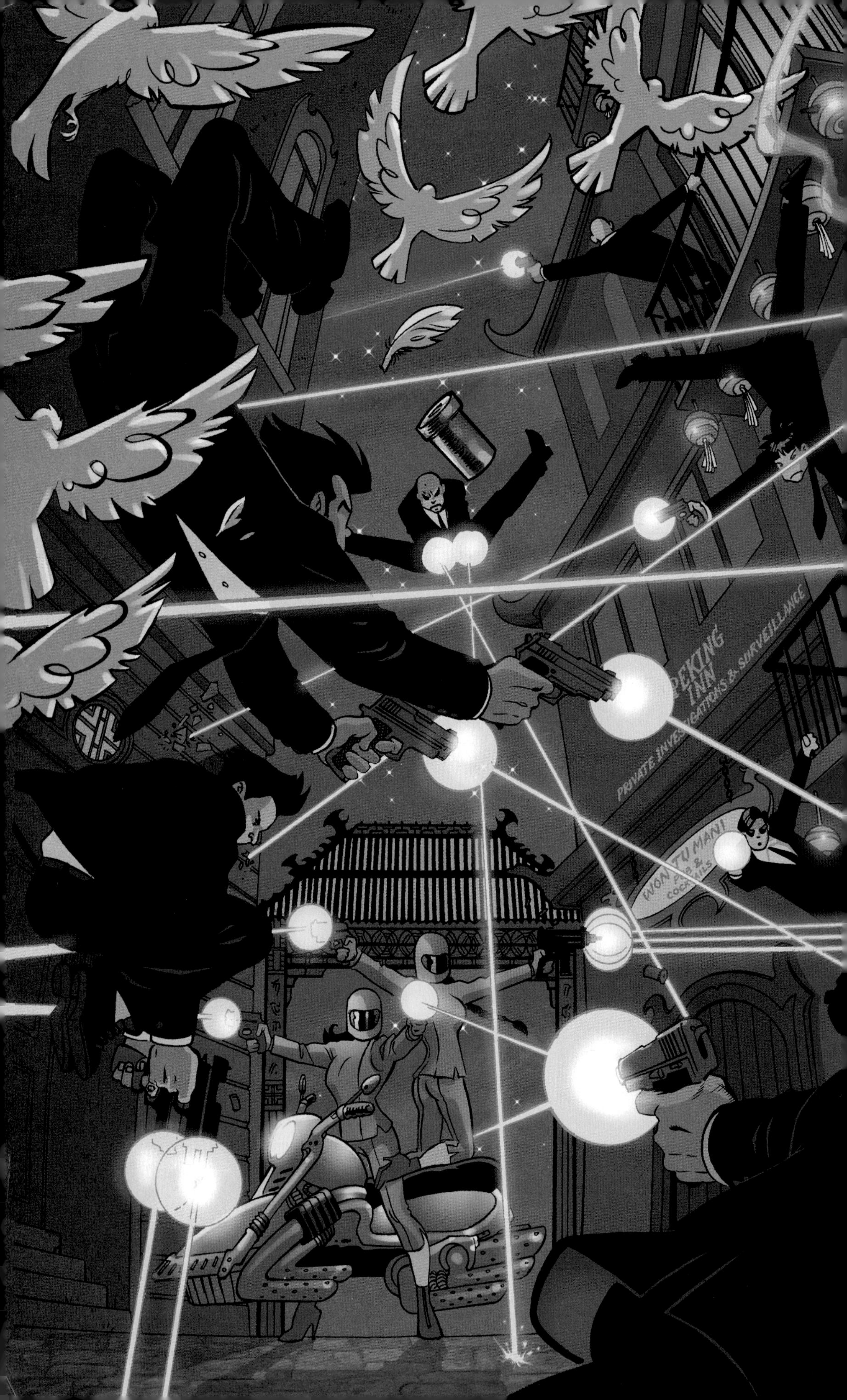
PEKING INN
SURVEILLANCE
WON TU MANI

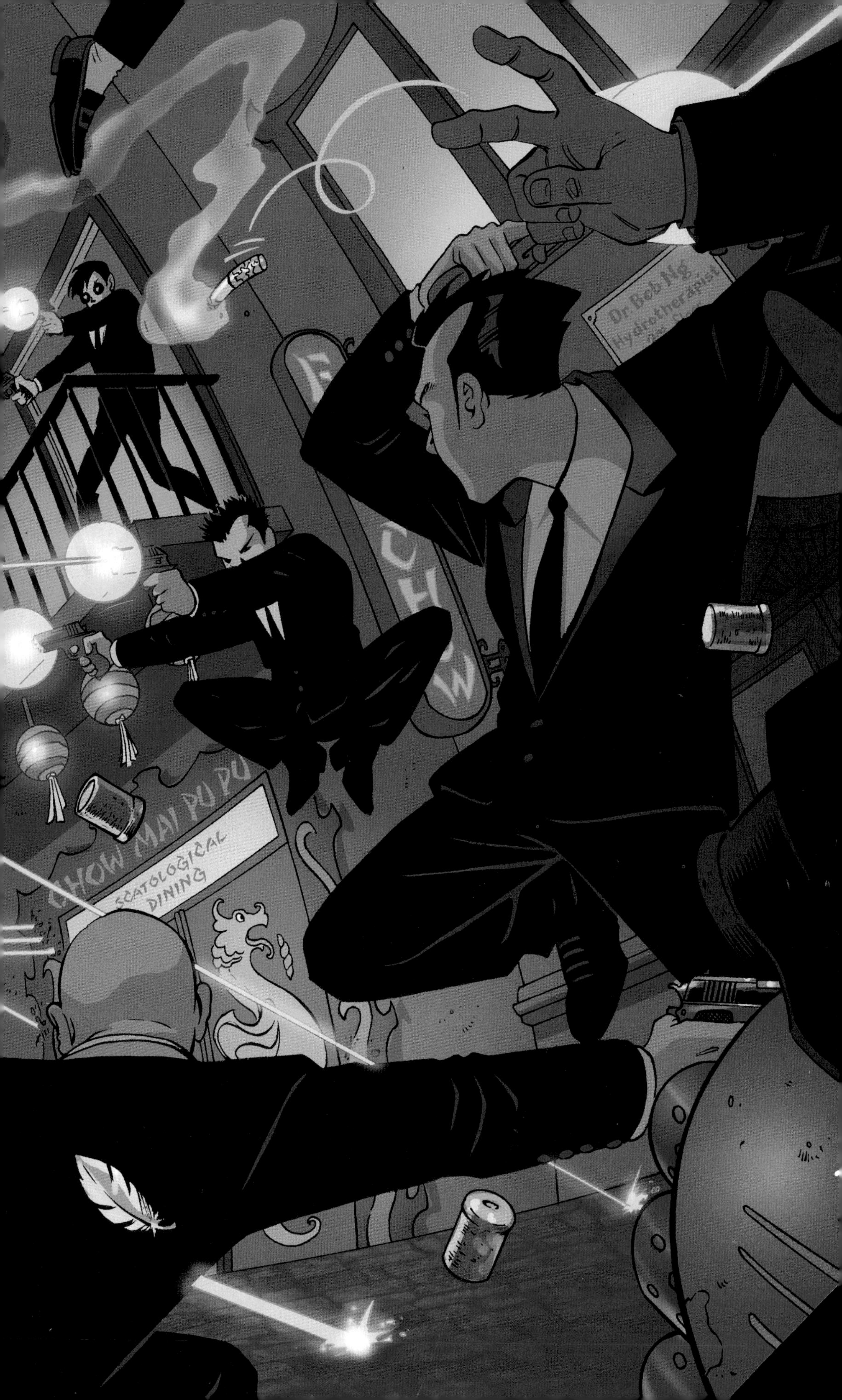
Dr. Bob Ng
Hydrotherapist
CHOW MAI PU PU
SCATOLOGICAL
DINING

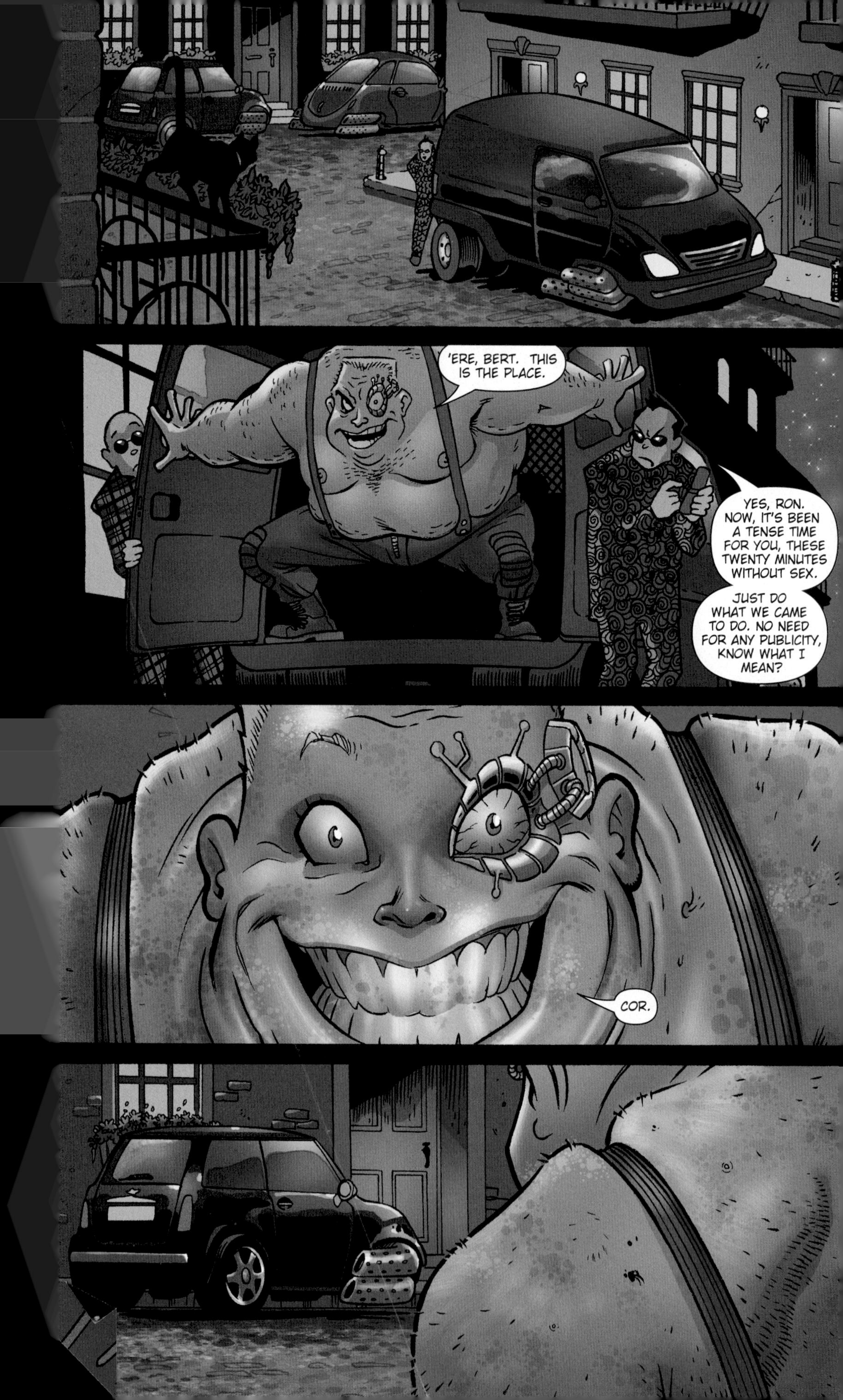
'ERE, BERT. THIS IS THE PLACE.
YES, RON. NOW, IT'S BEEN A TENSE TIME FOR YOU, THESE TWENTY MINUTES WITHOUT SEX.
JUST DO WHAT WE CAME TO DO. NO NEED FOR ANY PUBLICITY, KNOW WHAT I MEAN?
COR.

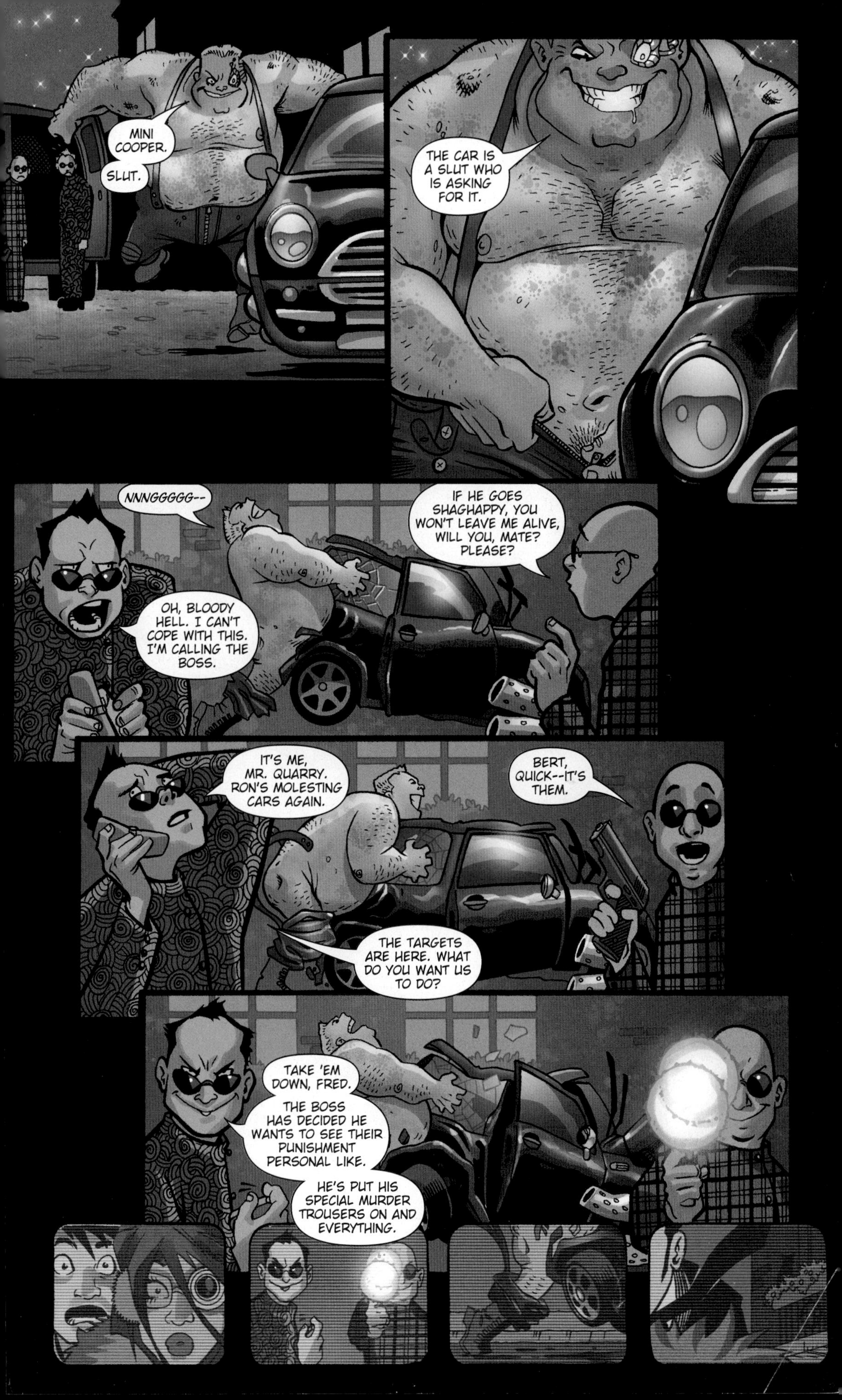
MINI COOPER.
SLUT.
THE CAR IS A SLUT WHO IS ASKING FOR IT.
NNNGGGGG--
IF HE GOES SHAGHAPPY, YOU WON'T LEAVE ME ALIVE, WILL YOU, MATE? PLEASE?
OH, BLOODY HELL. I CAN'T COPE WITH THIS. I'M CALLING THE BOSS.
IT'S ME, MR. QUARRY. RON'S MOLESTING CARS AGAIN.
BERT, QUICK--IT'S THEM.
THE TARGETS ARE HERE. WHAT DO YOU WANT US TO DO?
TAKE 'EM DOWN, FRED.
THE BOSS HAS DECIDED HE WANTS TO SEE THEIR PUNISHMENT PERSONAL LIKE.
HE'S PUT HIS SPECIAL MURDER TROUSERS ON AND EVERYTHING.

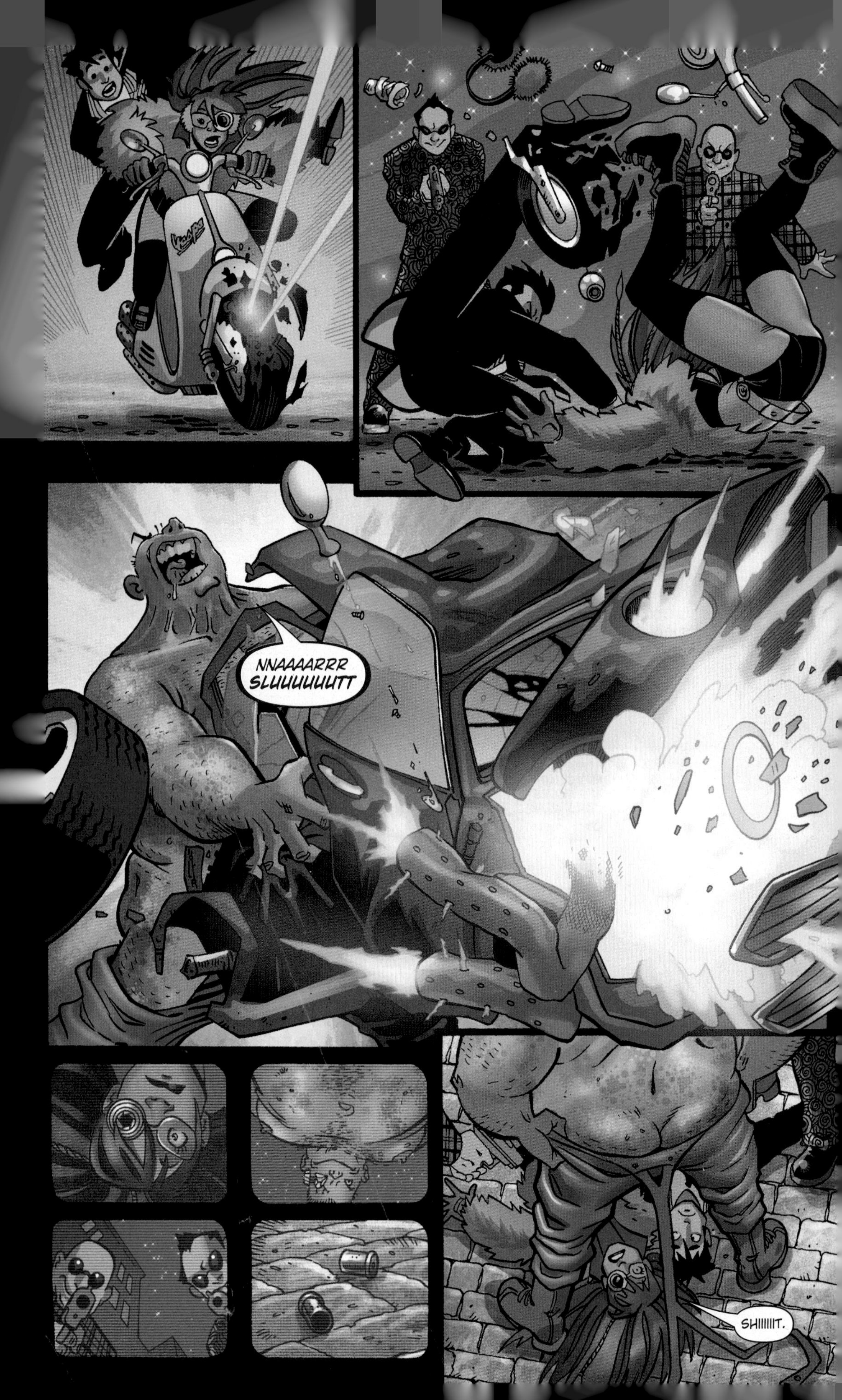
NNAAAARRR SLUUUUUUTT
SHIIIIIT.

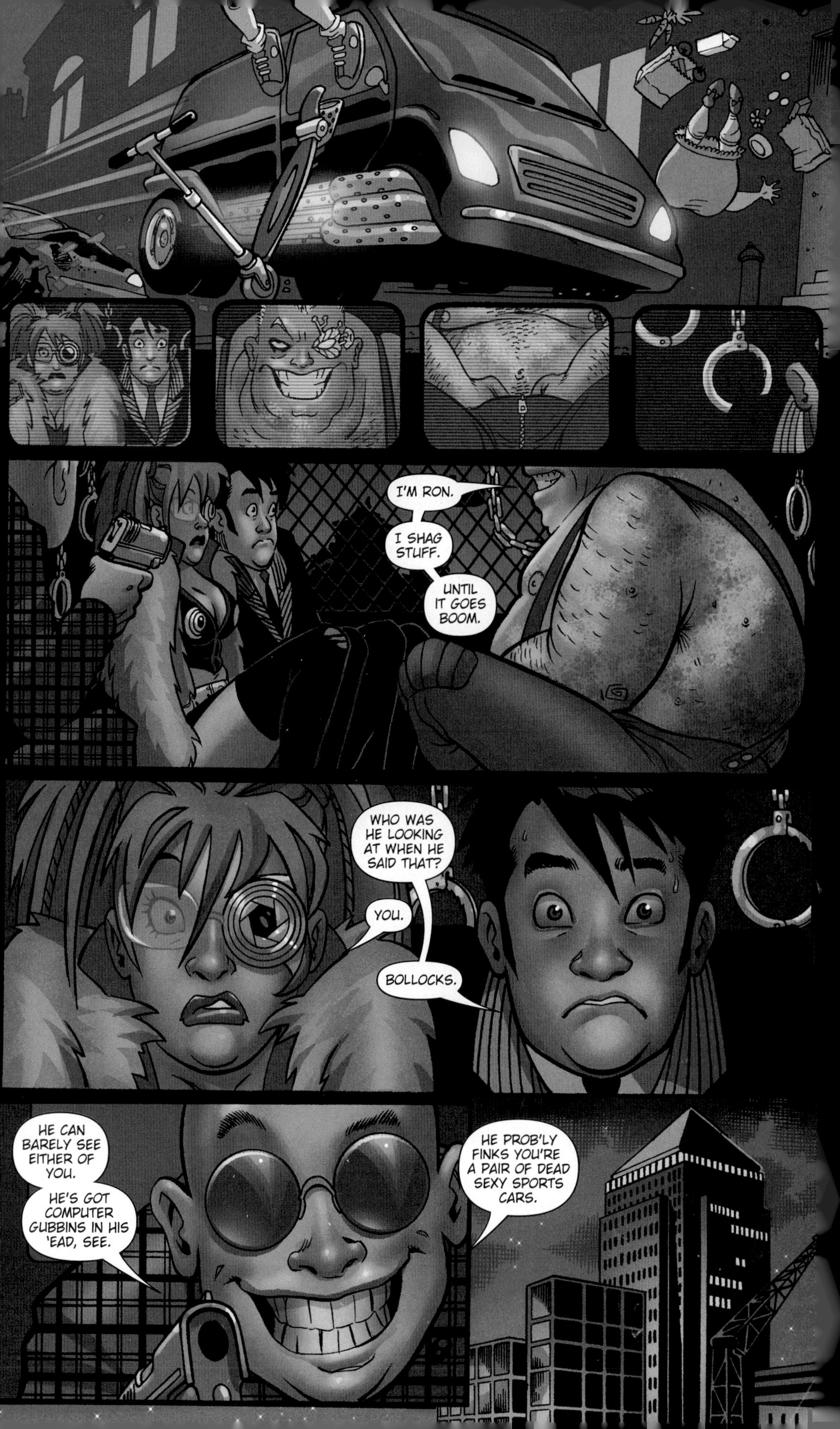

I'M RON.
I SHAG STUFF.
UNTIL IT GOES BOOM.
WHO WAS HE LOOKING AT WHEN HE SAID THAT?
YOU.
BOLLOCKS.
HE CAN BARELY SEE EITHER OF YOU.
HE'S GOT COMPUTER GUBBINS IN HIS 'EAD, SEE.
HE PROB'LY FINKS YOU'RE A PAIR OF DEAD SEXY SPORTS CARS.

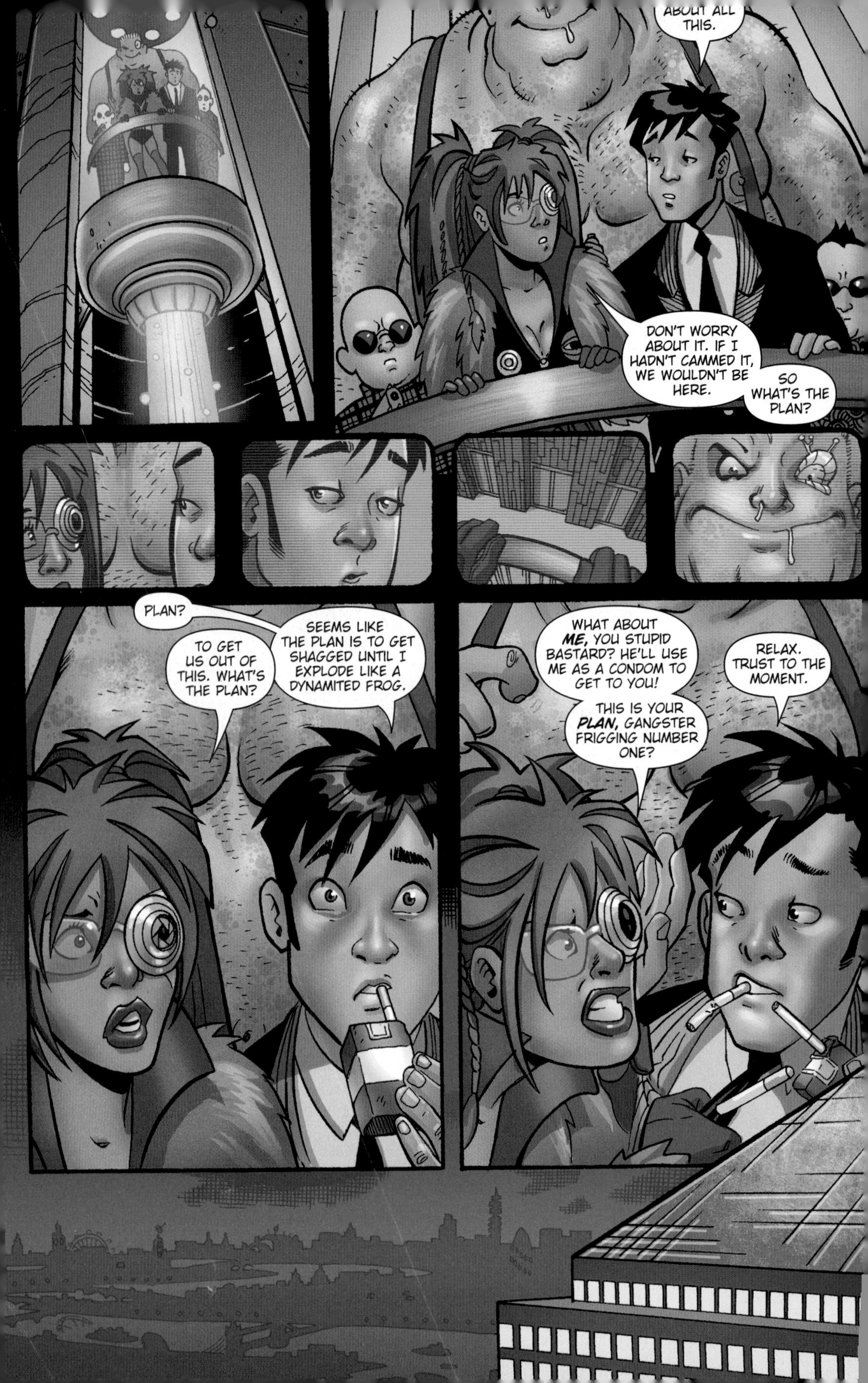

ABOUT ALL THIS.
DON'T WORRY ABOUT IT. IF I HADN'T CAMMED IT, WE WOULDN'T BE HERE.
SO WHAT'S THE PLAN?
PLAN?
TO GET US OUT OF THIS. WHAT'S THE PLAN?
SEEMS LIKE THE PLAN IS TO GET SHAGGED UNTIL I EXPLODE LIKE A DYNAMITED FROG.
WHAT ABOUT ME, YOU STUPID BASTARD? HE'LL USE ME AS A CONDOM TO GET TO YOU!
THIS IS YOUR PLAN, GANGSTER FRIGGING NUMBER ONE?
RELAX. TRUST TO THE MOMENT.

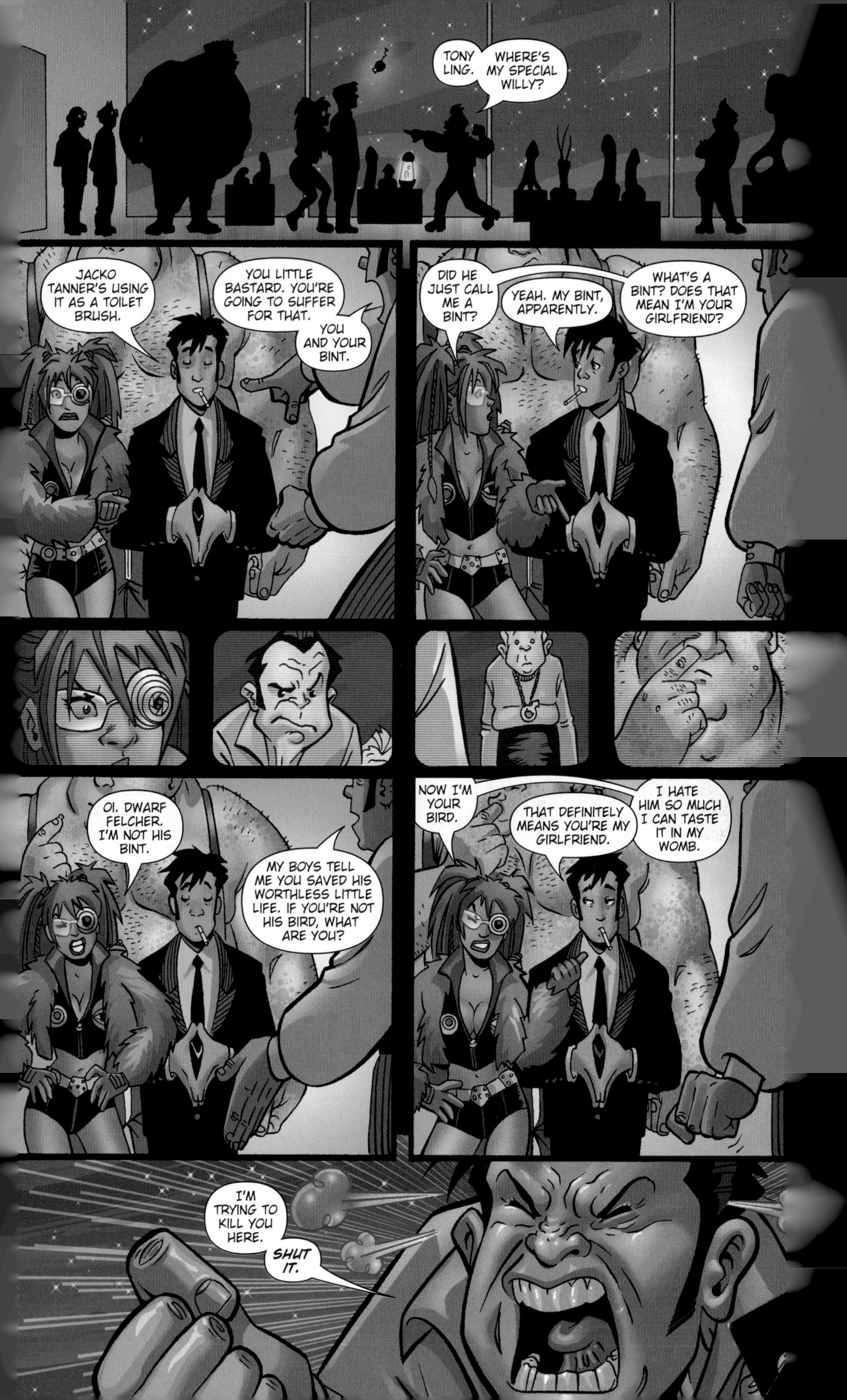
TONY LING.
WHERE'S MY SPECIAL WILLY?
JACKO TANNER'S USING IT AS A TOILET BRUSH.
YOU LITTLE BASTARD. YOU'RE GOING TO SUFFER FOR THAT.
YOU AND YOUR BINT.
DID HE JUST CALL ME A BINT?
YEAH. MY BINT, APPARENTLY.
WHAT'S A BINT? DOES THAT MEAN I'M YOUR GIRLFRIEND?
OI. DWARF FELCHER. I'M NOT HIS BINT.
MY BOYS TELL ME YOU SAVED HIS WORTHLESS LITTLE LIFE. IF YOU'RE NOT HIS BIRD, WHAT ARE YOU?
NOW I'M YOUR BIRD.
THAT DEFINITELY MEANS YOU'RE MY GIRLFRIEND.
I HATE HIM SO MUCH I CAN TASTE IT IN MY WOMB.
I'M TRYING TO KILL YOU HERE.
SHUT IT.

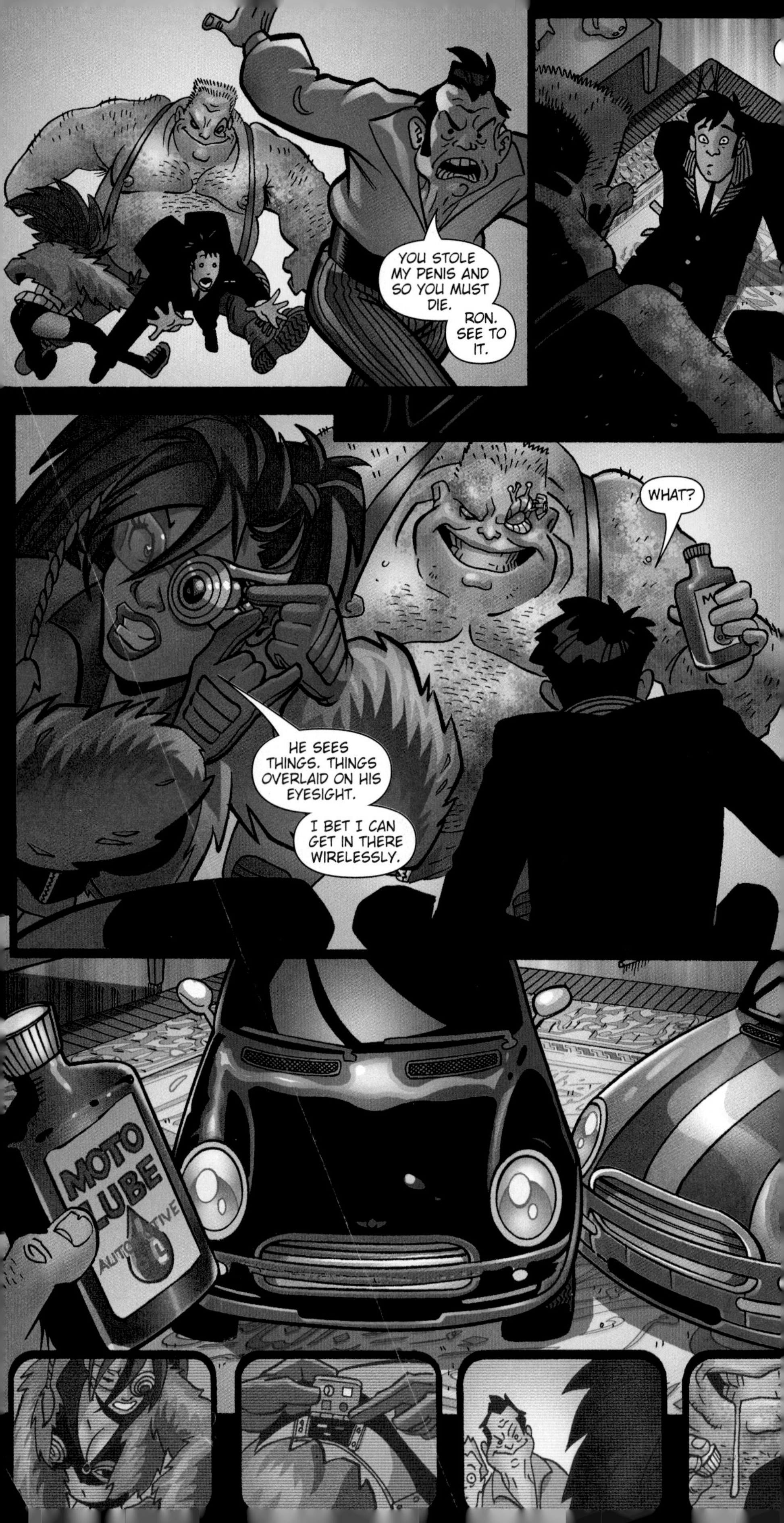
YOU STOLE MY PENIS AND SO YOU MUST DIE.
RON. SEE TO IT.
WHAT?
HE SEES THINGS. THINGS OVERLAID ON HIS EYESIGHT.
I BET I CAN GET IN THERE WIRELESSLY.
MOTO LUBE

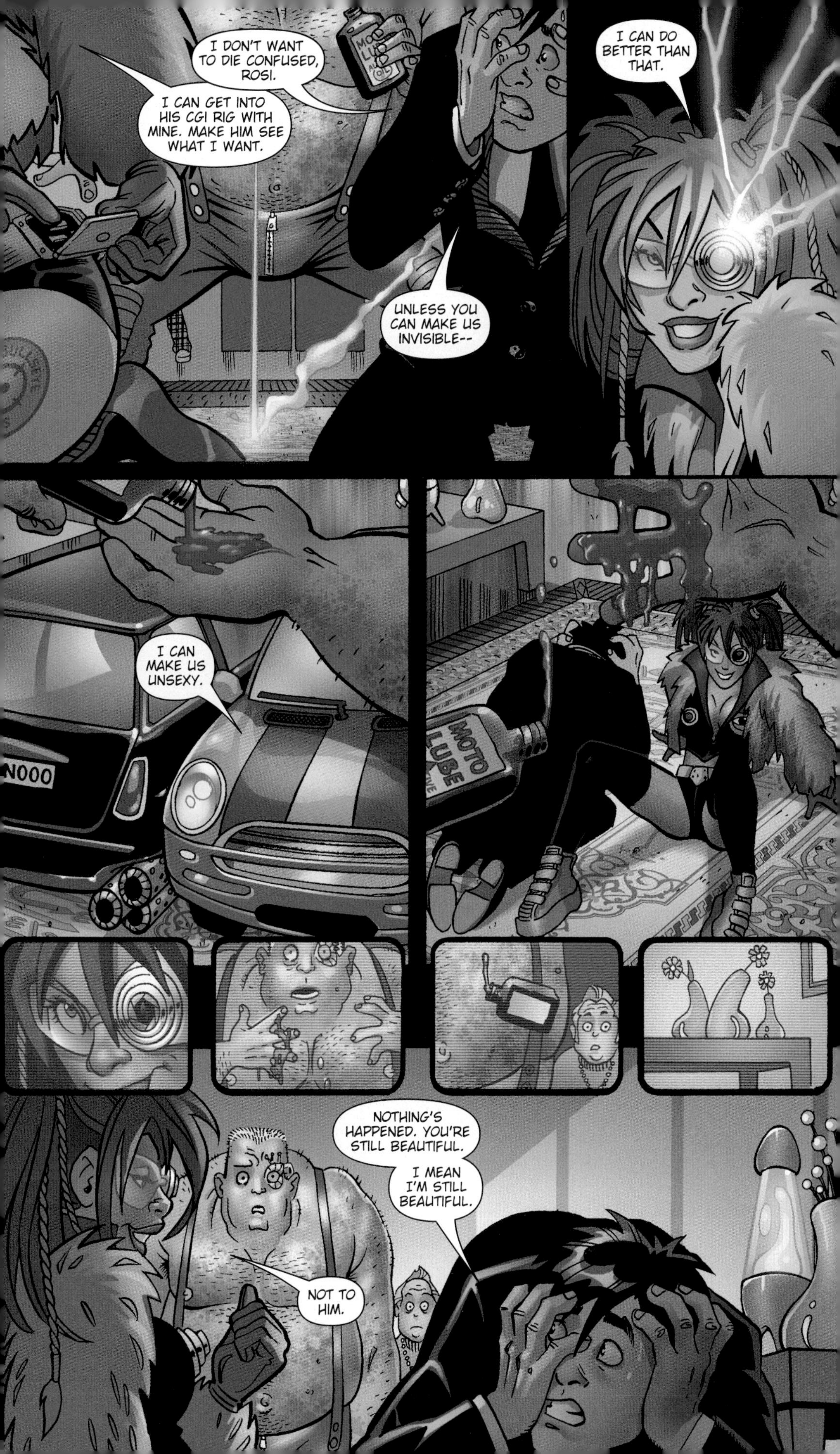
I DON'T WANT TO DIE CONFUSED, ROSI.
I CAN GET INTO HIS CGI RIG WITH MINE. MAKE HIM SEE WHAT I WANT.
UNLESS YOU CAN MAKE US INVISIBLE--
I CAN DO BETTER THAN THAT.
I CAN MAKE US UNSEXY.
MOTO LUBE
NOTHING'S HAPPENED. YOU'RE STILL BEAUTIFUL.
I MEAN I'M STILL BEAUTIFUL.
NOT TO HIM.

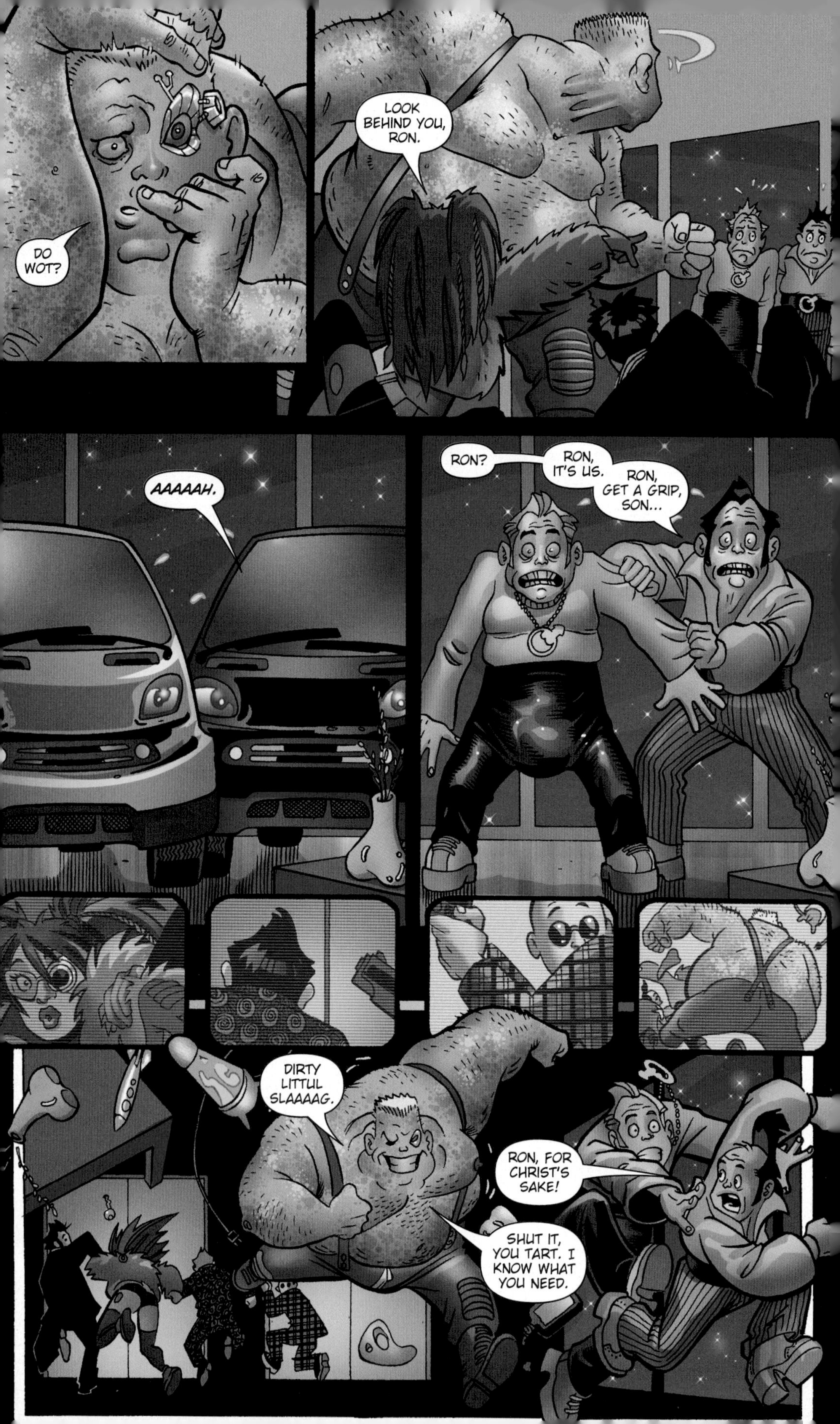
DO WOT?
LOOK BEHIND YOU, RON.
AAAAAH.
RON?
RON, IT'S US.
RON, GET A GRIP, SON...
DIRTY LITTUL SLAAAAG.
RON, FOR CHRIST'S SAKE!
SHUT IT, YOU TART. I KNOW WHAT YOU NEED.

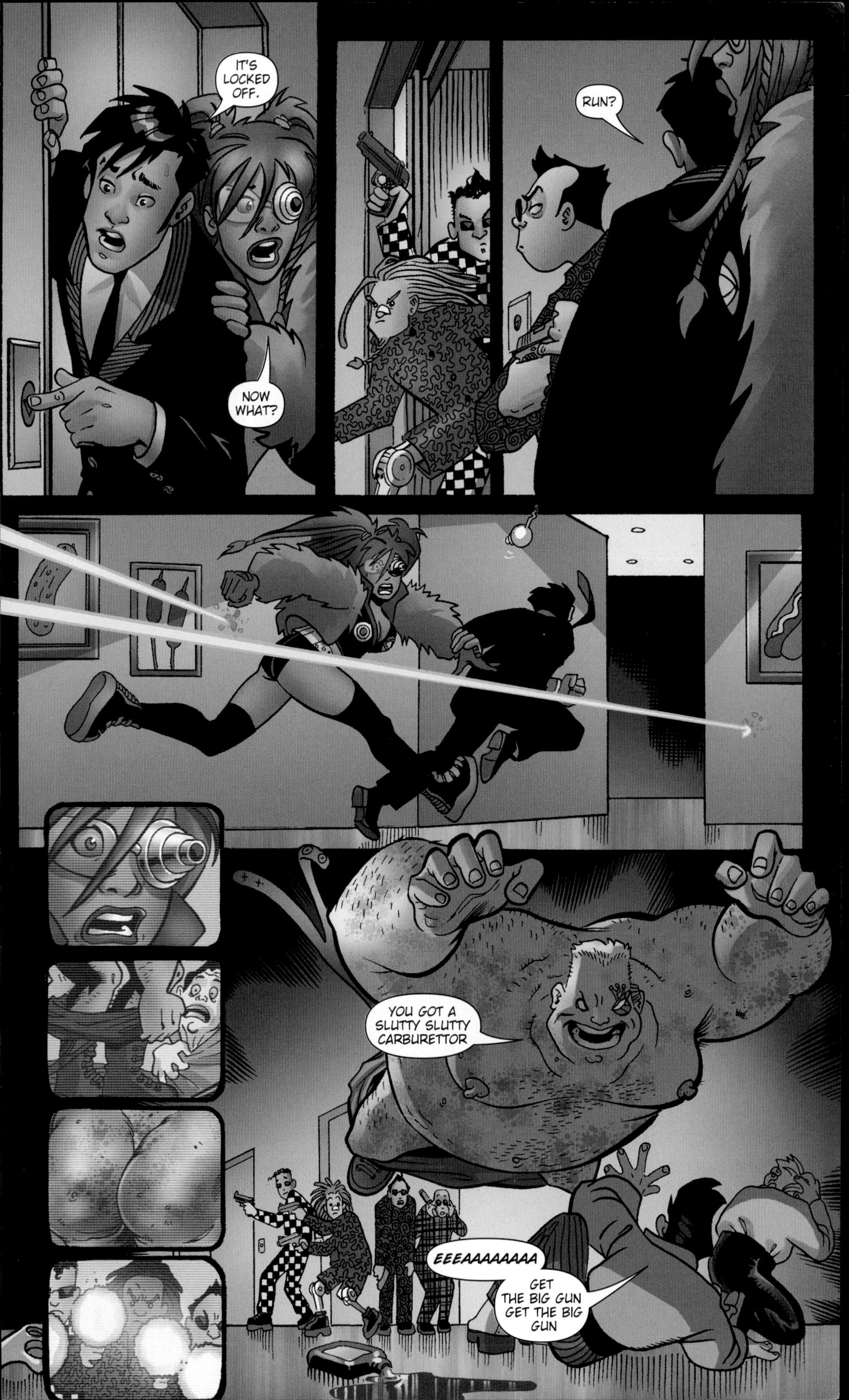
IT'S LOCKED OFF.
NOW WHAT?
RUN?
YOU GOT A SLUTTY SLUTTY CARBURETTOR
EEEAAAAAAAAA
GET THE BIG GUN GET THE BIG GUN

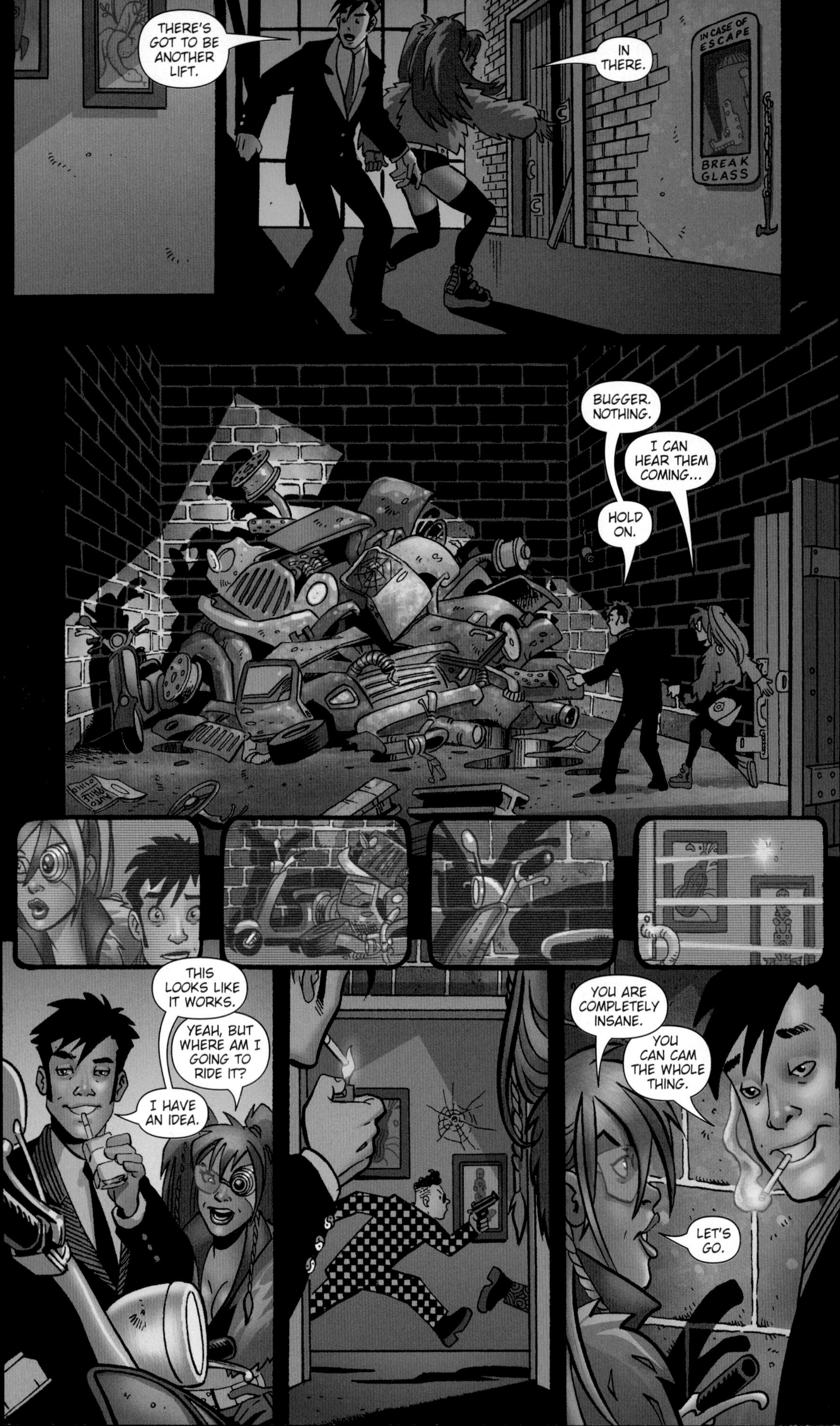
THERE'S GOT TO BE ANOTHER LIFT.
IN THERE.
IN CASE OF ESCAPE
BREAK GLASS
BUGGER. NOTHING.
I CAN HEAR THEM COMING...
HOLD ON.
THIS LOOKS LIKE IT WORKS.
YEAH, BUT WHERE AM I GOING TO RIDE IT?
I HAVE AN IDEA.
YOU ARE COMPLETELY INSANE.
YOU CAN CAM THE WHOLE THING.
LET'S GO.

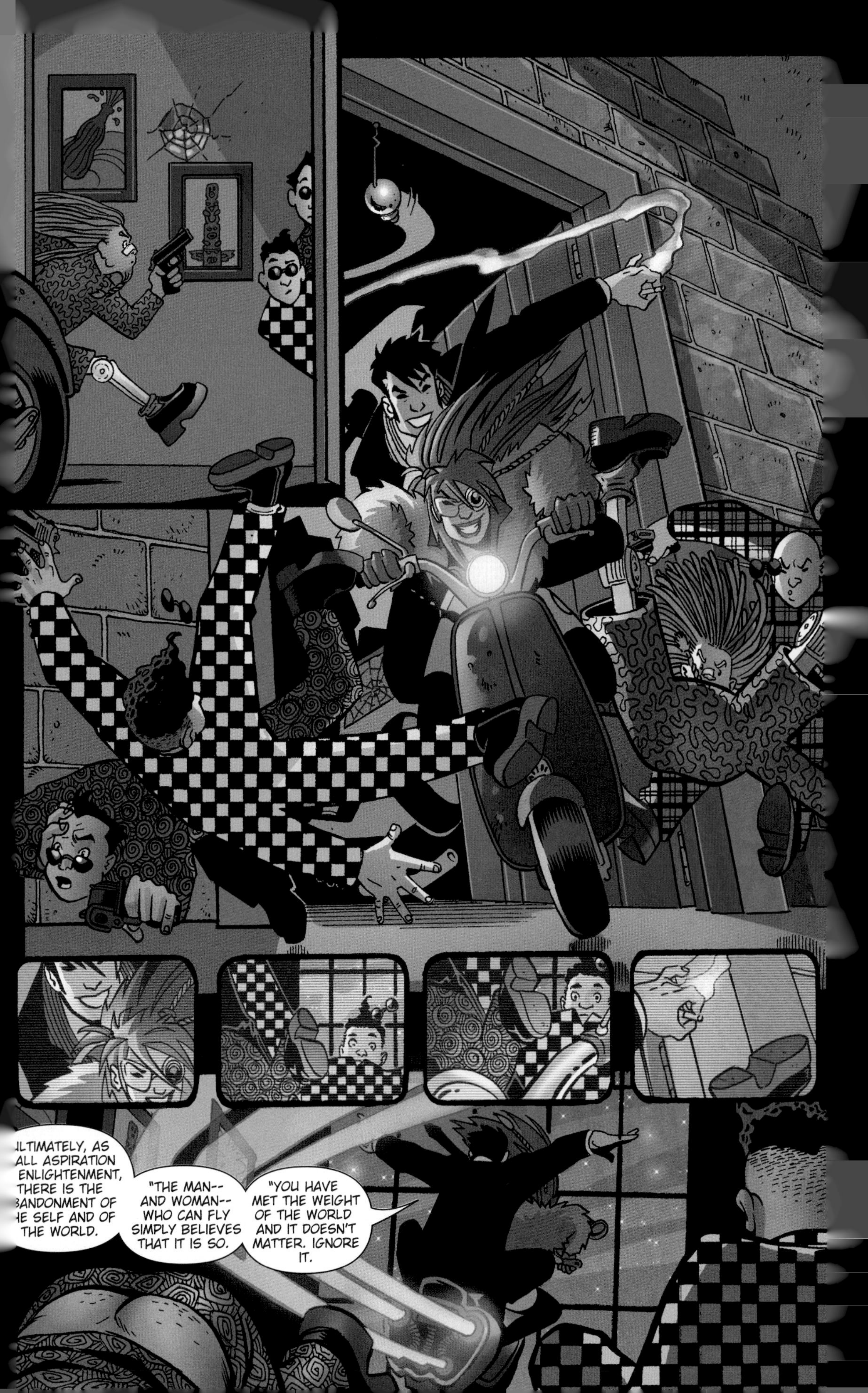
LTIMATELY, AS ALL ASPIRATION ENLIGHTENMENT, THERE IS THE BANDONMENT OF HE SELF AND OF THE WORLD.
"THE MAN-- AND WOMAN-- WHO CAN FLY SIMPLY BELIEVES THAT IT IS SO.
"YOU HAVE MET THE WEIGHT OF THE WORLD AND IT DOESN'T MATTER. IGNORE IT.

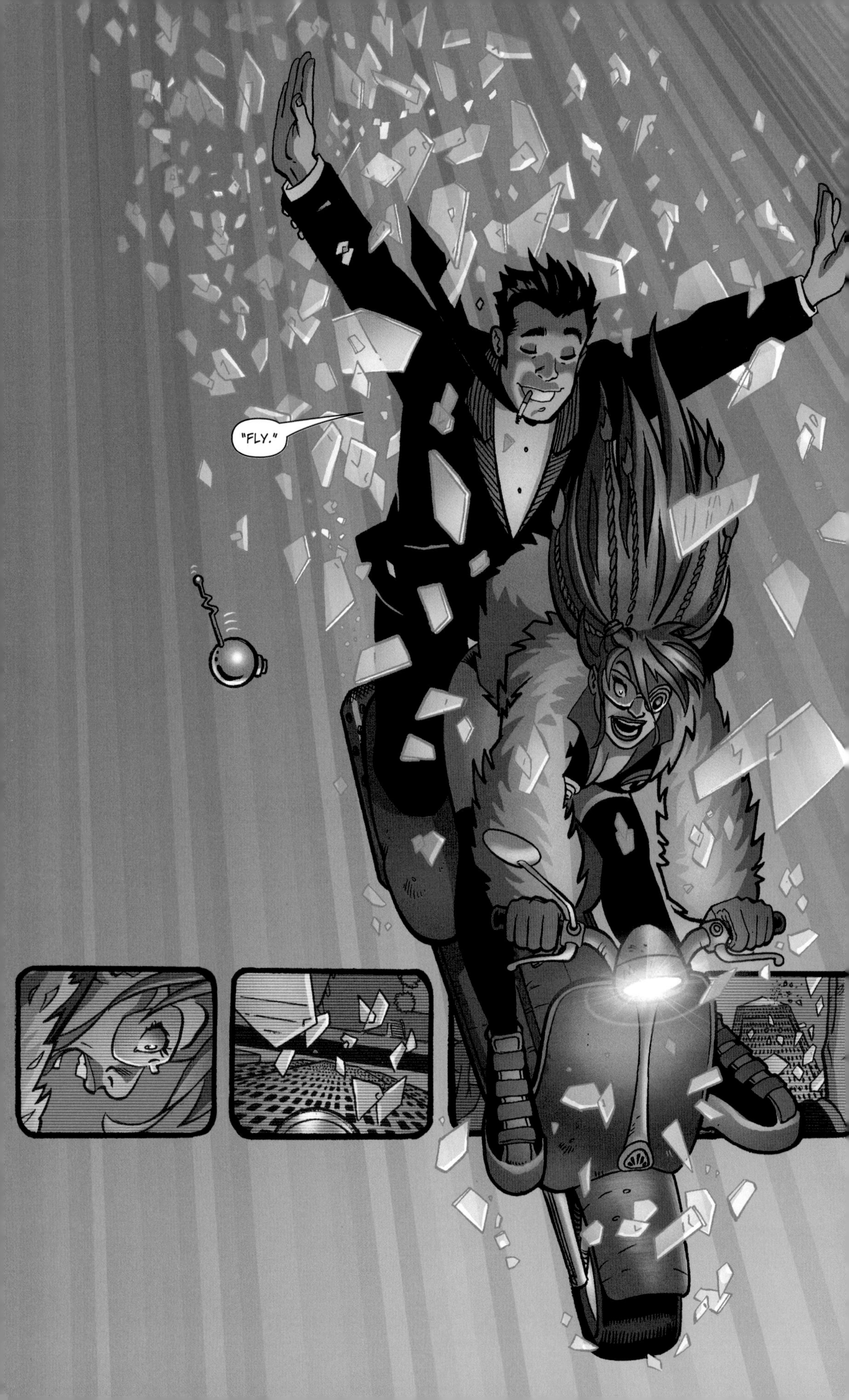
"FLY."

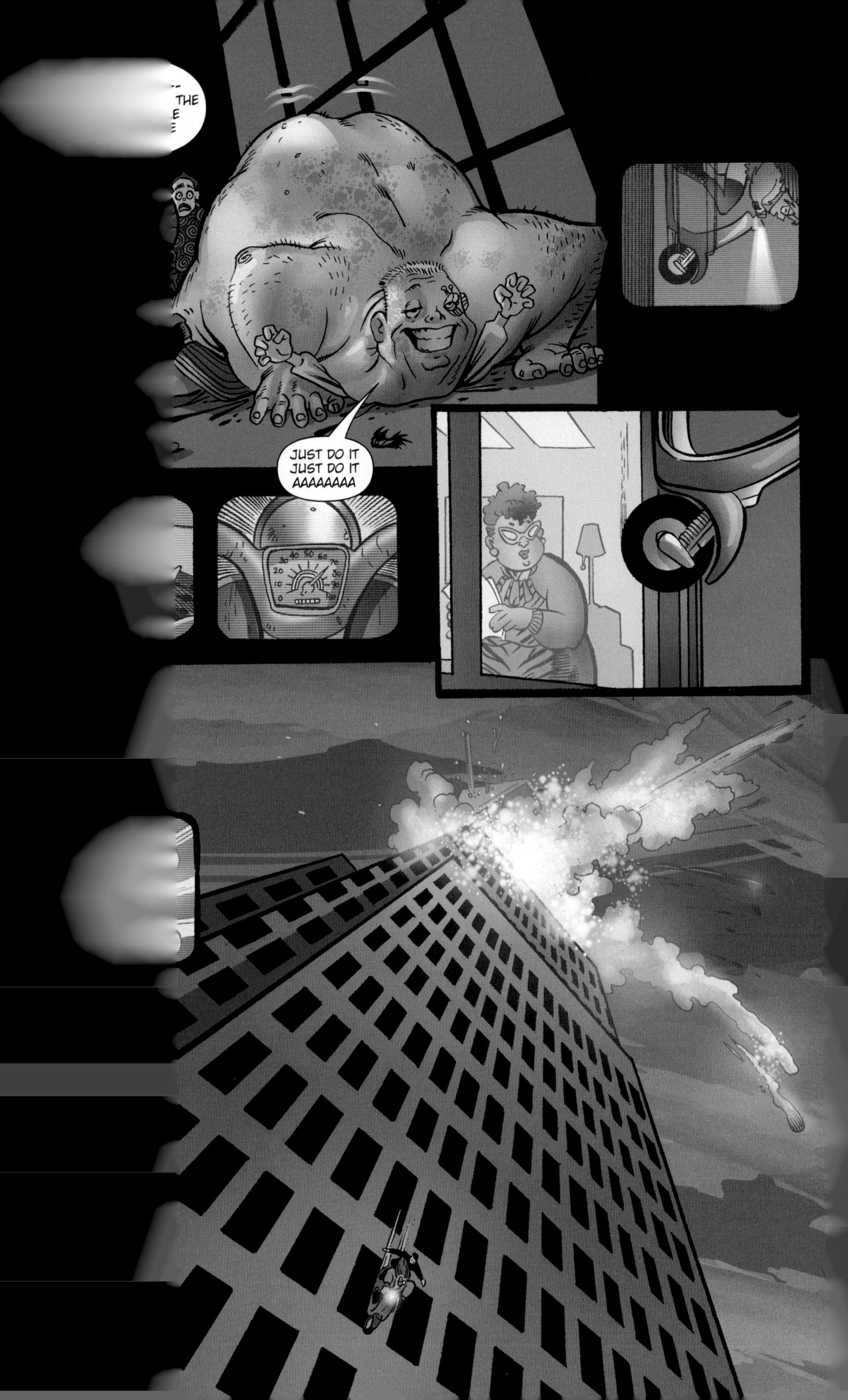
JUST DO IT
JUST DO IT
AAAAAAAA

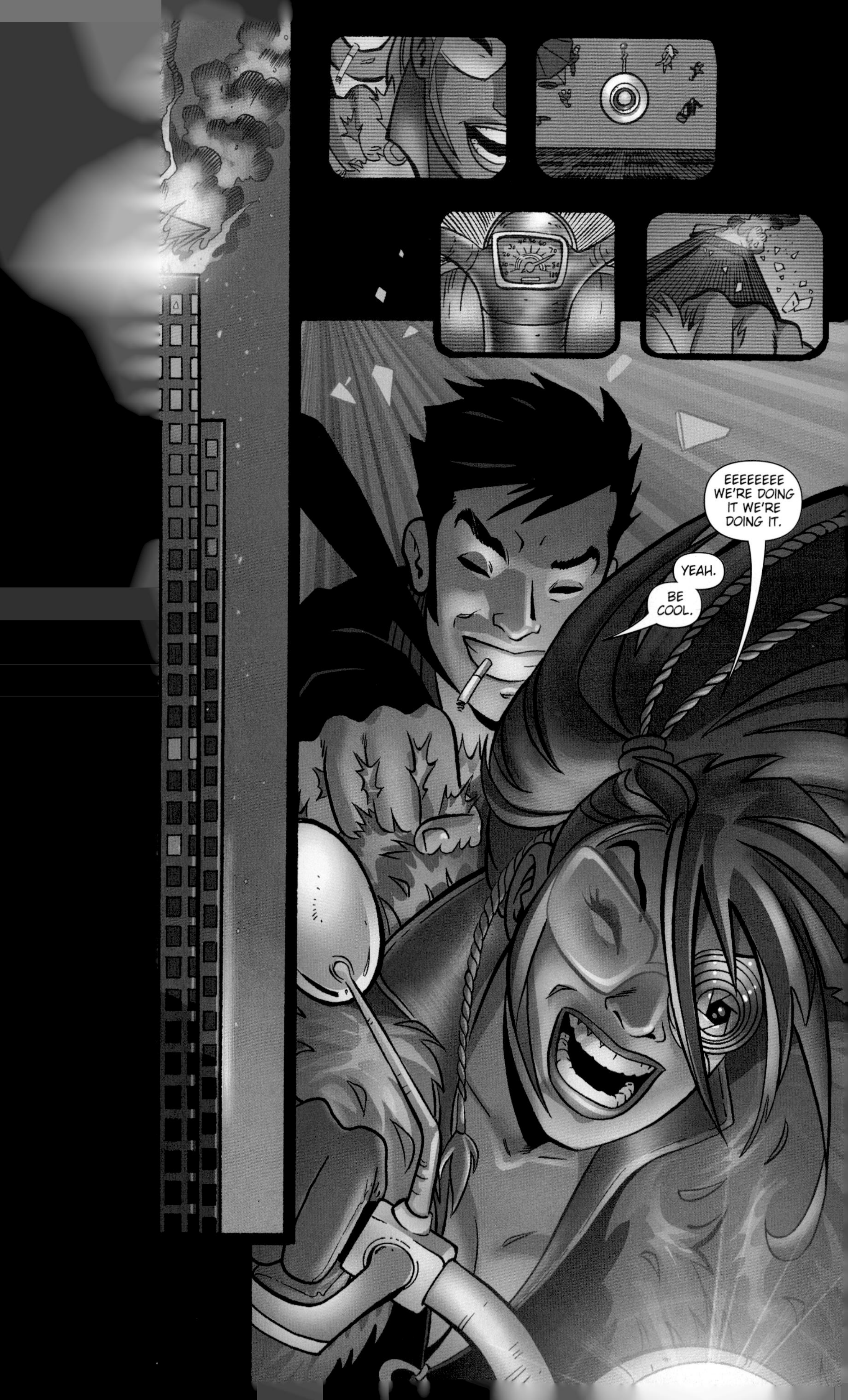
EEEEEEEE WE'RE DOING IT WE'RE DOING IT.
YEAH.
BE COOL.

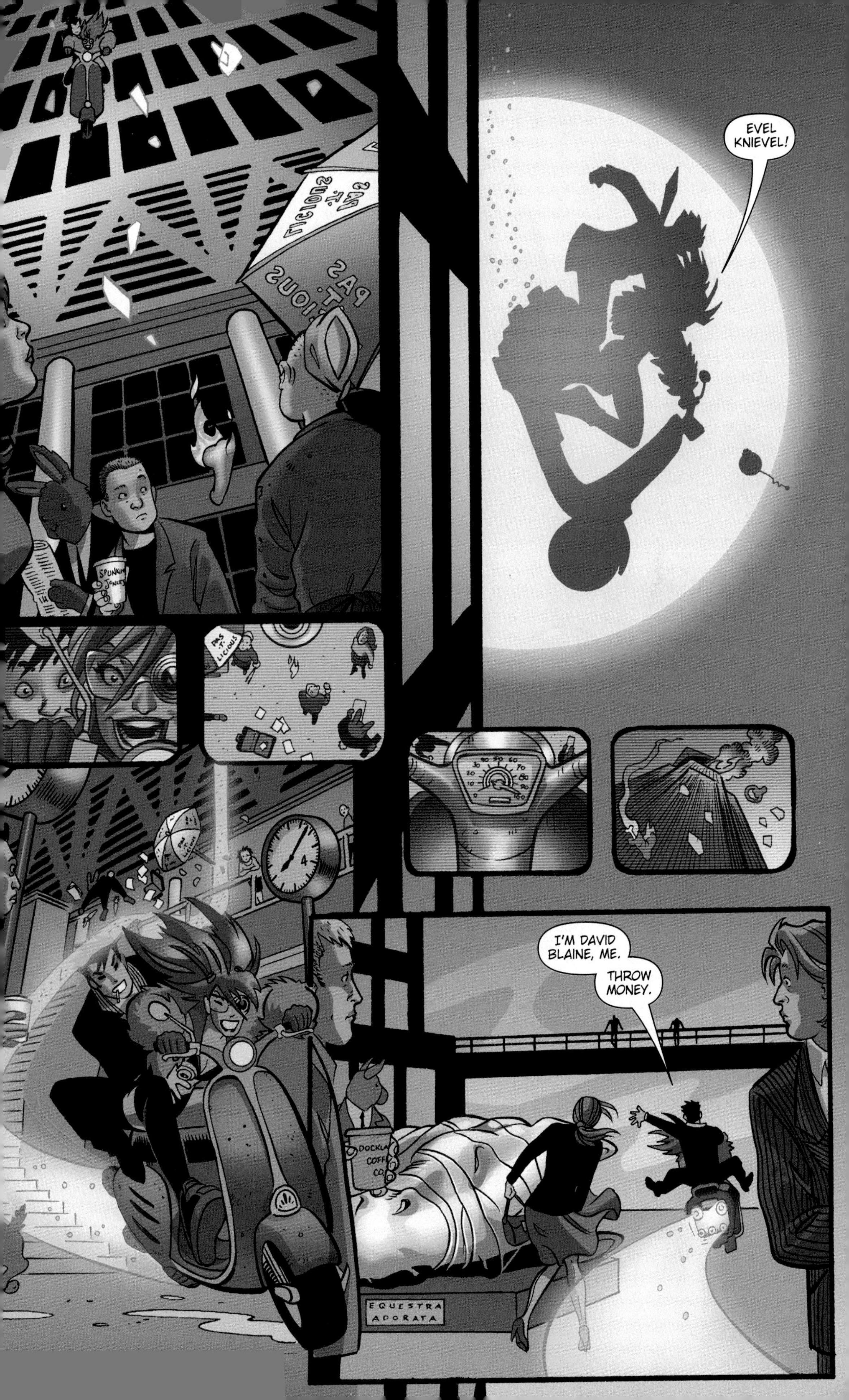
FICIOUS PAS 'T' LICIOUS
PAS 'T' LICIOUS
SPUNKIN' JONUTS
EVEL KNIEVEL!
PAS 'T' LICIOUS
I'M DAVID BLAINE, ME.
THROW MONEY.
EQUESTRA ADORATA

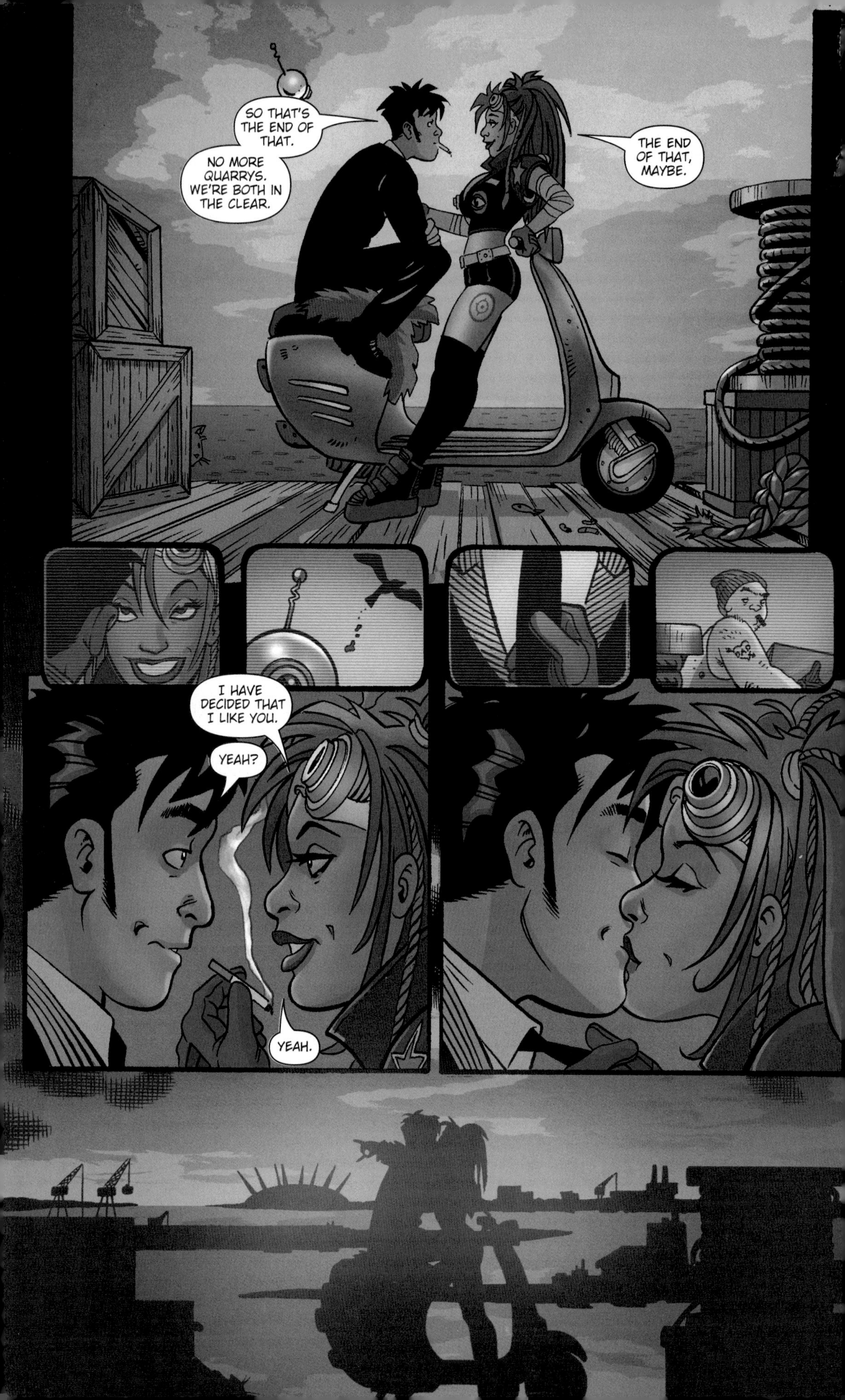
SO THAT'S THE END OF THAT.
NO MORE QUARRYS. WE'RE BOTH IN THE CLEAR.
THE END OF THAT, MAYBE.
I HAVE DECIDED THAT I LIKE YOU.
YEAH?
YEAH.

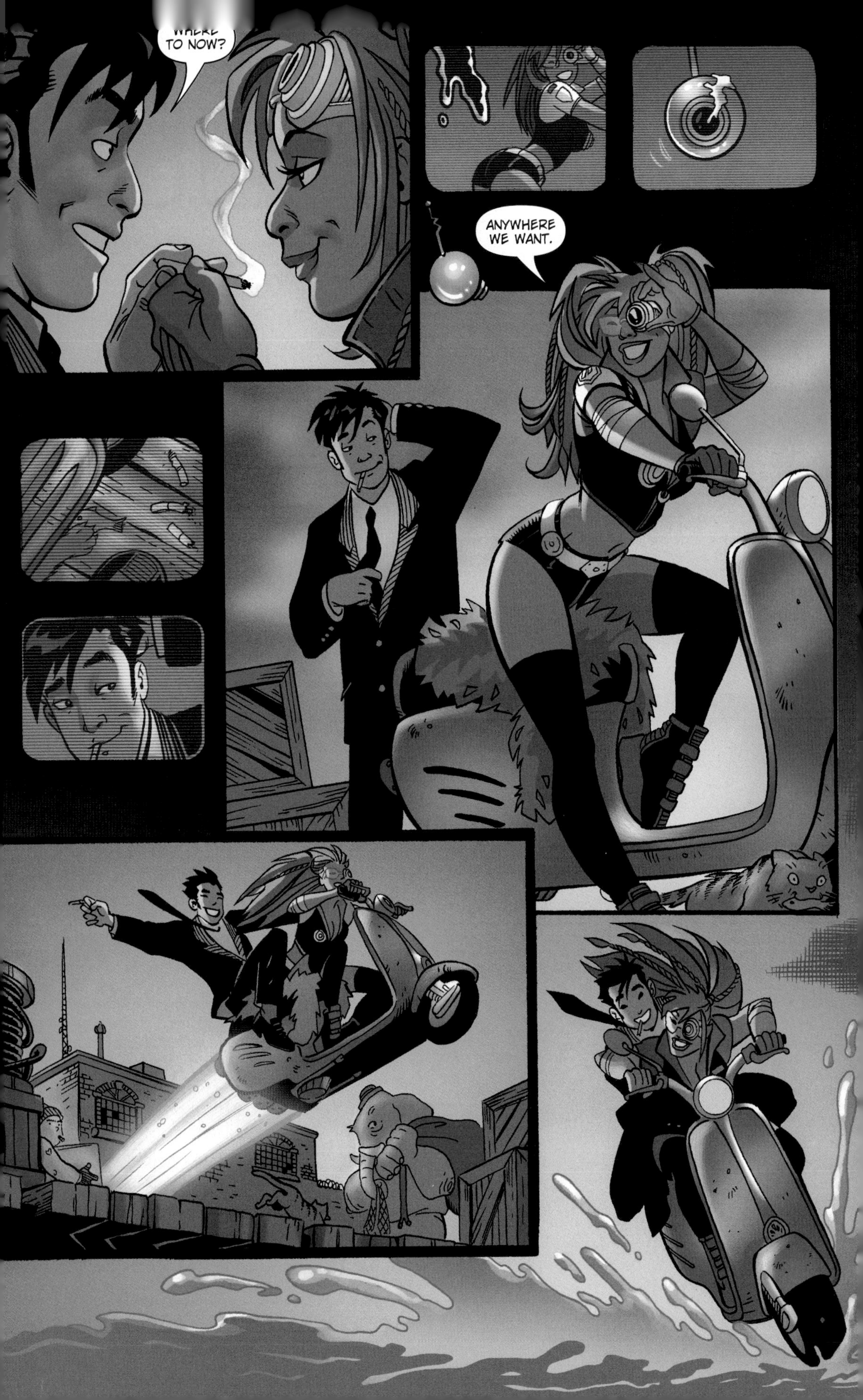
WHERE TO NOW?
ANYWHERE WE WANT.

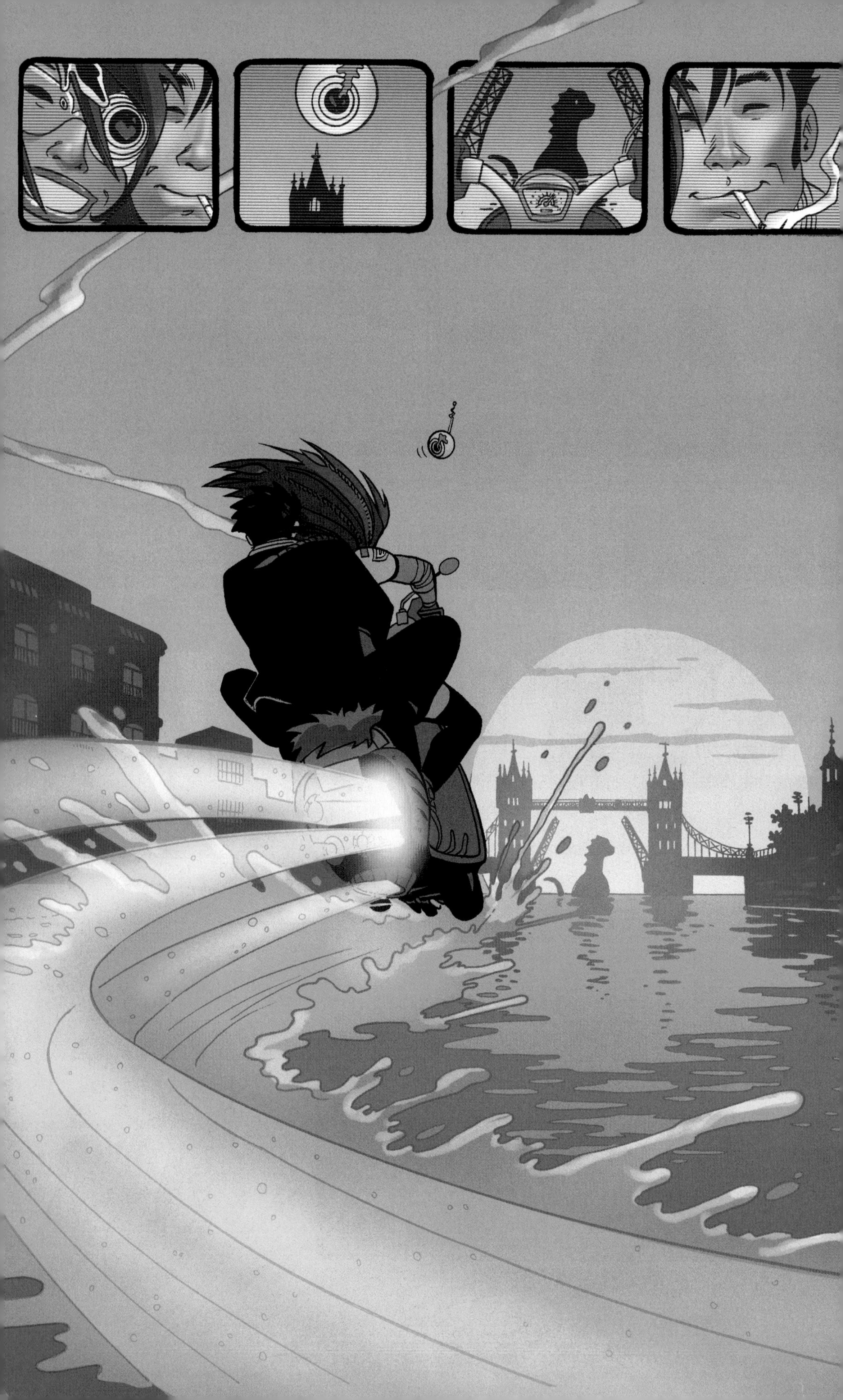

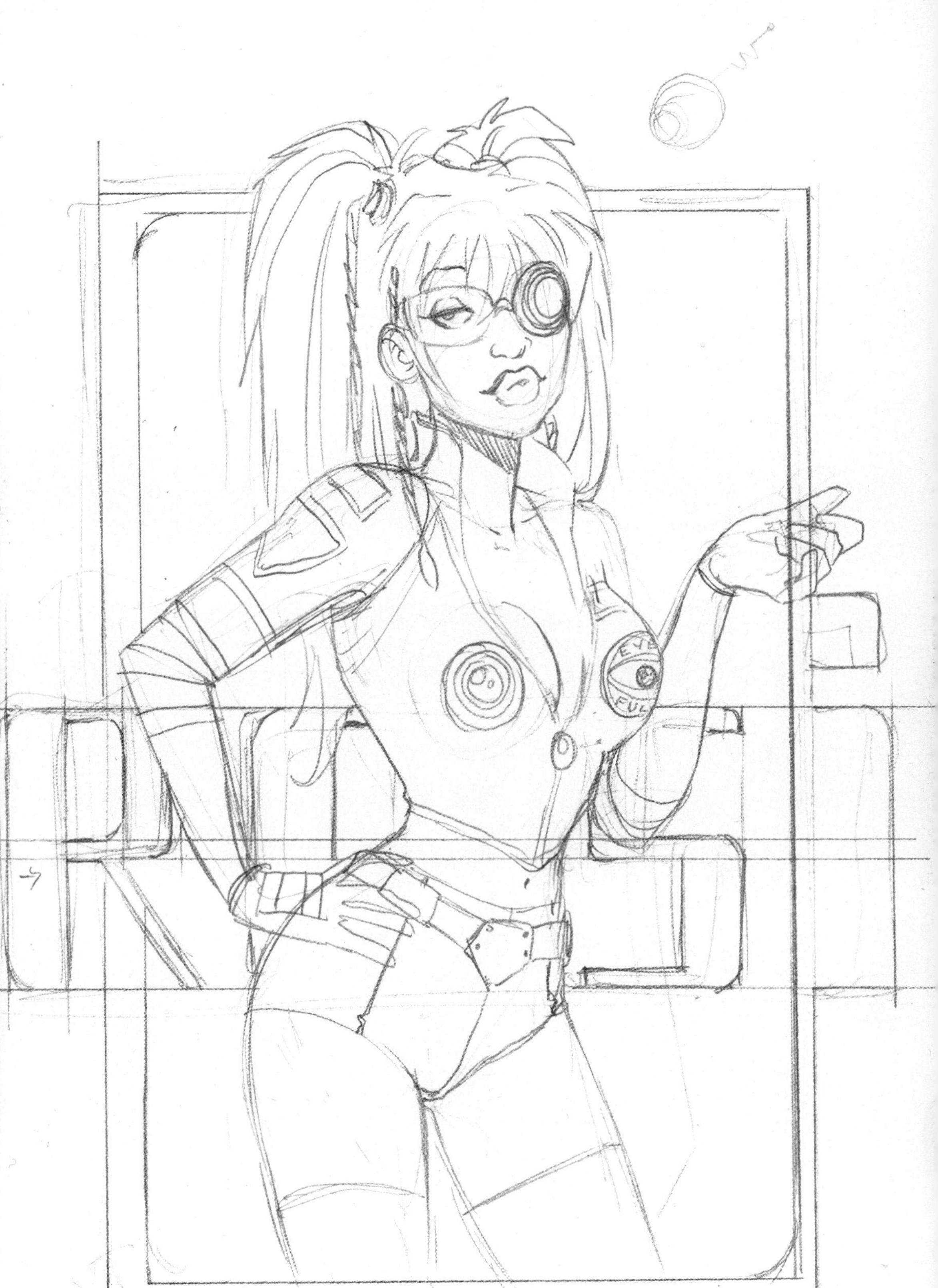
EYE
FUL

SKETCHBOOK

MAYBE SHE SUBSIDISES ALL OF HER VIDEO EQUIPMENT BY LETTING BIG COMPANIES STICK THEIR LOGOS ALL OVER HER (WHICH, I GUESS, ONLY WORKS IF SHE STANDS IN FRONT OF A MIRROR... THEN THEY'D HAVE TO BE WRITTEN BACKWARDS...)

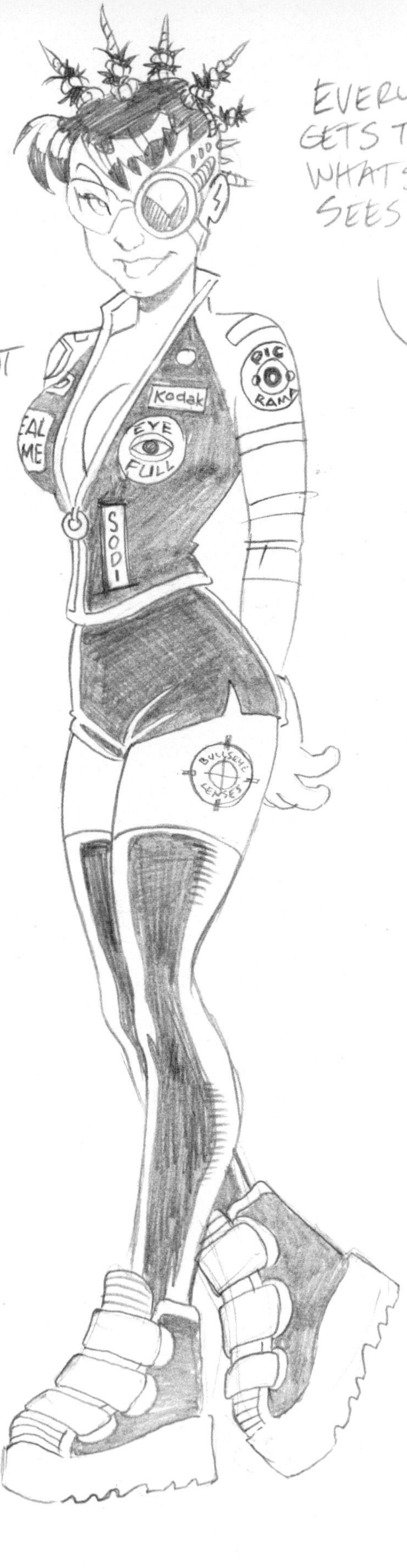
Kodak
EYE FULL
SODI
BIG O RAMA
BULLSEYE LENSES

EVERYBODY GETS TO SEE WHAT SHE SEES

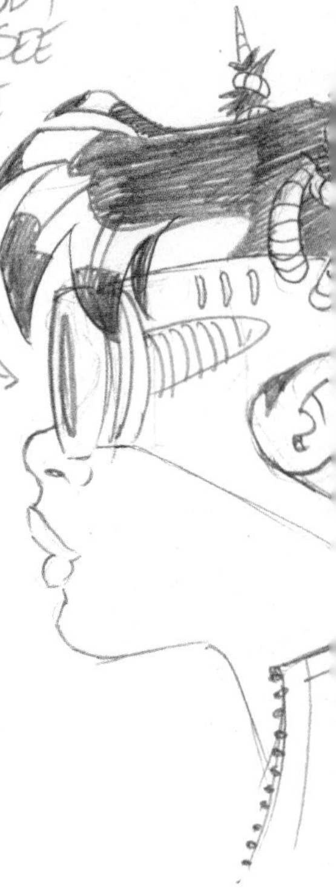

CAMGIRL

ANTENNAE COILED INTO HER HAIR TO PICK UP SAT. SIGNALS

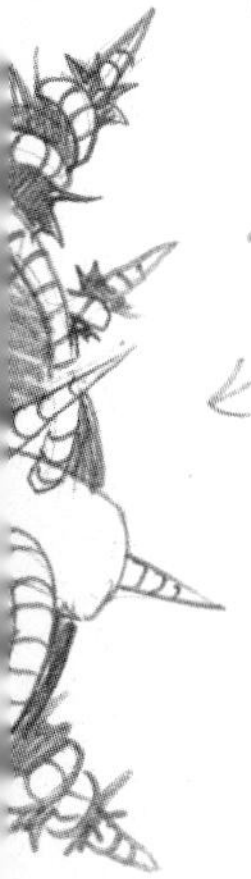

SHOULD WE MAYBE MAKE HER A BLACK GIRL?

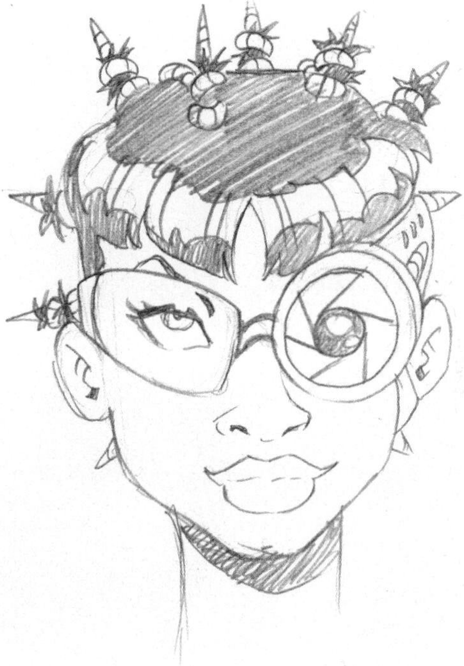

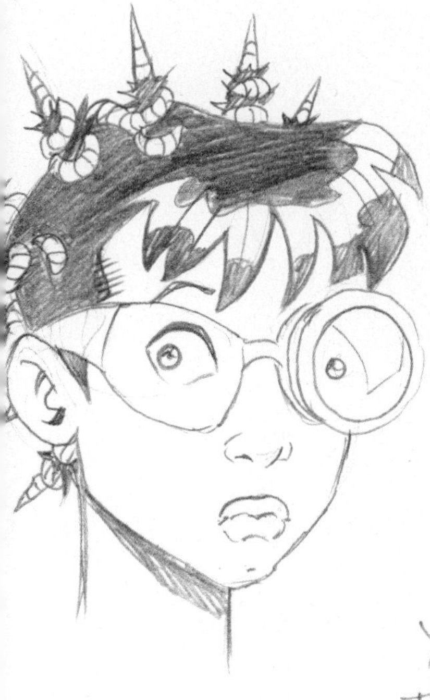

Warren.....

I HAVE NO IDEA WHAT YOU HAVE IN MIND FOR THE LOOK OF EITHER OF THE CHARACTERS SO I'M WINGING IT. I KEEP TRYING TO REMEMBER TO GIVE YOU A CALL, BUT EVERY TIME I THINK OF IT, IT'S ABOUT 2 AM YOUR TIME!

-A

Hmmm...
WHAT WOULD A ZEN GANGSTER WEAR?

GUYS SUITS HAVEN'T CHANGED THAT MUCH IN THE PAST CENTURY SO I DUNNO HOW MUCH THEY'RE GONNA CHANGE IN THE FUTURE.....

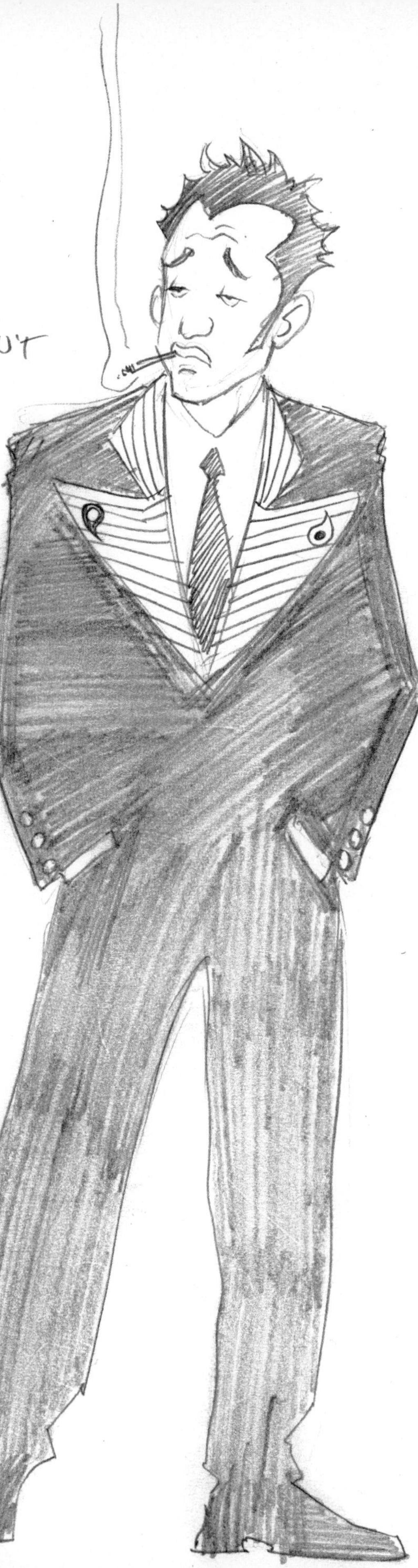

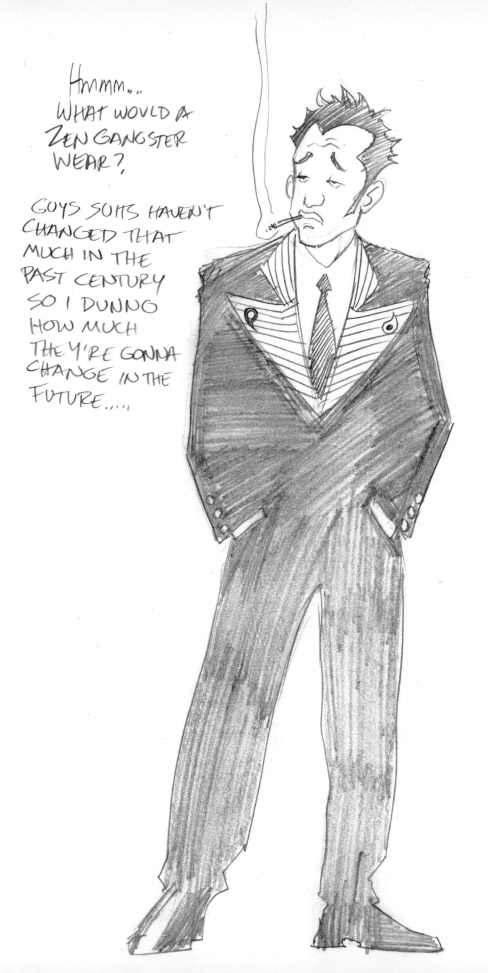

ZENBOY

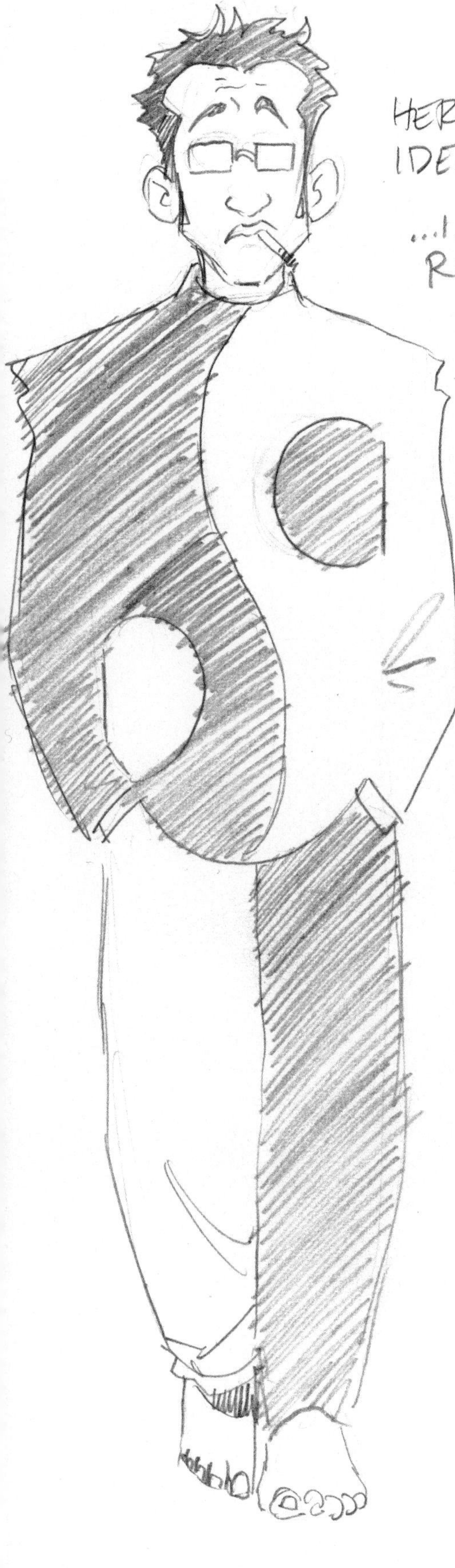

HERE'S ANOTHER IDEA.....

...IS THIS TOO RIDICULOUS?

WRINKLED BROW FROM EXCESSIVE CONTEMPLATING COUPLED WITH THE BORED LOOK OF SOMEONE WHO KILLS FOR A LIVING...

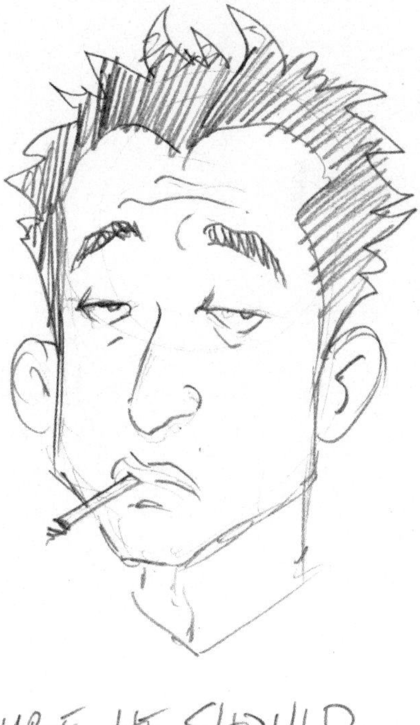

MAYBE HE SHOULD JUST BE NAKED OR IN A LOINCLOTH!

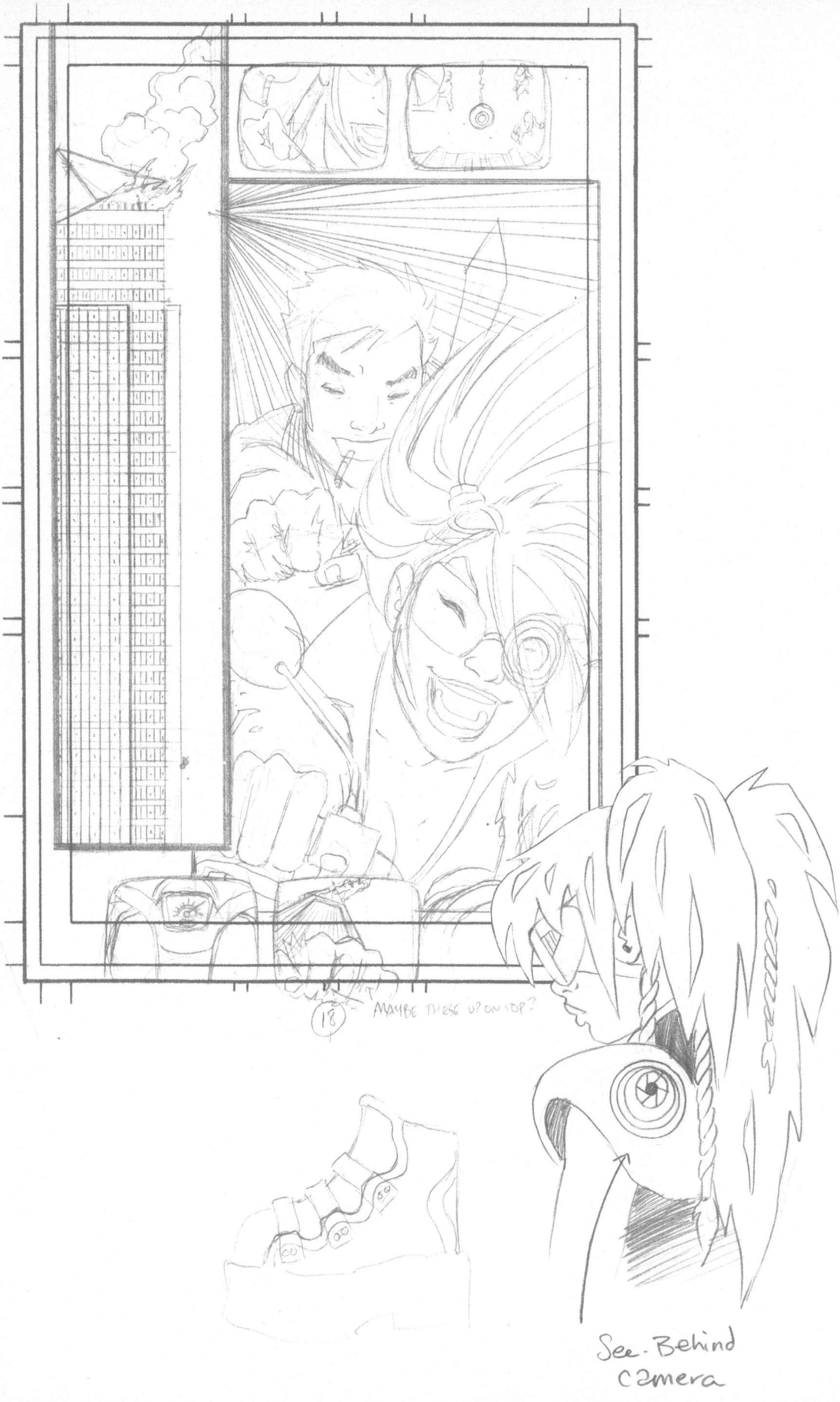
18
MAYBE THESE UP ON TOP?
See-Behind camera

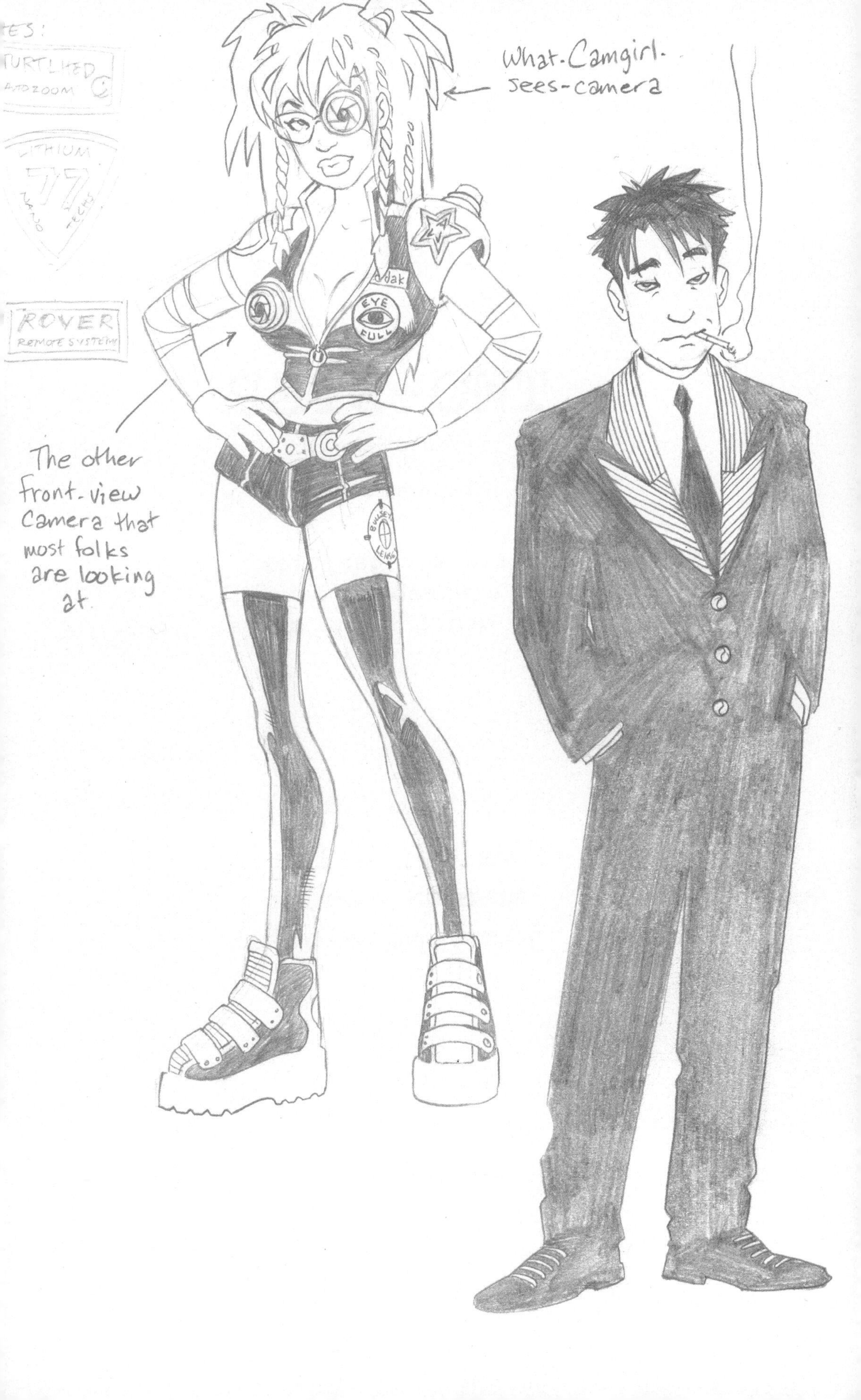

TES:
TURTLHED
AUTOZOOM
LITHIUM
77
ROVER
REMOTE SYSTEMS
What-Camgirl-
sees-camera
odak
EYE
FULL
BULLSEYE
LENS
The other
front-view
camera that
most folks
are looking
at.

TWO-STEP

a weird romance
with guns
in three issues

He's a Zen gangster.
She's a wirehead camgirl.
They don't fight crime.

warren ellis
amanda conner
jimmy palmiotti

It's set in London, but no London you'd ever recognise. Like an
alternate-world London, full of sci-fi shit and wildly multicultural.
Most scenes open with a signpost reading LONDON, written in a different
ethnic script every time. Cloned flocks of Bollywood chorus girls
walking the streets, hordes of Chinese men in black suits constantly
shooting at each other in Chinatown, giant robots fucking on the banks
of the Thames at low tide.

The boy is a young London gangster with a Zen attitude, waiting for
trouble to find him. The girl is a mobile camgirl, wirelessly hooked
up to the net and broadcasting everything she sees, looking for trouble
to boost her hit count and give her a reason to be interested in life.

He's a Zen gangster. She's a bored camgirl. They don't fight crime.

They meet when she thinks he's being assaulted by another gangster. He
was actually doing the mugging, intercepting a specially-created
artificial penis for transplant onto one of the principles of the
Quarry gang, a berserk mob of congenital dwarves living in the
pyramidal summit of the riverside Canary Tower and obsessed with
possessing monstrous dongs (never seen, of course). By lifting this
foul high-tech member that plays Ride Of The Valkyries when aroused,
our boy has damaged the rep of the gang. At least, as far as they're
concerned. They have lost face. The honour of the Quarry Gang and
their immense artificial cocks must be avenged.

Dirty Ron, Quarry enforcer, he who can kill Volvos by shagging them, is
released upon our couple -- a couple who genuinely can't stand each
other, but are completely fascinated by each other.

Mob gunfights in a fair on a frozen River Thames. The logistics of
riding a Vespa down the side of a hundred-storey building. And two
people whose careers kind of depend on them never falling in love.
Two-step.

PAGE ONE

Pic 1:
Three page-wide panels.

By the edge of a highway, there's a low sign. It reads WELCOME TO LONDON, but it's in Indian script -- by Indian, I mean subcontinental India, not Injuns.

DISPLAY LETT;   TWO-STEP
            part one

Pic 2;
Jump/zoom – and the highway has changed into a city street, and we're blitzing past curry houses and cinemas showing Bollywood musicals.

DISPLAY LETT;   by WARREN ELLIS and AMANDA CONNER and JIMMY
            PALMIOTTI

Pic 3;
CUT TO; A welter of undulating blue arms, a close-in shot on them, like a cropped image of Kali posing, only probably with more arms…

DISPLAY LETT;   with colours by *** and lettering by **** and *** as the editor

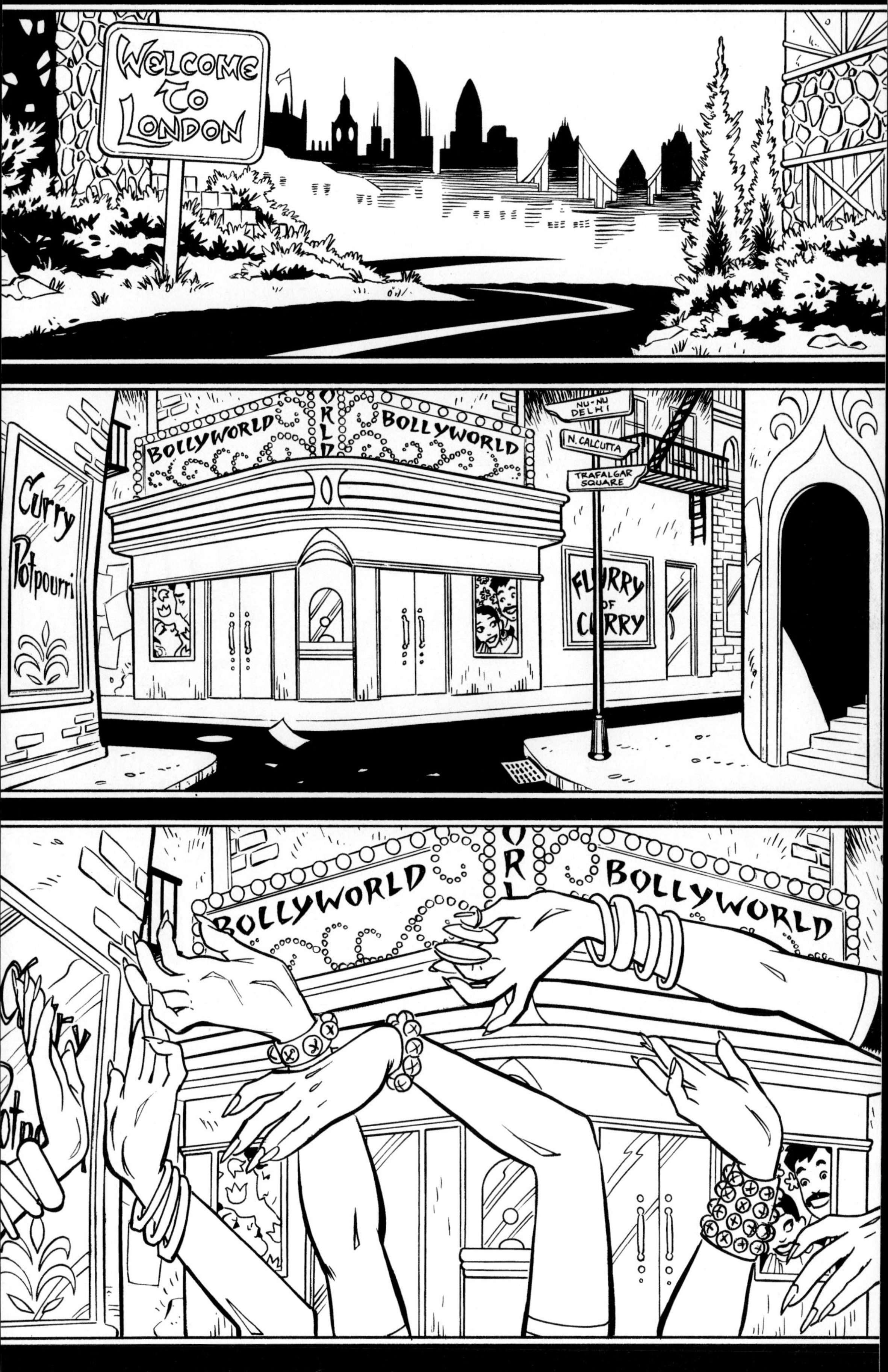
WELCOME TO LONDON
BOLLYWORLD
BOLLYWORLD
NU-NU DELHI
N. CALCUTTA
TRAFALGAR SQUARE
Curry Potpourri
FLURRY OF CURRY
BOLLYWORLD
BOLLYWORLD

PAGES TWO and THREE

Pic 1;
And we pull back on a London junction, all the buildings being either cinemas or nightclubs, and a flock of cloned Kali-blue Bollywood dancing girls flow past us, revealing the buildings behind them, and the kids dancing, the multiracial weird beautiful sci-fi kids of London.

And on the fire escape on the side of one of the buildings, sitar heroes play, Indian men in leather jackets or Hendrix tie-dyes striking poses with their sitars, doing Pete Townsend arm-whirls…

It's a wild night in London.

DISPLAY LETT; LONDON, ENGLAND; 2001

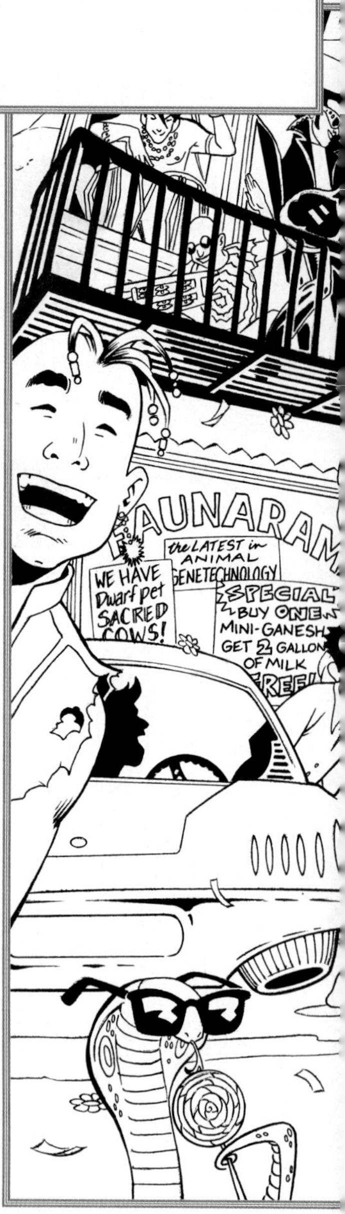

the LATEST in ANIMAL GENETECHNOLOGY
WE HAVE Dwarf pet SACRED COWS!
SPECIAL
BUY ONE
MINI-GANESH
GET 2 GALLON
OF MILK

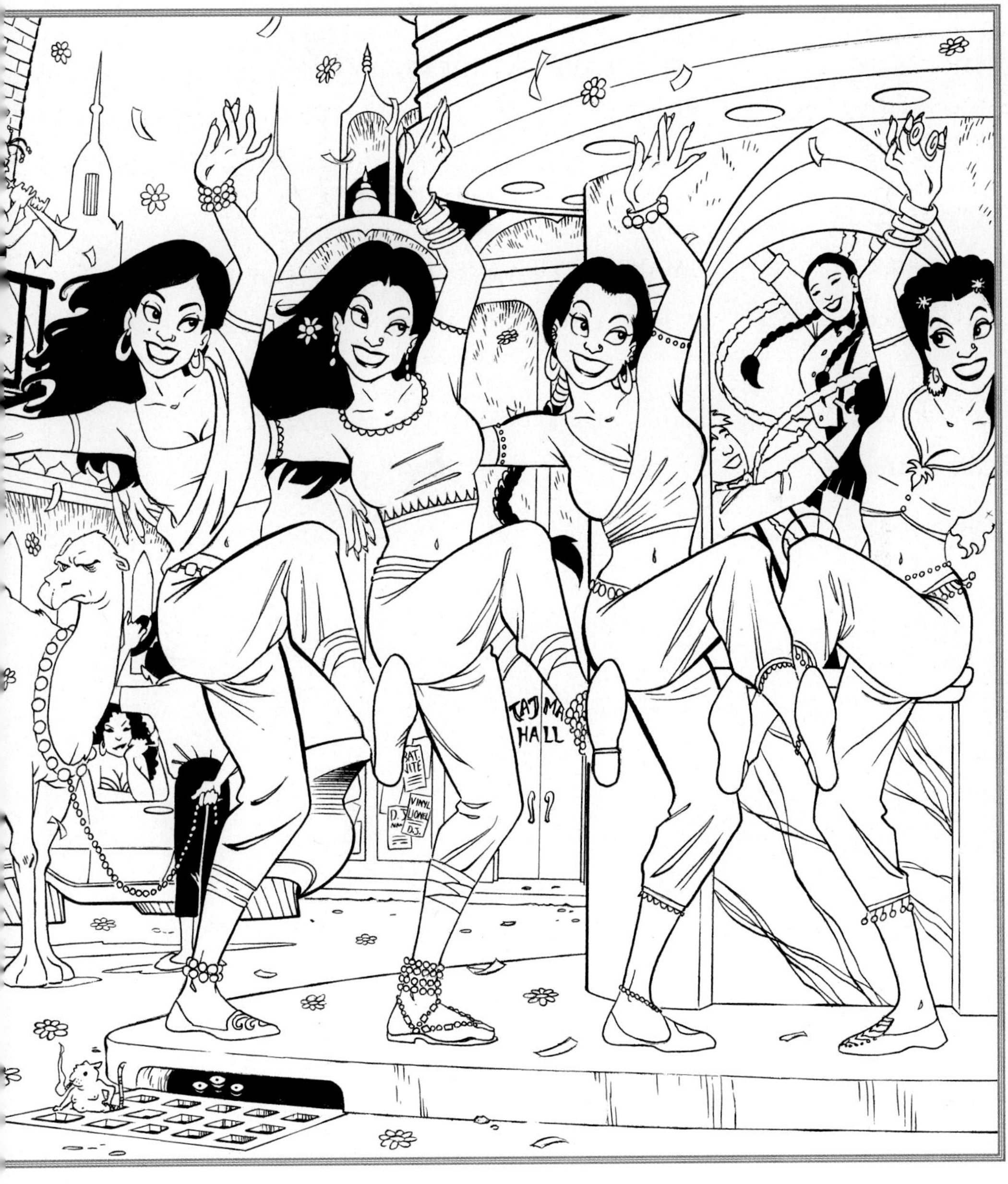
TAJ MA
HALL
VINYL
LIONEL
D.J.

PAGE FOUR

Pic 1;
Call out some sections of the whole – the Greek chorus of blue girls
sliding past us and smiling, all making the same motions, all with the
same smiles --

CHORUS GIRLS;   UP AND DOWN THE CITY ROAD

CHORUS GIRLS;   IN AND OUT THE EAGLE

CHORUS GIRLS;   THAT'S THE WAY THE MONEY GOES

Pic 2;
CUT TO; one of our guitar/sitar heroes, bashing his instrument – maybe
make him an Indian Elvis impersonator, I dunno, have some fun with
this…

SITAR HERO;   MAYBE IT'S BECAUSE I'M A LONDONER

SITAR HERO;   THAT I LOVE LONDON TOWN

Pic 3;
Aerial view, looking down on this street-party junction…

(no dialogue)

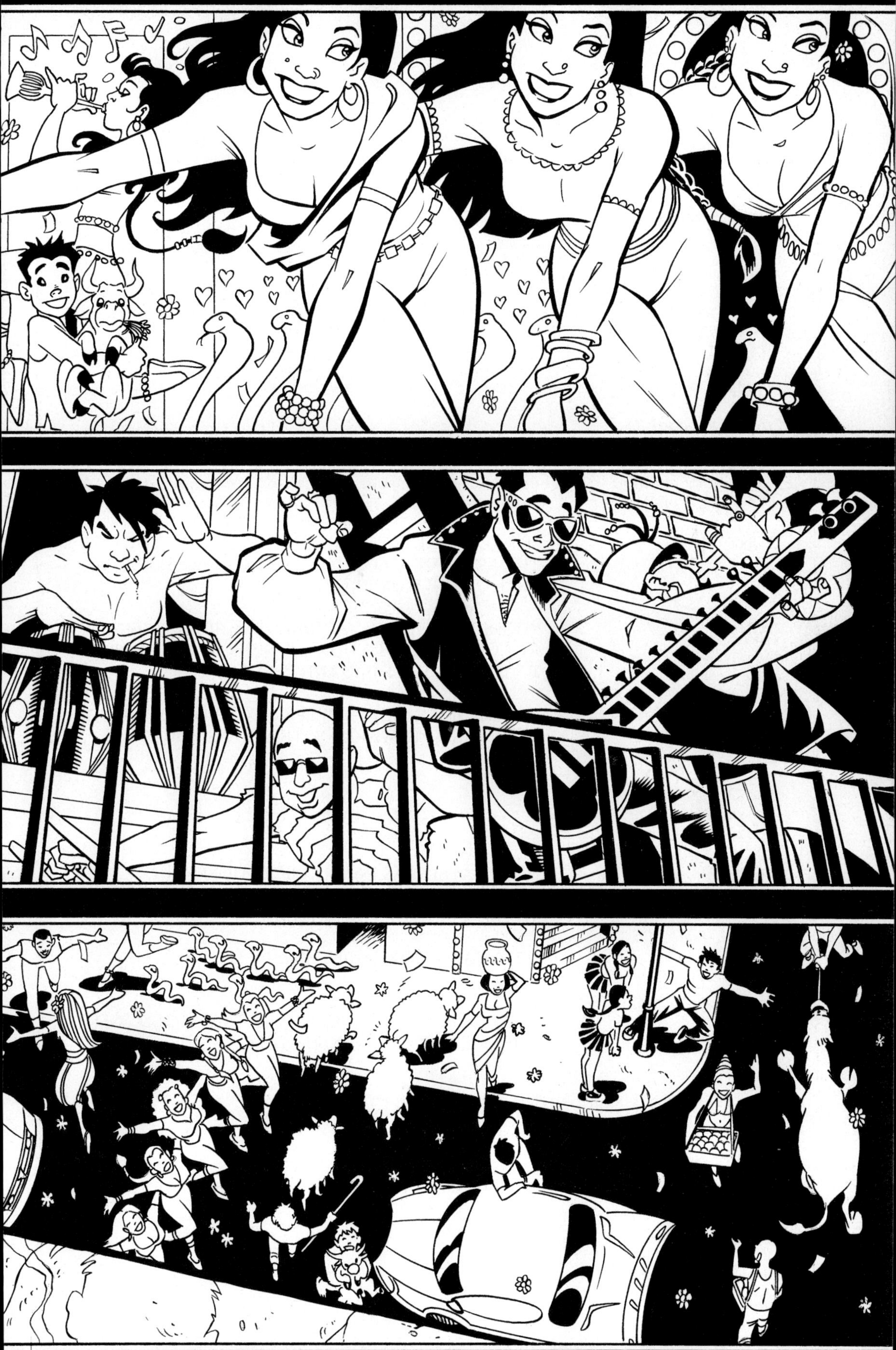

PAGE FIVE

Pic 1;
…finding ourselves on one building's roof.

On the edge of which, our Zen Gangster sits. His name is TONY LING.
Ling means zero in Cantonese, which I like, for reasons you'll see in a
sec.

Reading a book.

(no dialogue)

Pic 2;
Pan round on him; cigarette lazily hanging from his lips as he studies
his book, the cover of which reads: ZEN FLIGHT.

TONY:	"FIRST, THERE IS THE TRAINING WITH WEIGHTS ON THE ARMS AND LEGS, TO UNDERSTAND FULLY THE PULL OF THE WORLD.
TONY:	"THEN THERE IS THE DIGGING OF A HOLE, ITSELF AN ACT OF CONTEMPLATION. AT SUNRISE AND SUNSET, JUMP FROM THE HOLE AND RETURN.
TONY;	"AS THE HOLE GROWS DEEPER, CONSIDER YOUR CHI, AND HURL IT UPWARDS WITH YOU AS YOU JUMP.

Pic 3;
He stands up, an effortless flow, still with his eyes glued to the
book, still on the very edge of the flat roof.

TONY:	"ULTIMATELY, AS IN ALL ASPIRATION TO ENLIGHTENMENT, THERE IS THE ABANDONMENT OF THE SELF AND OF THE WORLD.
TONY;	"THE MAN WHO CAN FLY SIMPLY BELIEVES THAT IT IS SO."
TONY;	"YOU HAVE MET THE WEIGHT OF THE WORLD AND IT DOESN'T MATTER. IGNORE IT. FLY."

Pic 4;
He pushes the book into one jacket pocket, frowning.

TONY;	JUST LET IT HAPPEN.
TONY;	STORY OF MY LIFE, THAT.

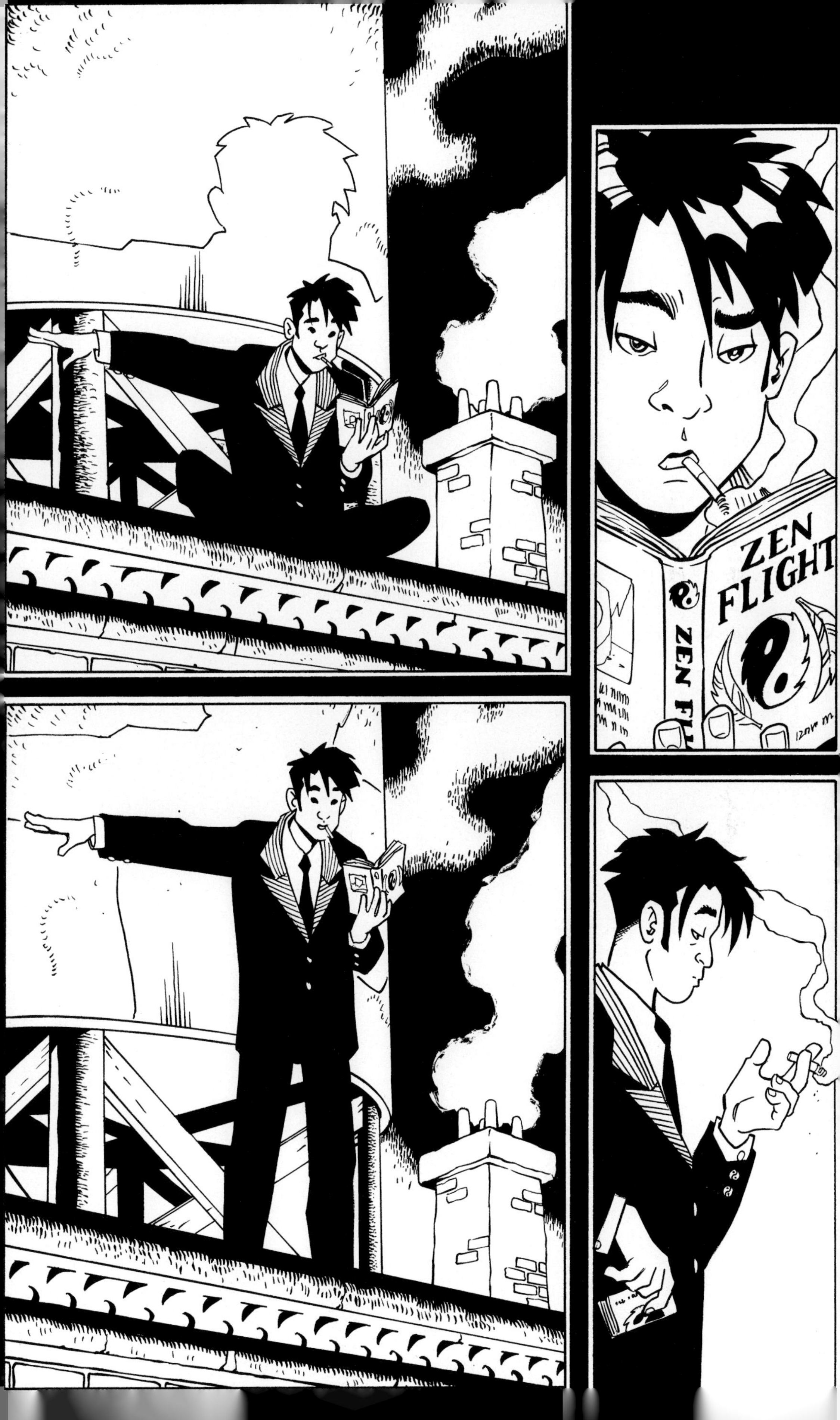
ZEN
FLIGHT

PAGE SIX

Pic 1;
Pan around, so he has his back to us… slight wind up here whipping his tie around, pushing smoke off his cigarette.

TONY;   WELL, OBVIOUSLY I'D HAVE TO BE BLOODY MAD TO BELIEVE I COULD LEARN TO FLY FROM A BOOK I PICKED UP DOWN BRICK LANE.

Pic 2;
And in the next pic, he's gone - all we see is his tie disappearing over the edge of the roof and a skein of cigarette smoke. The silly bastard's jumped.

(no dialogue)

Pic 3;
We lunge to the edge of the roof, looking down --

(no dialogue)

Pic 4;
-- and we don't see him, but from above we see our CAMGIRL moving through the crowds at the street junction.

(no dialogue)

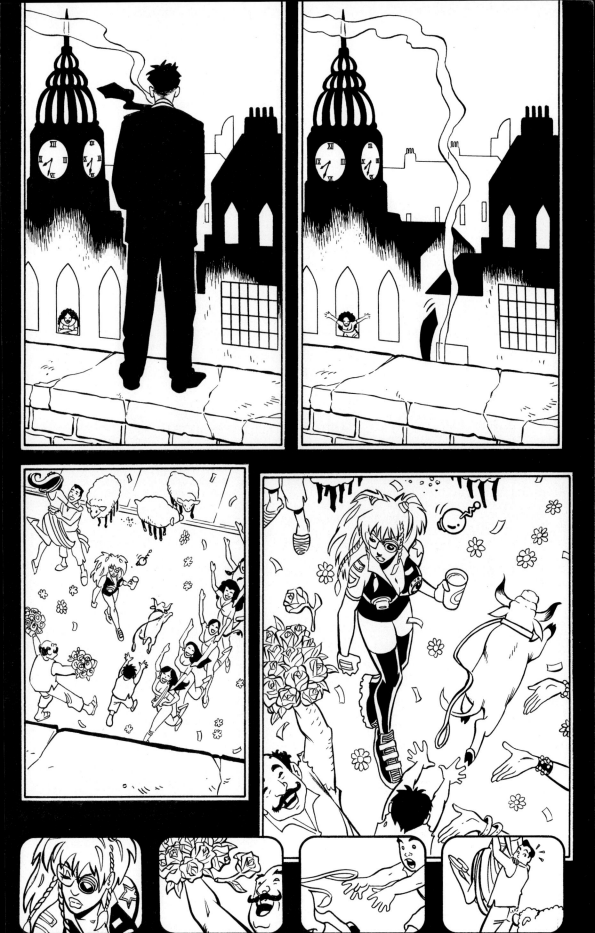

Pic 1;
And she looks up at us, right into our eyes: (and her NAME is ROSI
BLADES)

ROSI;   I AM SO BORED I COULD **FART BLOOD**.

Pic 2;
Pan down, to capture her walking towards us. One other addition to her
– she needs to have a tiny floating camera facing her at all times.
She's walking through the crowds, pissed off, not really seeing
anything around her, not really giving a shit either way…

ROSI;   THIS IS THE VOICE OF ROSI BLADES, MOST-CLICKED
                               CAMGIRL IN LONDON, AND YOU'RE LOOKING AT ME
                               AS WELL AS WHAT I SEE --

ROSI;   -- AND WHAT I SEE BORES MY TITS OFF.

Pic 3;
CUT TO; A small dark apartment, and a bank of computer monitors on a
low table. One shows Rosi in the floating cam's POV, and the image is
called ROSICAM. One shows one angle of what's in front of her, and
that's called ROSIPOV1. The next shows the scene around her from a
slightly different angle, and it's called ROSIPOV2. And in front of
all that, two cats are having sex.

JAGGED (NO TAIL);   TWENTY THOUSAND OF YOU BASTARDS ON THE
                               INTERNET WATCHING ME BE PISS-BORED WITH THIS
                               CITY AND EVERYTHING IN IT.

JAGGED (NO TAIL);   STREET-BOLLYWOOD IS SO LAST SEASON THAT IT'S
                               NOT EVEN PATHETIC.

JAGGED (NO TAIL);   IT'S JUST KIND OF YEAH, COULD YOU MAYBE JUST
                               DIE NOW AND GET OUT OF MY SODDING WAY?

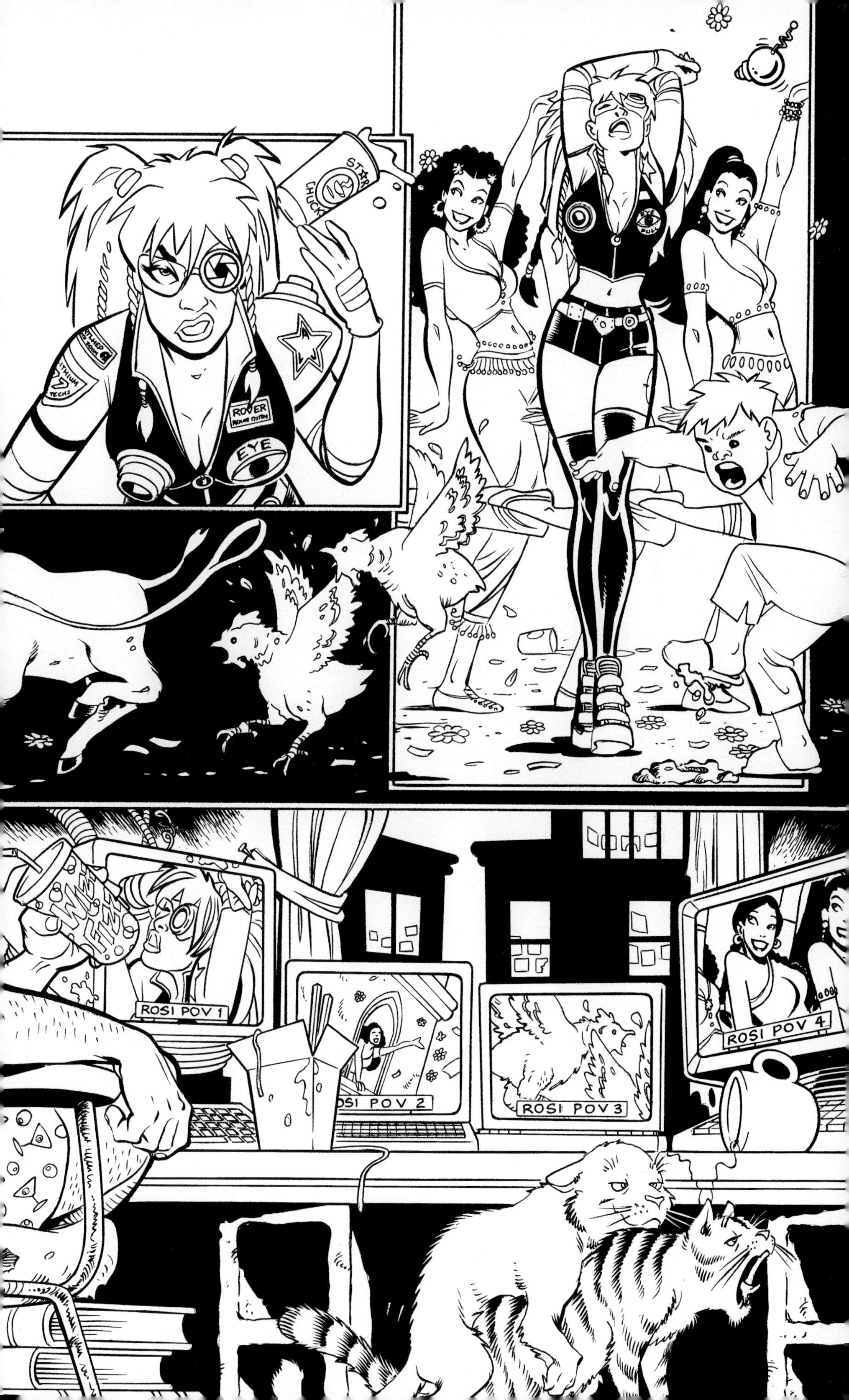

ROVER
EYE
ROSI POV 1
OSI POV 2
ROSI POV3
ROSI POV 4

PAGE EIGHT

Pic 1;
CUT TO: Rosi strolling along, scowling at all the people having fun,
scratching idly at one piece of tech mounted on her eye-cam.

ROSI;　　　　　　　IT'S GETTING SO I'M THINKING ABOUT ACTUALLY
　　　　　　　　　USING THIS CGI RIG TO STITCH FAKE STUFF INTO MY
　　　　　　　　　LIVE CAMS JUST TO BRIGHTEN MY DAY.

ROSI;　　　　　　　MAKE EVERYONE WALK AROUND WITH MASSIVE
　　　　　　　　　HAIRY CARTOON NIPPLES OVER THEIR FACES FOR A
　　　　　　　　　DAY.

Pic 2;

I AM SO BORED IT'S UNTRUE, IT REALLY IS.

I FEEL LIKE STABBING MYSELF REPEATEDLY IN THE BRAIN JUST FOR THE
NOVELTY VALUE.

I'VE BEEN WIRED UP FOR A FULL YEAR, NOW, AND I JUST FEEL WASTED.

YOU ALL GET MORE SEX THAN I DO.

YOU KNOW YOU DO - AT LEAST TEN PERCENT OF YOU STILL LOG ON EVERY NIGHT
LOOKING FOR A BIT OF THE OLD IN-OUT/IN-OUT ACTION.

YOU HOPELESS BASTARDS.

YOU ALL GET SOMETHING OUT OF THIS, THIS CONSTANT WATCHING OF WHATEVER I
WATCH, MY SUPPOSED COMMENTARY ON WHEREVER I AM.

YOU MUST DO, YOU PAY GOOD MONEY FOR IT SO I DON'T HAVE TO GET A PROPER
JOB.

BUT I'VE WALKED ALL OVER LONDON AND THERE'S NOTHING LEFT OF IT FOR ME.

ALL WALKED OUT.

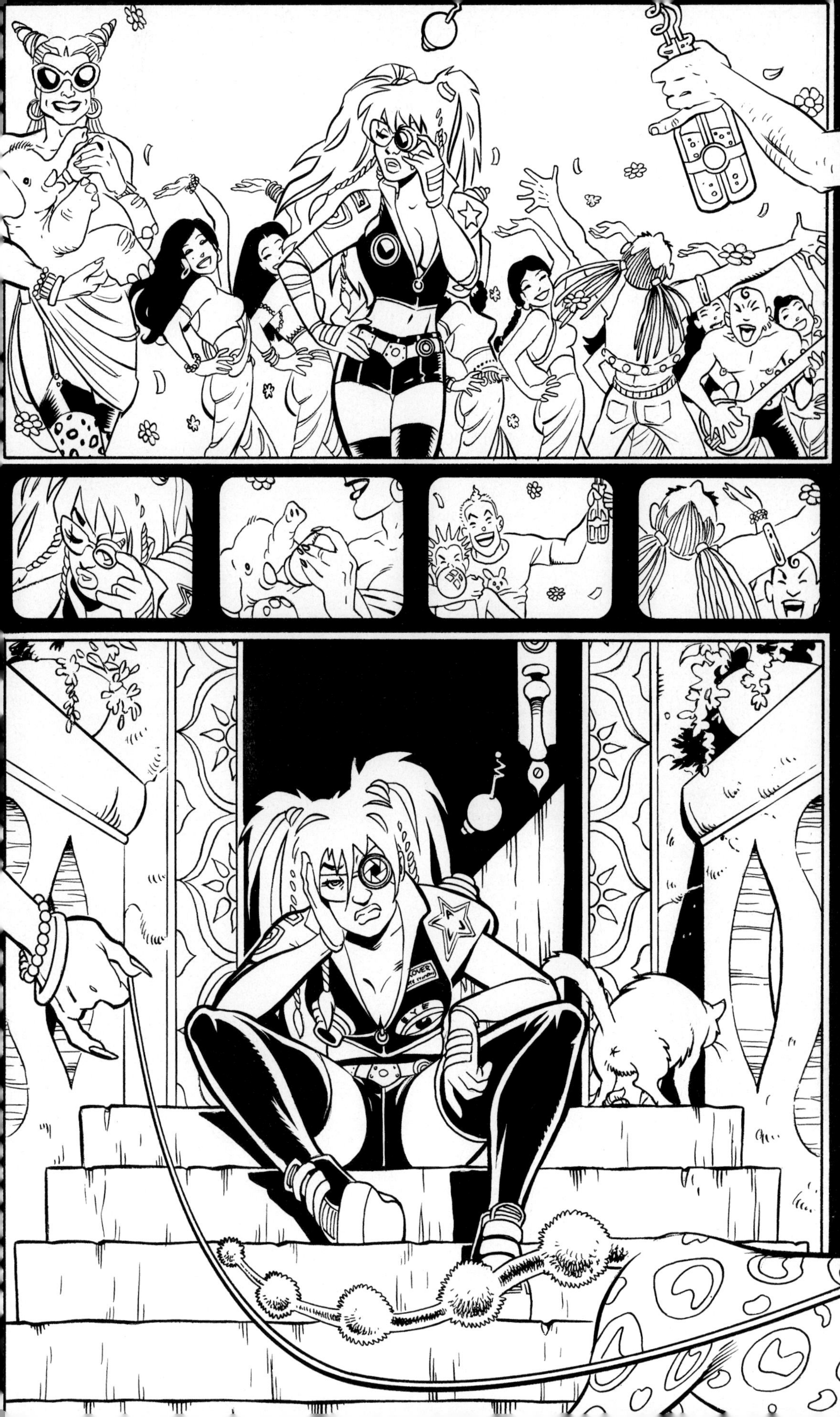

PAGE NINE

Pic 1;
A guy we'll refer to as a QUARRYMAN -- a soldier of the Quarry Mob --
barrels past Rosi, knocking her to one side. He carries a case --
looks like a pool cue case, maybe a little wider. Maybe two feet long.
Trainers and tracksuit bottoms, a puffy flourescent plastic jacket, t-
shirt underneath, plastic hair extensions.

ROSI: OI!

QUARRYMAN: BOLLOCKS --

Pic 2;
TONY LING races past her, in hot pursuit of the Quarryman.

TONY: I'LL HAVE YOUR BOLLOCKS **OFF**, YOU LITTLE
                         BASTARD --

TONY;   -- GIVE ME THAT SODDING THING BACK!

Pic 3;
Rosi looks up, grinning.

ROSI: THAT'S MORE LIKE IT.

Pic 4;
The pair of men tear off down the street -- and Rosi runs to follow.

(no dialogue)

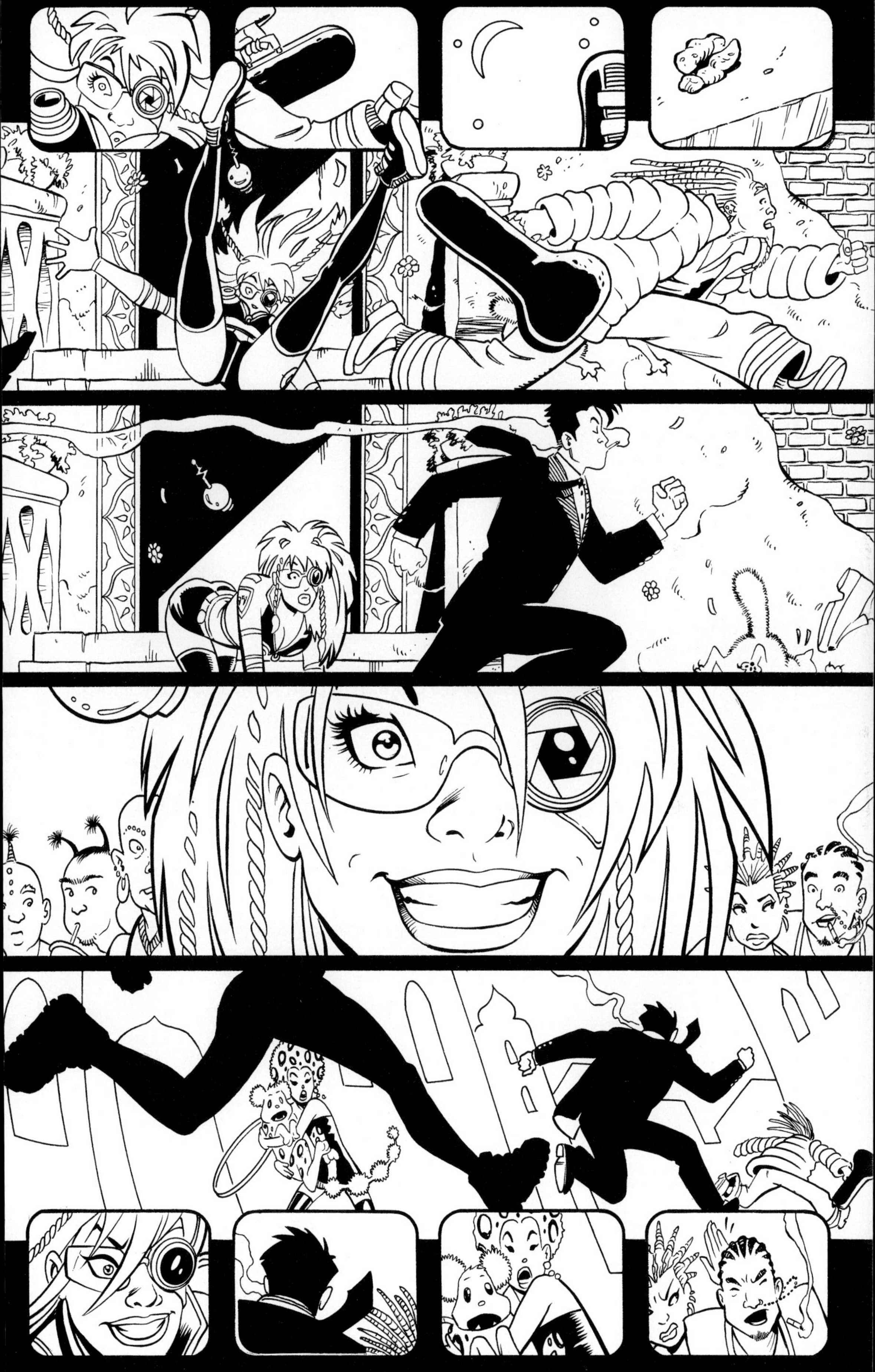

PAGE TEN

Pic 1;
The Quarryman runs like Satan's on his arse, sweat pouring off his
face, eyes wide.

(no dialogue)

Pic 2;
Tony pursues easily, focussed, no sweat -- a Zen sprinter.

(no dialogue)

Pic 3;
The Quarryman ducks into an alley.

QUARRYMAN;   LEAVE ME ALONE --

QUARRYMAN;   -- I'M WITH THE **QUARRY GANG,** YOU RETARD --

Pic 4;
Tony tears after him.

TONY: ASK ME IF I CARE, YOU DISGUSTING LITTLE TOERAG.

Pic 5;
Rosi runs after them.

ROSI;   THIS IS WHAT THEY WANT. A SPIT OF THE OLD TRUE
CRIME.

ROSI;   RAMPANT THIEVERY ON THE STREETS OF THE
LONDON.

ROSI;   AND THE ONE IN FRONT OF ME'S GOT A NICE BUM ON
HIM.

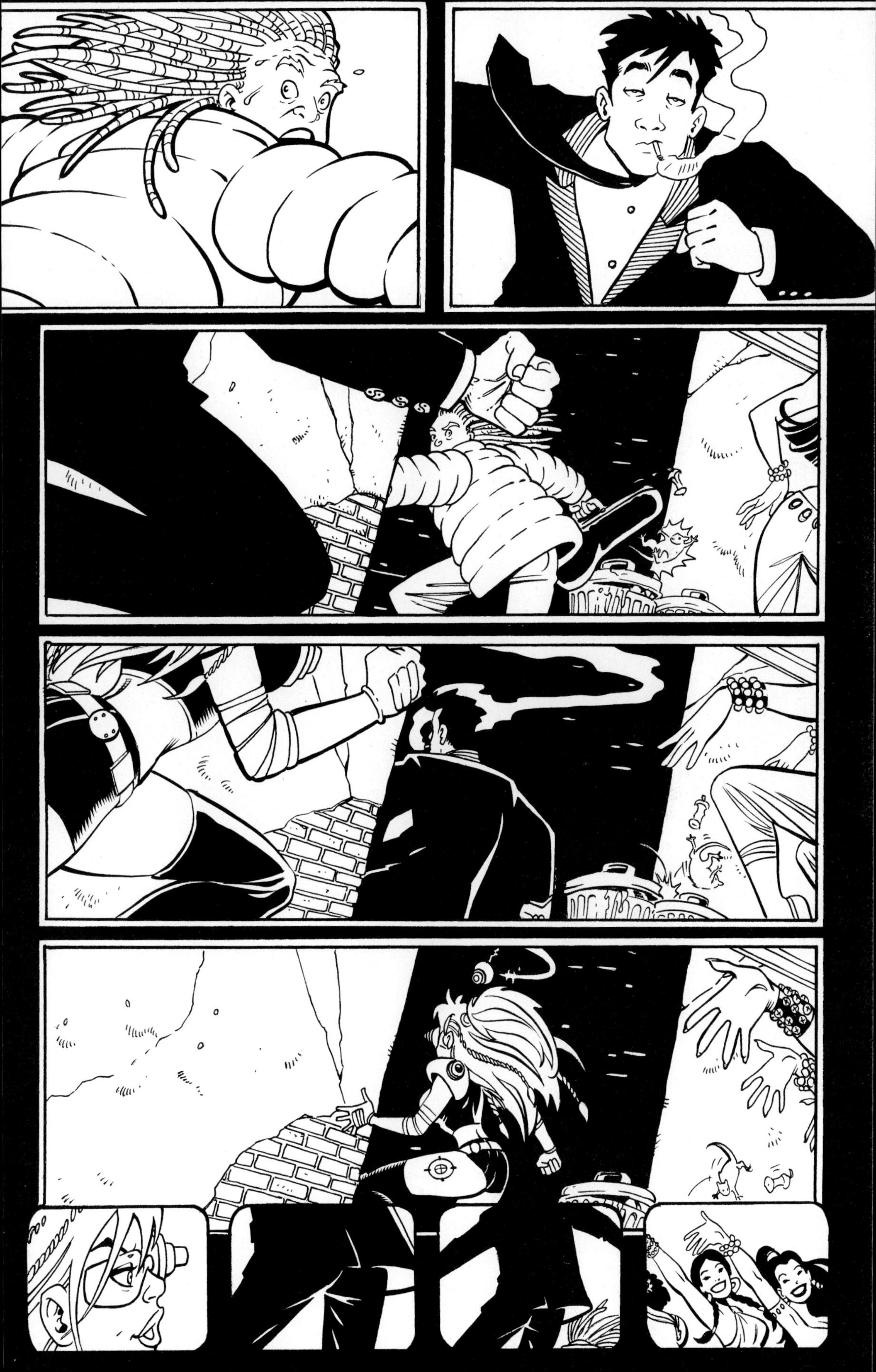

PAGE ELEVEN

Pic 1;
In the alley -- the Quarryman leaps up for the base of a fire escape, nine feet up, reaching out for its lip with his free hand --

(no dialogue)

Pic 2;
-- and Tony gives him a flying kick in the back as he tries to pull himself up.

(no dialogue)

Pic 3;
His face slams into the edge of the fire escape.

QUARRYMAN;   **AOWWW!**

Pic 4;
He tumbles down messily as Tony picks himself up.

(no dialogue)

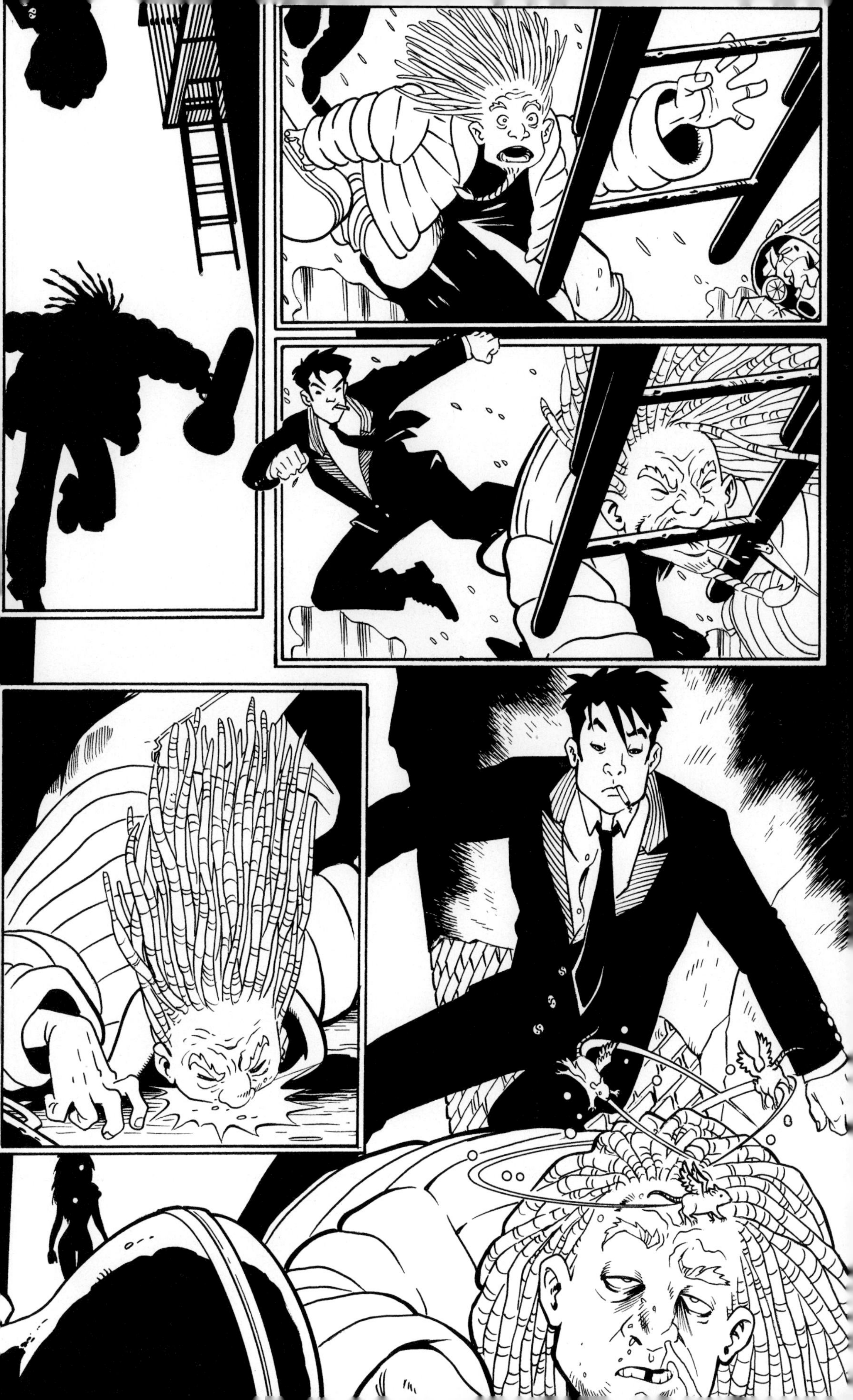

PAGE TWELVE

Pic 1;
Tony walks over to him.

TONY: COME ON NOW, SON. LET'S DON'T BE SILLY. HAND IT
                         OVER.

Pic 2;
And the Quarryman smacks him in the nuts with one end of the case.

(no dialogue)

Pic 3;
The Quarryman takes off down the alley as Tony clutches his punished
scrote.

QUARRYMAN: RIGHT IN THE DADPASTE DISPENSER --

TONY: your mum'll be disappointed

Pic 4;
Tony straightens up, trying to put the pain away, as Rosi catches up
with him.

ROSI;   TRUE CRIME, CHASE SCENE AND NOW TODGER
                         ULTRA-VIOLENCE. YOU ALL RIGHT?

TONY;   I WILL BE ONCE I'VE BROKEN A LAMPOST OFF IN HIS
                         ARSE.

TONY;   DO I KNOW YOU?

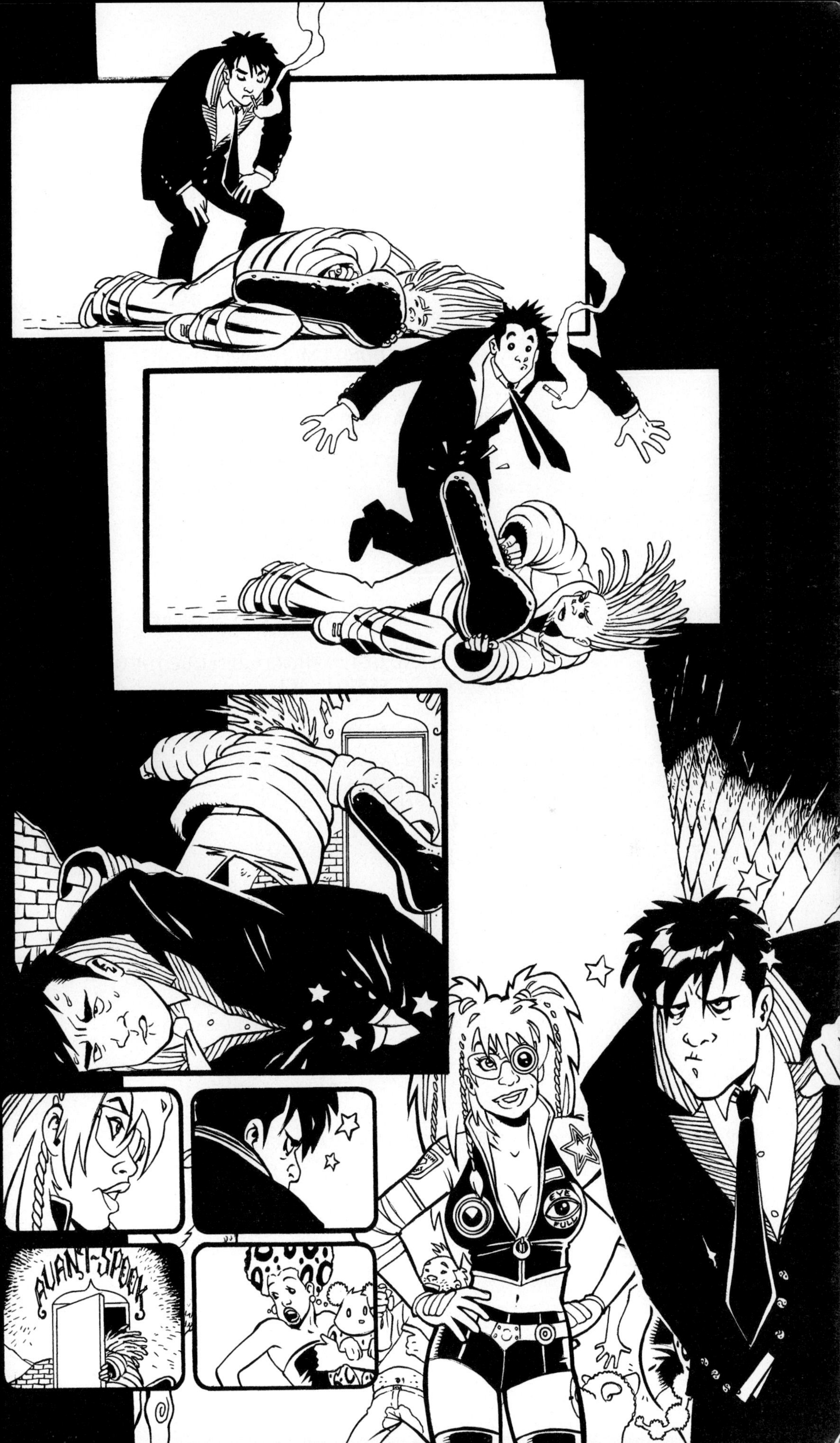
AVANT-SPOOK
EYE FULL

PAGE THIRTEEN

Pic 1;
Tony takes off, Rosi keeping up with him.

ROSI;   I GUESS YOU DON'T USE THE WEB MUCH.

TONY;   ONLY FOR PORN. WHAT, ARE YOU ONE OF THOSE
                         TITS-OUT CAMGIRLS?

ROSI;   I'VE DECIDED THAT YOU'RE HORRIBLE.

Pic 2;
At the end of the alley is the entrance to a nightclub -- its signage
proclaims it as AVANT-SPOOK.

TONY;   YOU AND THE REST OF THE WORLD.

TONY;   BUGGER. HE MUST'VE DUCKED IN THERE.

ROSI;   HE'LL STAND OUT IN THERE -- HE'LL BE THE ONLY
                         ONE NOT WEARING BLACK.

Pic 3;
They get inside the door -- Rosi's eyes go wide as she sees him draw a
gun from a hidden shoulder holster.

TONY;   GOOD.

ROSI;   WHO ARE YOU?

TONY;   I AM A ZEN GUNMAN. PULLING THE TRIGGER IS MY
                         ACT OF CONTEMPLATION.

Pic 4;
He pulls the safety off.

TONY;   SHOOTING TOERAGS IS MY ACT OF STAND-UP
                         COMEDY.

Pic 5;
She watches him go.

ROSI;   I DON'T THINK I'M LAUGHING YET.

TONY (off):   WAIT TIL YOU SEE WHERE I SHOOT HIM.

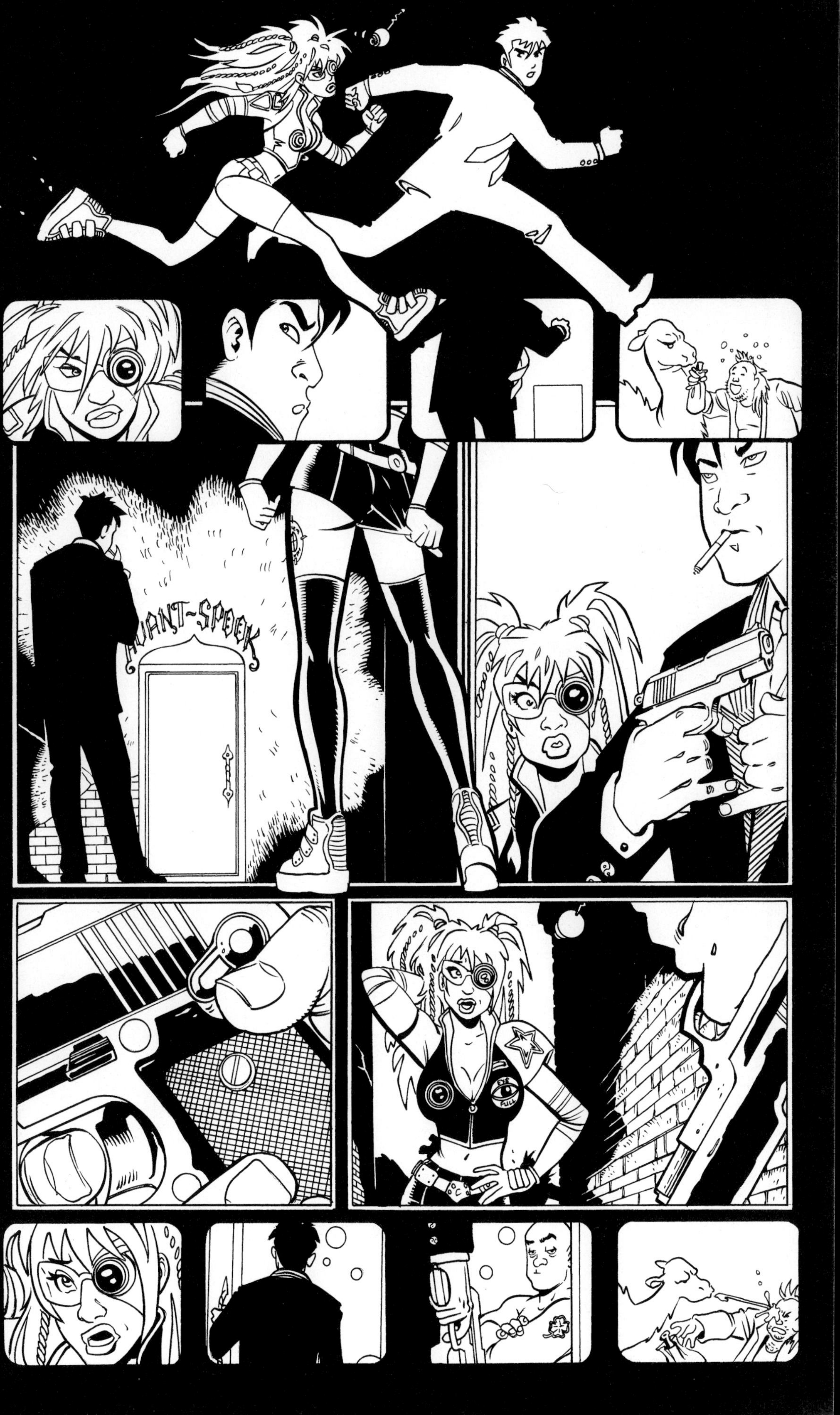
AVANT~SPOOK
EYE FULL

PAGE FOURTEEN

Pic 1;
Int. club: it's a goth haunt. And most of the people here have had
body modification. People with actual sparking bolts in their necks,
green and blue skins, real fangs, actual batwings growing down their
arms, you get the idea... no visual idea is too nuts or too stupid
here, have fun with it... (two-thirds of the page)

(no dialogue)

Pic 2;
...and, in the middle, standing out bright as day, the Quarryman,
getting accosted by a GOTH GIRL.

GOTH GIRL: I VANT TO ZUCK YOUR BLUDD.

QUARRYMAN;   COULD I LIKE TEXT YOU LATER OR SOMETHING?

GOTH GIRL;   COMMITMENTPHOBE.

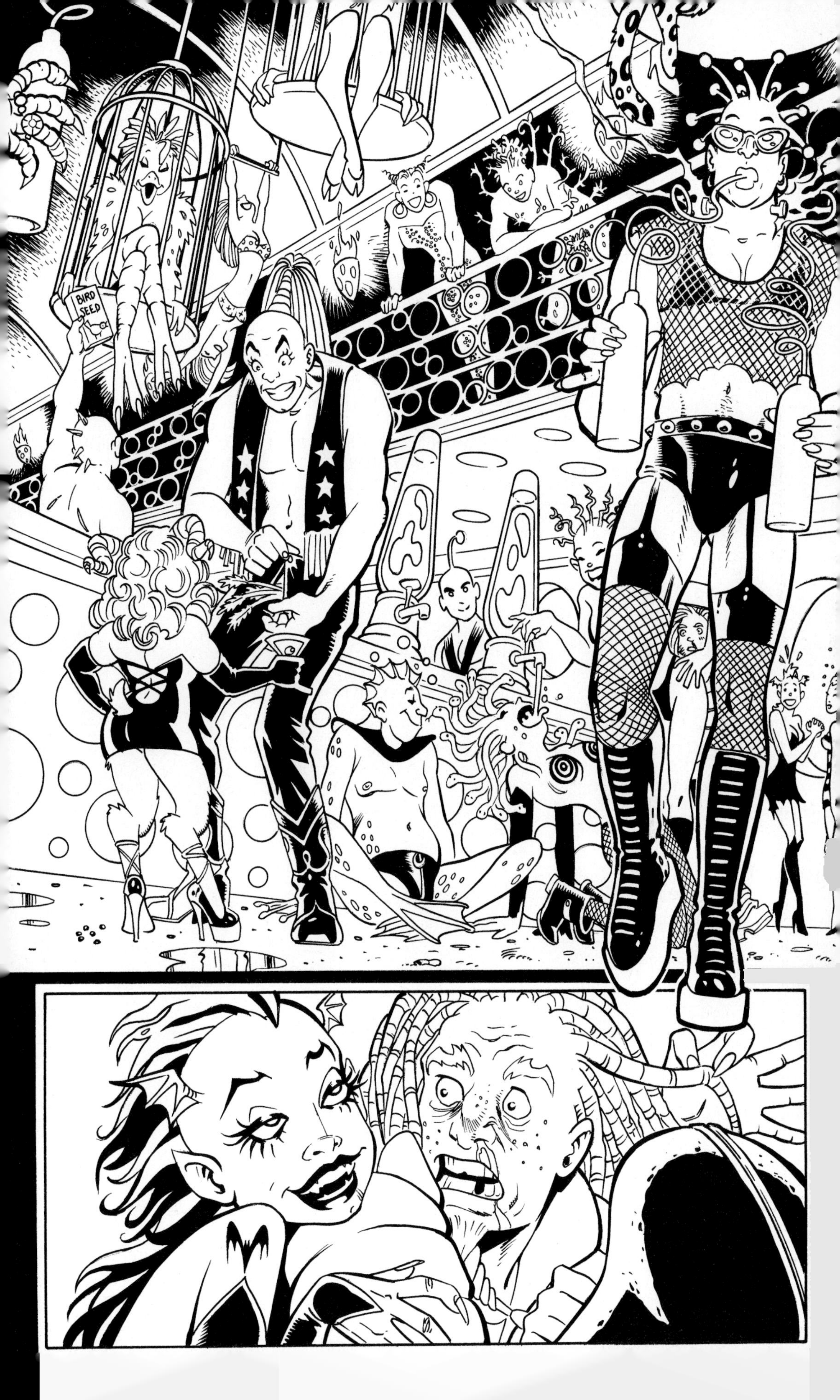
BIRD SEED

PAGE FIFTEEN

Pic 1;
On the other side of the club, a space clears around Rosi and Tony, who is aiming his gun.

TONY: YOU WERE RIGHT. CLEAR SHOT.

ROSI;   YOU'RE GOING TO KILL HIM FOR STEALING?

TONY;   WELL, THEY DON'T SEND PEOPLE TO AUSTRALIA FOR STEALING ANY MORE.

Pic 2;
Close in on Tony, concentrating.

TONY: BESIDES, THIS IS KINDER.

Pic 3;
The Quarryman notices, grabs the Goth Girl by the wrist.

QUARRYMAN: SHIT --

GOTH GIRL;   OH YEAH, HOLD ME DOWN --

Pic 4;
--pulls her in front of him, hand on her throat, making her face Tony.

QUARRYMAN;   BACK OFF, TONY -- YOU KNOW THIS IS HOW IT HAS TO BE --

GOTH GIRL;   I AM SO HORNY.

Pic 5;
Tony is still aiming his gun, eyes closed now. Contemplation.

(no dialogue)

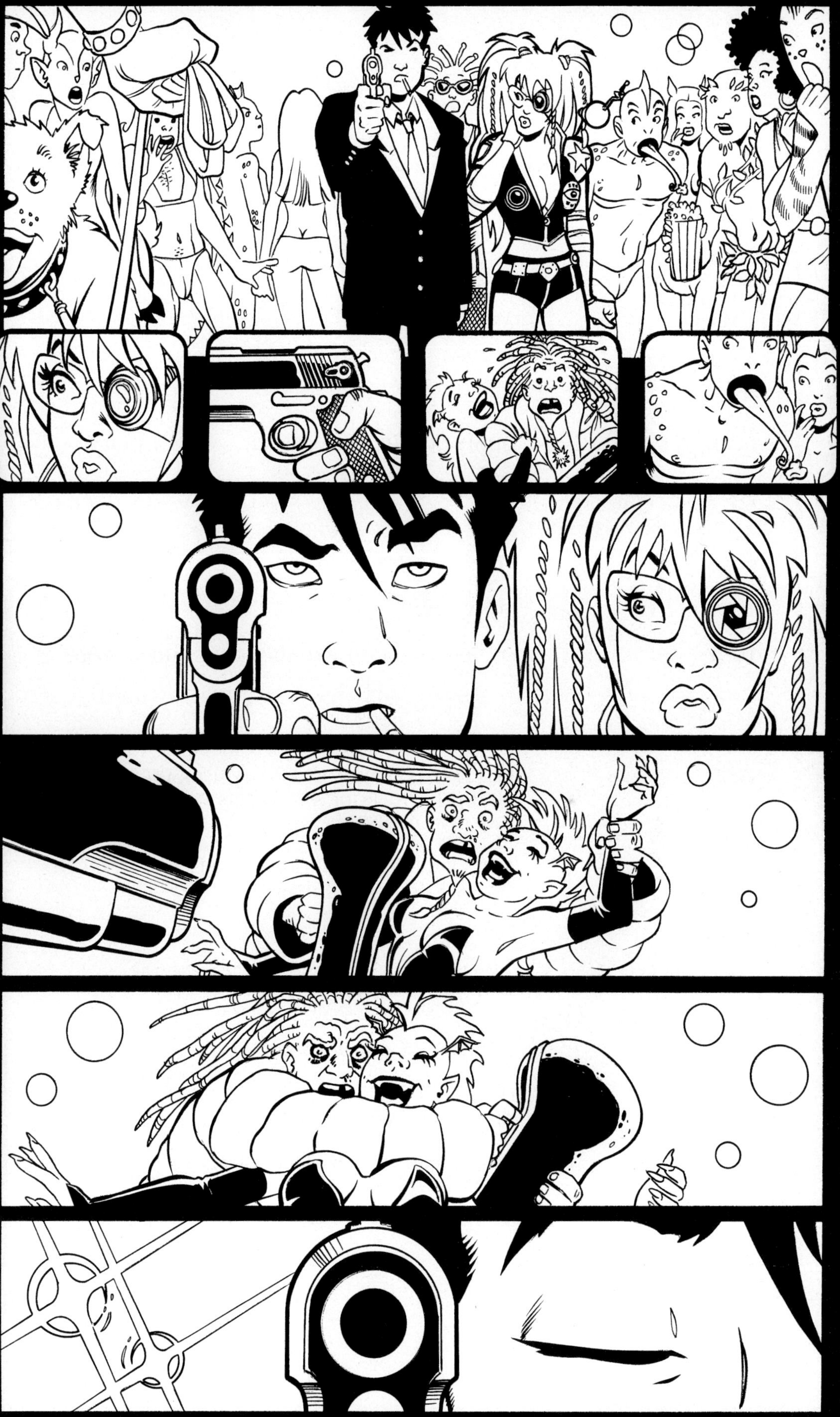

PAGE SIXTEEN

Pic 1;
Tony hangs up his gun, scowling.

TONY;   ARSEHOLE.

Pic 2;
The Quarryman takes off, leaving the Goth Girl standing there, right in
the way --

GOTH GIRL;   OH MY GOD, HE'S DUMPED ME -- VODKA, QUICK --

Pic 3;
Tony and Rosi run after them.

ROSI;   TONY WHAT?

TONY;   TONY LING.

TONY;   OH, HELL -- YOU'RE BROADCASTING, AREN'T YOU?

Pic 4;
They bump past bouncers, scowling at each other.

ROSI;   DO I LOOK STUPID TO YOU? MY HIT RATE'S GOING
                           THROUGH THE ROOF AND THIS IS THE MOST FUN I'VE
                           HAD IN MONTHS.

TONY;   YOU REALLY NEED TO GET YOURSELF A BOYFRIEND
                           OR A GIRLFRIEND OR SOMETHING.

Pic 5;
Out on to the street through the club entrance -- they see the
Quarryman across the street, just finished sprinting across the road --
there's another alleyway over there he could disappear into --

ROSI;   HOW DO YOU KNOW I DON'T HAVE A BOYFRIEND?

TONY: ONE, YOU'RE OUT HERE FOLLOWING STRANGE MEN
                           AND BITCHING A LOT.

TONY;   TWO, YOU HAVE THE PERSONALITY OF A WEASEL
                           WITH PAINTSTRIPPER ON ITS NIPPLES.

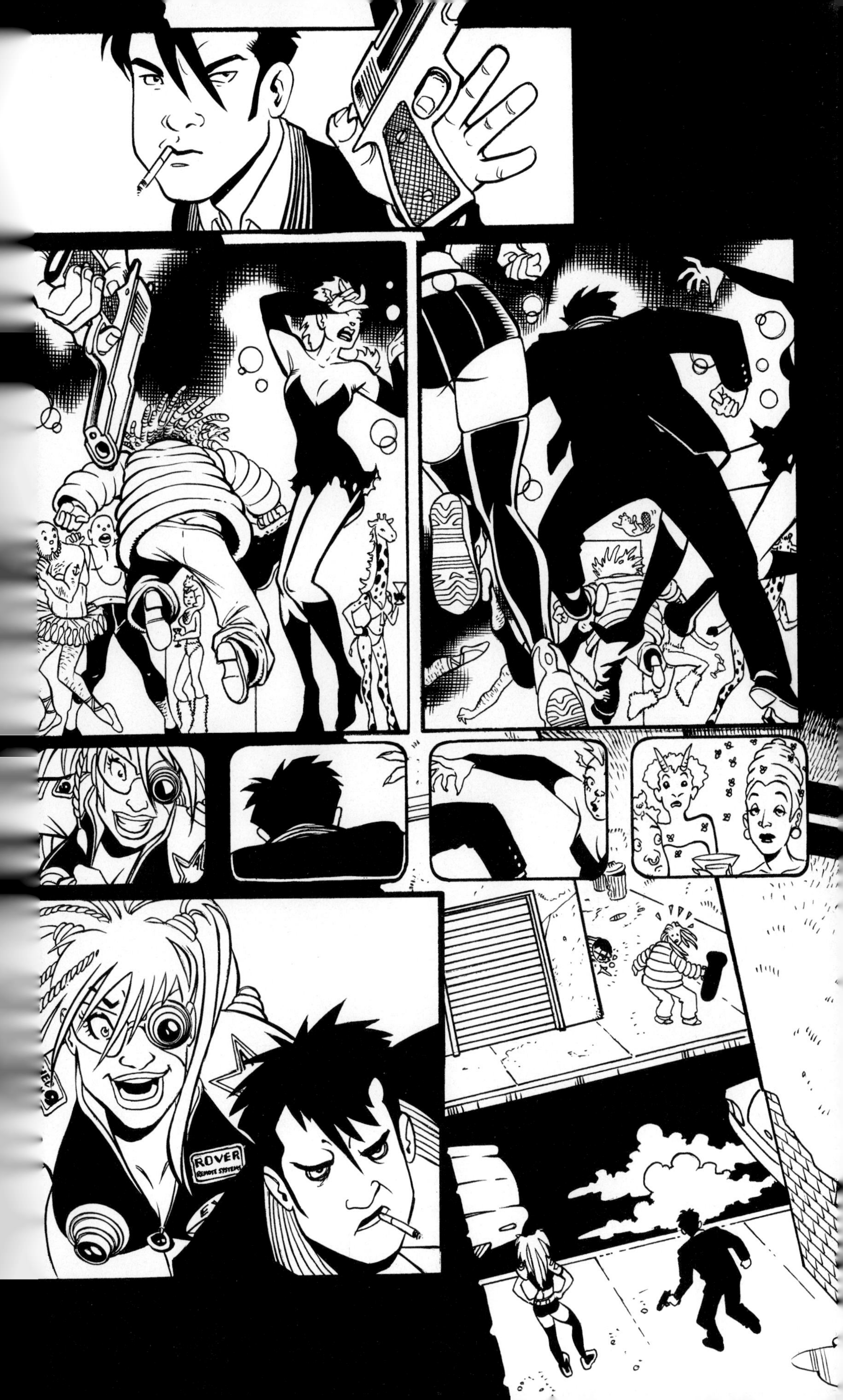
ROVER
REMOTE SYSTEMS

PAGE SEVENTEEN

Pic 1;
Tony launches himself out into the street -- there's a car coming --

(no dialogue)

Pic 2;
-- Tony jumps on top of it --

(no dialogue)

Pic 3;
-- jumps off, spinning in the air -

(no dialogue)

Pic 4;
-- and, upside down, he cracks off two shots with the gun --

(no dialogue)

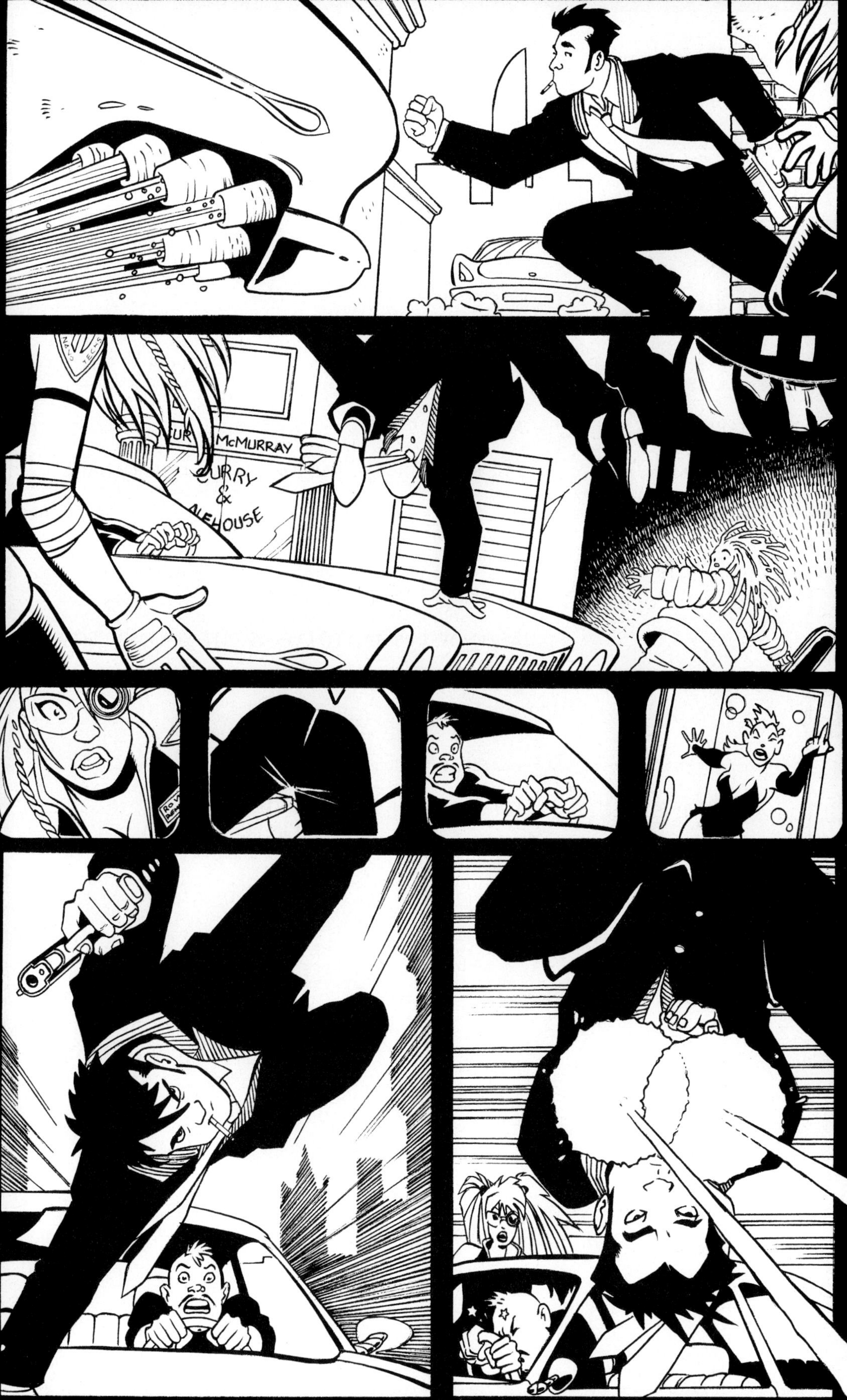
McMURRAY
CURRY & ALEHOUSE

PAGE EIGHTEEN

Pic 1;
-- The Quarryman, just headed into the alley, has the interesting experience of getting both his kneecaps blown off from behind.

(no dialogue)

Pic 2;
Tony tumbles down on the other side of the street. Rosi passes him at speed, headed for the Quarryman.

(no dialogue)

Pic 3;
Who's down on his face in the alley, sobbing, the case on the ground in front of his head.

QUARRYMAN;   ME KNEES

QUARRYMAN;   I'LL NEVER BE A CHAMPION FARTCATCHER AGAIN

Pic 4;
Rosi picks up the case. Tony's at his feet. The Quarryman turns painfully to face Tony, therefore turning away from Rosi.

TONY: I WARNED YOU, YOU DAFT SOD.

TONY;   AND NOW I'VE HAD TO CONFISCATE YOUR KNEECAPS.

QUARRYMAN: STOAT FELCHER.

Pic 5;
Tony turns around. The Quarryman's hand goes inside his jacket.

TONY;   OKAY, NO-ONE'S WATCHING...

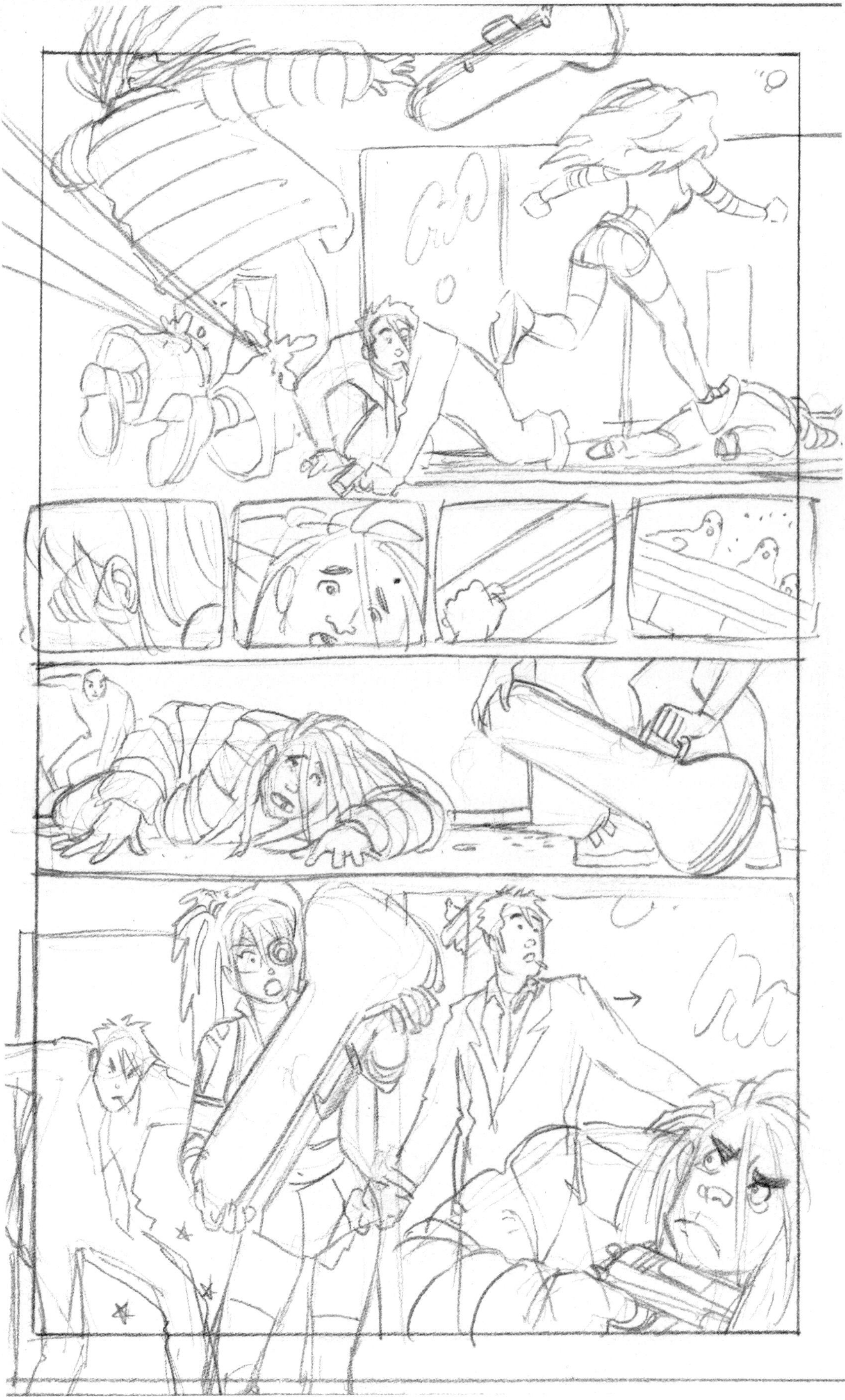

PAGE NINETEEN

Pic 1;
The Quarryman draws a gun on Tony.

QUARRYMAN;   NO. NO-ONE.

Pic 2;
And Rosi stamps on his head. Hard.

(no dialogue)

Pic 3;
Tony stares. Rosi stares at the unconscious Quarryman.

TONY;   I DON'T BELIEVE IT.

ROSI;   ME NEITHER.

ROSI;   I WOULD'VE MADE A SHITLOAD OF HITS IF I'D LET HIM
                         SHOOT YOU.

Pic 4;
She tosses the case to Tony.

ROSI;   SO THIS IS WHAT HE STOLE FROM YOU?

TONY;   GOD, NO.

Pic 5;
Tony catches the case.

TONY;   IT'S WHAT I WAS TRYING TO STEAL FROM HIM.

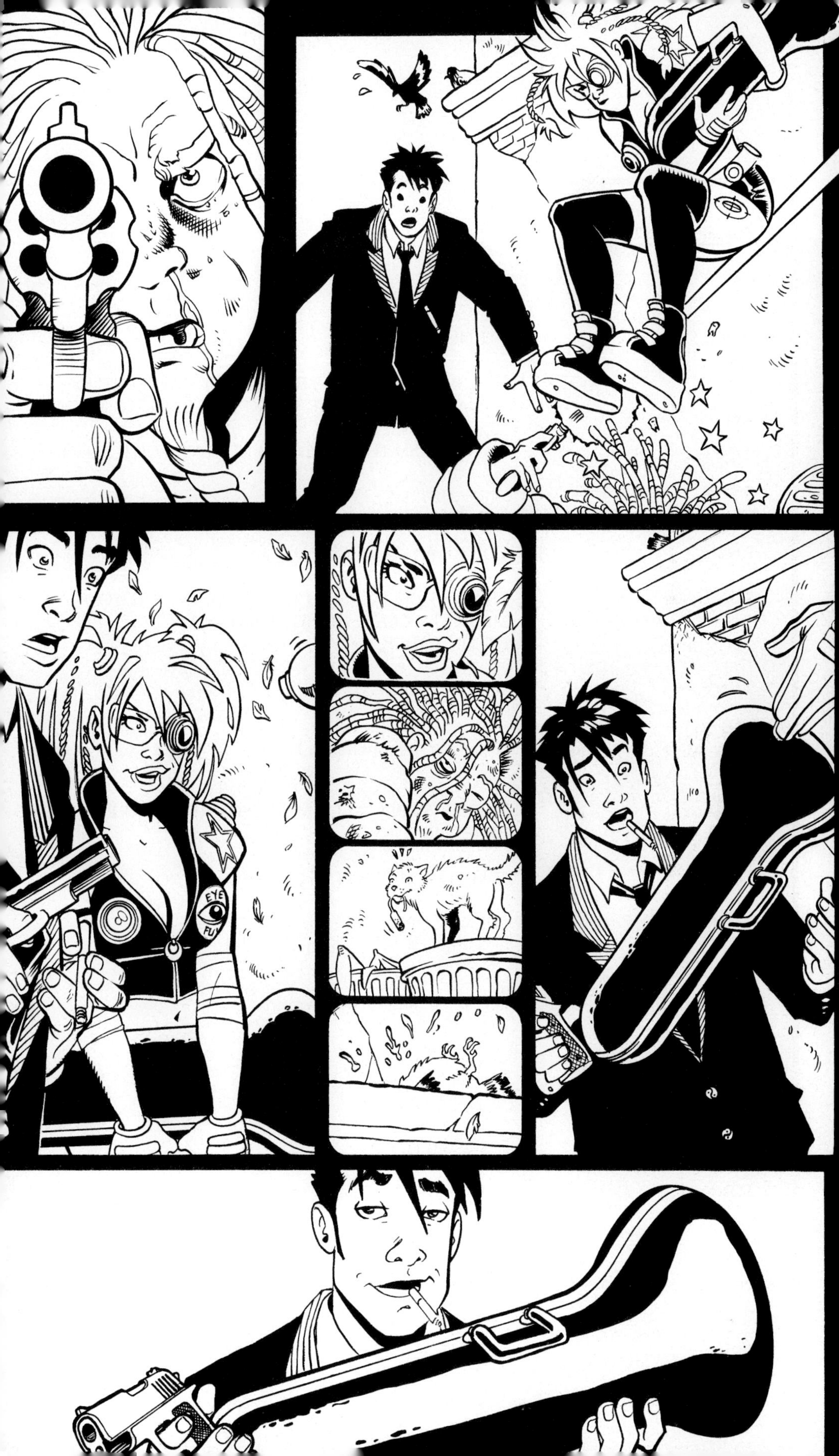
EYE
FU

Pic 1;
Rosi gazes at him.

ROSI;   I THOUGHT -

TONY;   HE'S A COURIER FOR THE QUARRY GANG, OUT OF
                               CANARY WHARF -- BRINGING THIS BACK TO THEM.

TONY: I WAS HIRED TO MAKE SURE IT NEVER GOT THERE.

Pic 2;
He smiles, goes to open the case.

ROSI;   YOU'RE A GANGSTER?

TONY;   THAT'S A BIT HARSH. I'M A FREELANCE BLACK
                               MARKET AGENT. BEING IN A GANG IS...
                               PREDICTABLE.

TONY;   WANT TO SEE?

Pic 3;
They stand together facing us as he opens it. We don't see what's in
it.

TONY;   THIS WAS SPECIALLY MADE FOR REG QUARRY. VERY
                               EXPENSIVE.

TONY;   IT SUITED MY EMPLOYERS THAT HE NOT RECEIVE IT.

ROSI;   OPEN IT, OPEN IT...

Pic 4;
And she kind of wishes she hadn't said that, you can see it in her
face. All these are going to be same-POV, Amanda…

(no dialogue)

Pic 5;
She looks at Tony.

ROSI;   IT'S A WILLY.

TONY;   YEP.

ROSI;   A VERY VERY BIG WILLY.

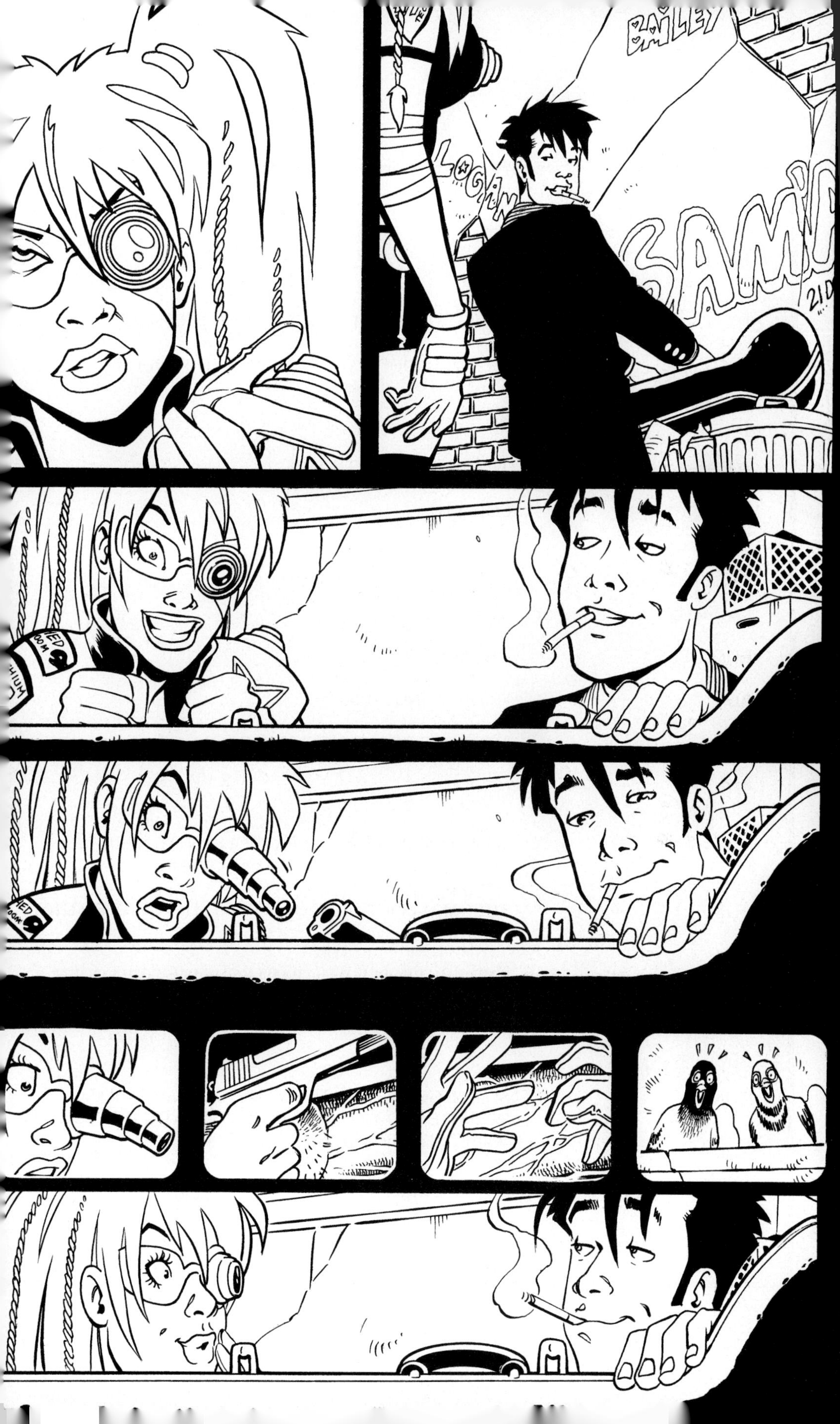
BAILEY

PAGE TWENTY-ONE

Pic 1;
He points inside with his gun.

TONY;   TOUCH THAT LITTLE BUTTON UNDER THERE.

ROSI;   I'M NOT BLOODY TOUCHING IT. YOU TOUCH IT.

Pic 2;
He pokes the gun inside.

TONY;   I'LL TOUCH IT WITH THIS.

ROSI;   COWARD.

TONY;   SHUT UP.

Pic 3;
She screws her face up.

ROSI;   OH MY GOD.

ROSI;   IT'S PLAYING MUSIC.

TONY;   "THE RIDE OF THE VALKYRIES."

Pic 4;
He snaps it shut.

TONY;   THE QUARRYS HAVE A PATHOLOGICAL NEED TO BE
                                                THE BEST-ENDOWED GANG IN LONDON.

TONY;   THE SMALLER THEIR EQUIPMENT, THE QUIETER THEY
                                                ARE.

ROSI;   AND THE PEOPLE WHO PAID YOU LIKE THEM QUIET.

Pic 5;
He sticks the case under his arm, she heads out of the alley, all
attitude..

TONY;   SO I'VE GOT WHAT I NEED, AND YOU GOT A RAVE
                                                WEBSITE SHOW OR WHATEVER IT IS YOU DO. YOU
                                                WON'T SEE ME AGAIN.

ROSI;   I DON'T WANT TO SEE YOU AGAIN. YOU'RE HORRIBLE.

TONY   EXCELLENT.

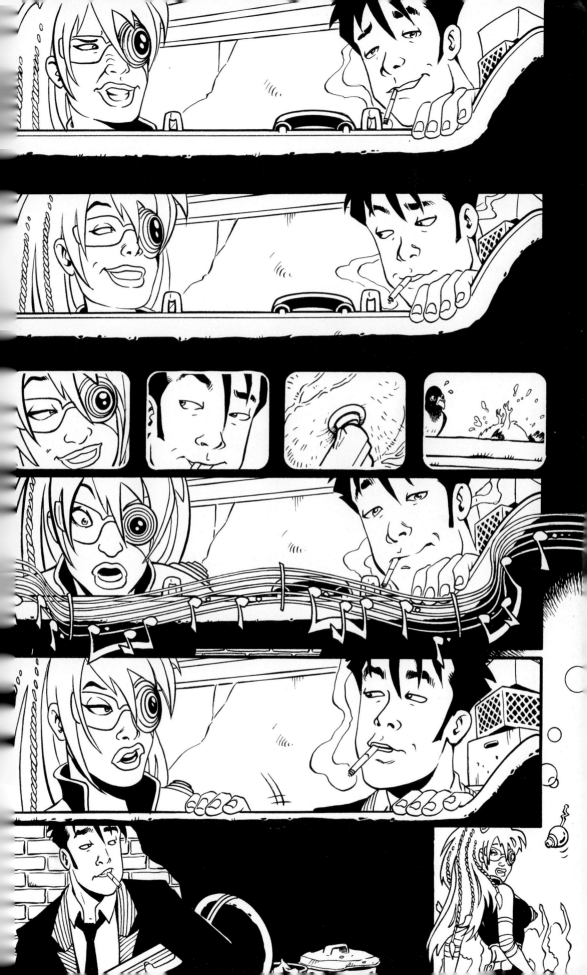

PAGE TWENTY-TWO

Pic 1;
She stops, as he reaches the alley mouth with her.

ROSI;   WHY AREN'T YOU IN A GANG, GANGSTER?

TONY;   IT'S A ZEN THING.

TONY;   I LIKE TO JUST LET THINGS HAPPEN.

Pic 2;
He smiles. When he relaxes, he has a good smile.

TONY;   INTERESTING THINGS COME TO YOU, IF YOU WAIT.

Pic 3;
And they head off in opposite directions.

(no dialogue)

Pic 4;
Tony stops, turns his head to check her out as she walks off.

(no dialogue)

Pic 5;
And Rosi stops and turns to check him out as he turns and walks off.

(no dialogue)

To be continued

##

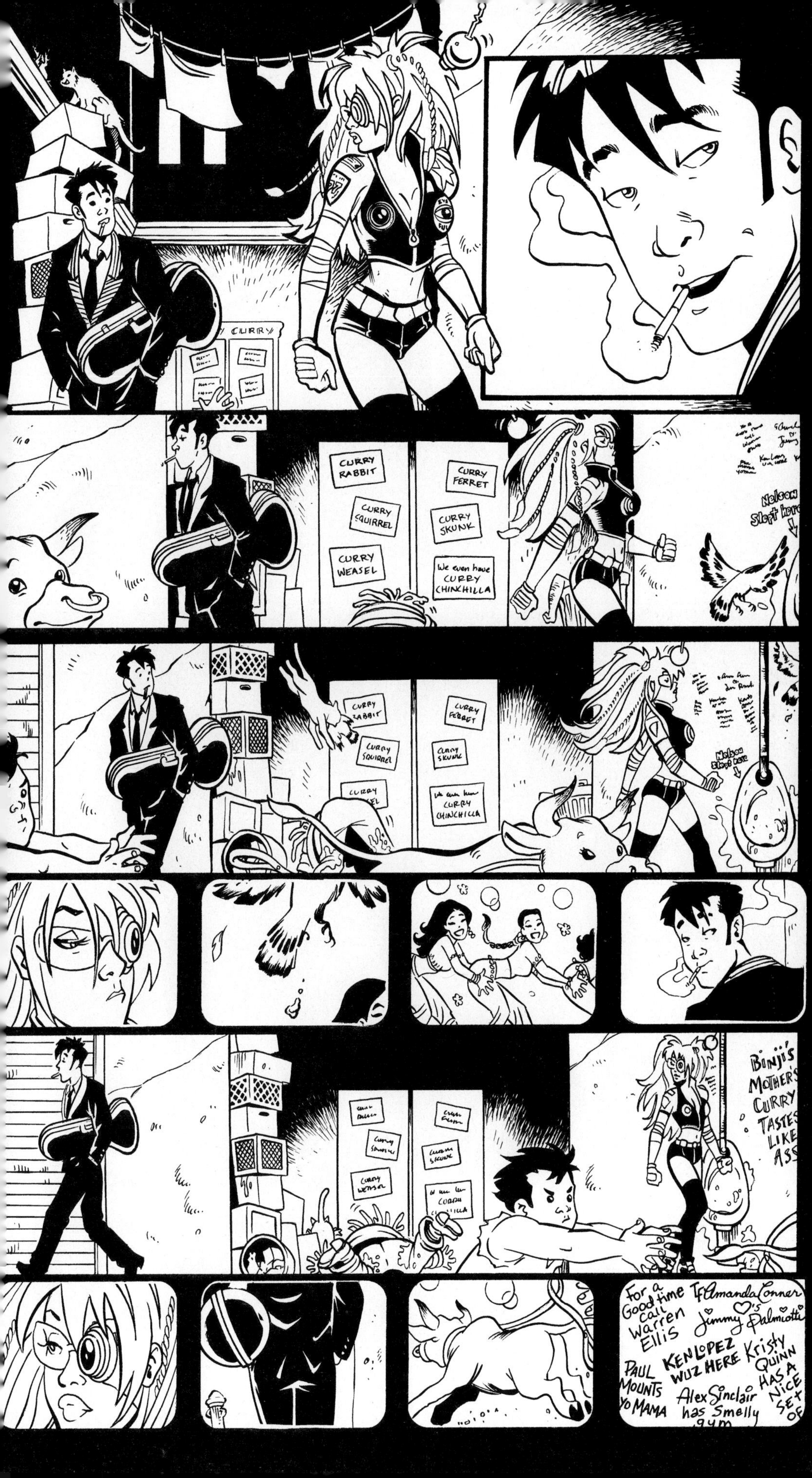

CURRY
CURRY RABBIT
CURRY SQUIRREL
CURRY WEASEL
CURRY FERRET
CURRY SKUNK
We even have CURRY CHINCHILLA
Nelson Slept here
CURRY RABBIT
CURRY SQUIRREL
CURRY FERRET
CURRY SKUNK
CURRY CHINCHILLA
BINJI'S MOTHER'S CURRY TASTES LIKE ASS
For a Good time call Warren Ellis
Amanda Conner ♡'s Jimmy Palmiotti
PAUL MOUNTS YO MAMA
KEN LOPEZ WUZ HERE
Kristy QUINN HAS A NICE SET OF
Alex Sinclair has Smelly gum

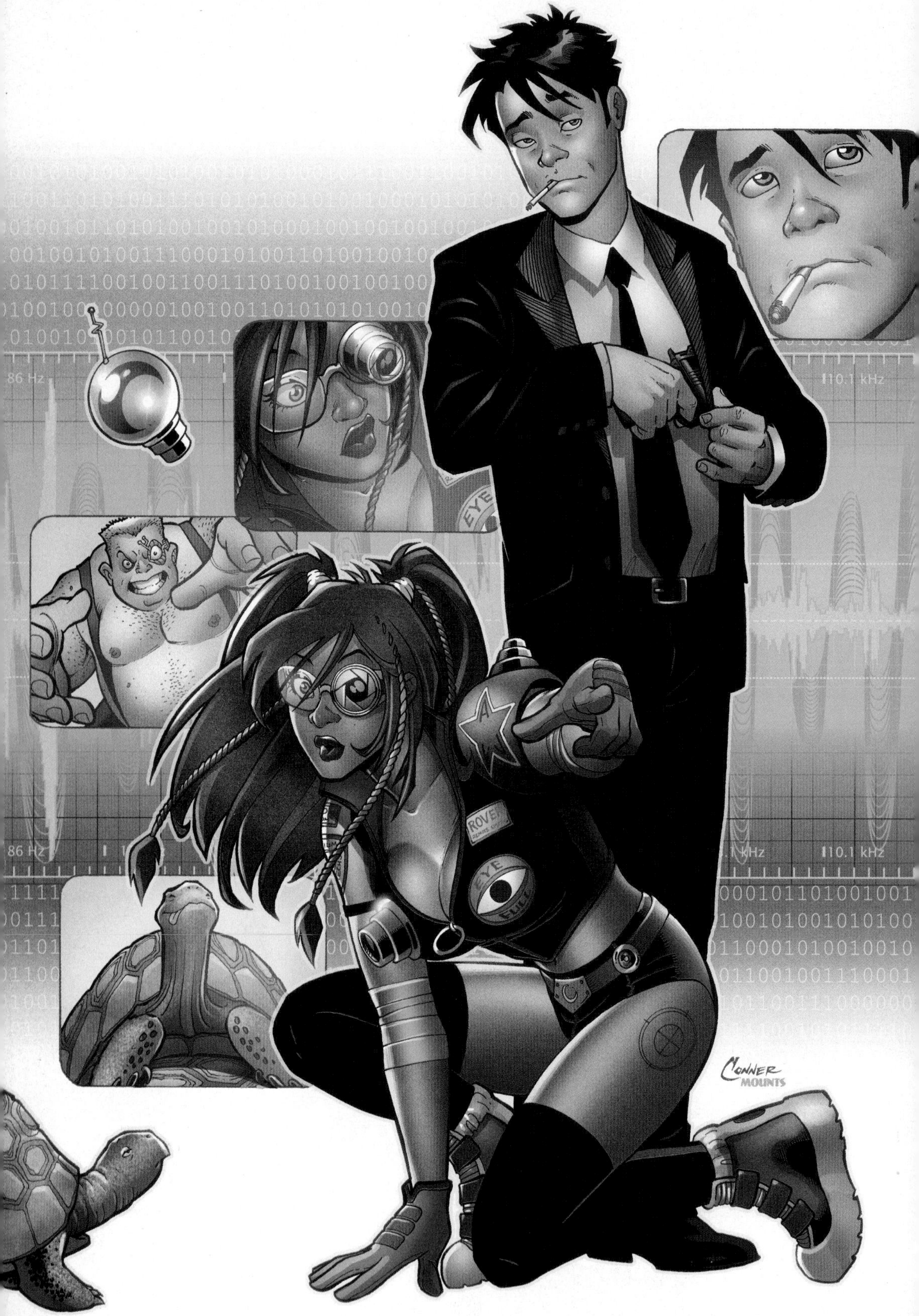
86 Hz
10.1 kHz
ROVER
EYE
CONNER
MOUNTS

WARREN ELLIS

GLOBAL FREQUENCY

1001 agents on the Global Frequency are all that stand between the people of Earth and the horrors the technological advances of the past century have seeded around the planet. When G.F. leader Miranda Zero has Aleph activate you, you'd best be prepared to lend your expertise...or face the end of the world. Can you handle the pressure?

In PLANET ABLAZE and DESOLATION RADIO, Warren Ellis teams up with twelve of comics' brightest talents to bring you his unique vision of the future.

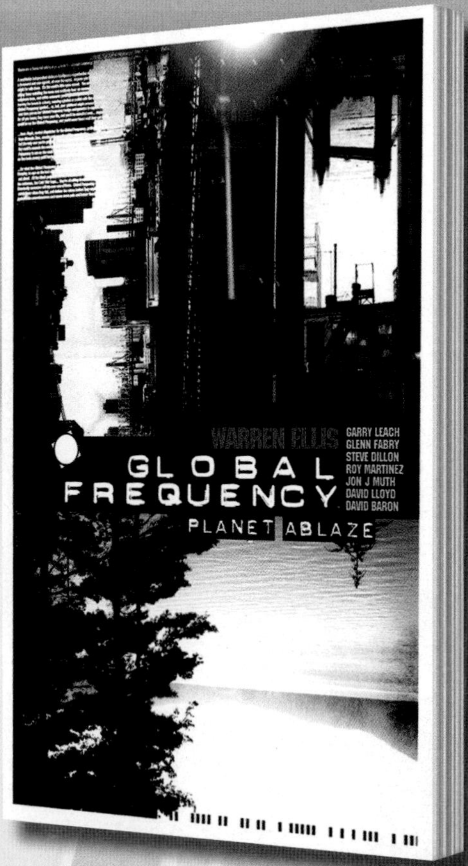
WARREN ELLIS
GARRY LEACH
GLENN FABRY
STEVE DILLON
ROY MARTINEZ
JON J MUTH
DAVID LLOYD
DAVID BARON
GLOBAL
FREQUENCY
PLANET ABLAZE

Explore more worlds with these creators...

DESOLATION JONES: MADE IN ENGLAND

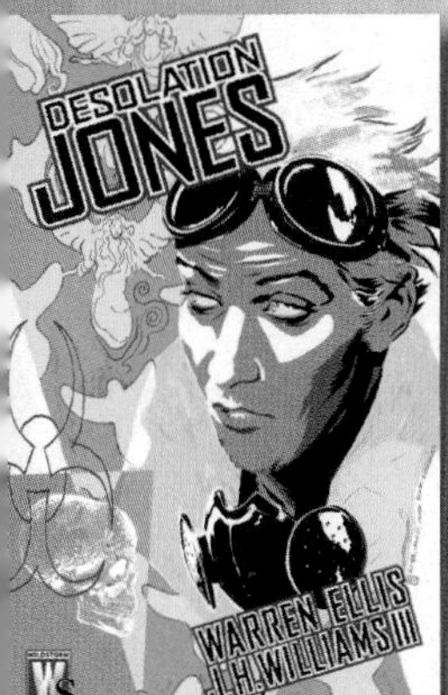
DESOLATION
JONES
WARREN ELLIS
J.H. WILLIAMS III

Ellis • Williams III

POWER GIRL Books 1-2

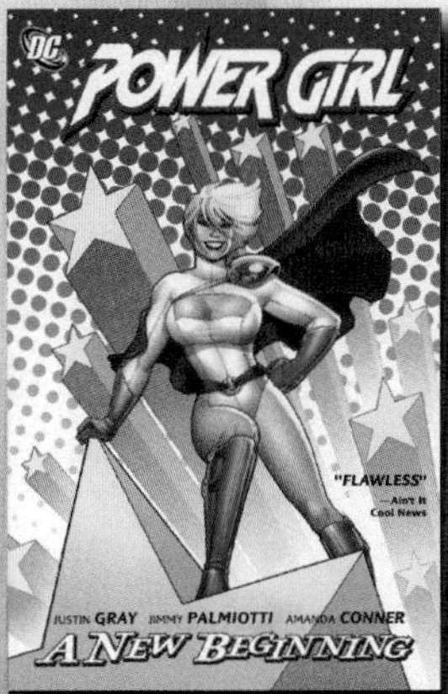
POWER GIRL
"FLAWLESS"
—Ain't It Cool News
JUSTIN GRAY JIMMY PALMIOTTI AMANDA CONNER
A NEW BEGINNING

Gray • Palmiotti Conner

RED

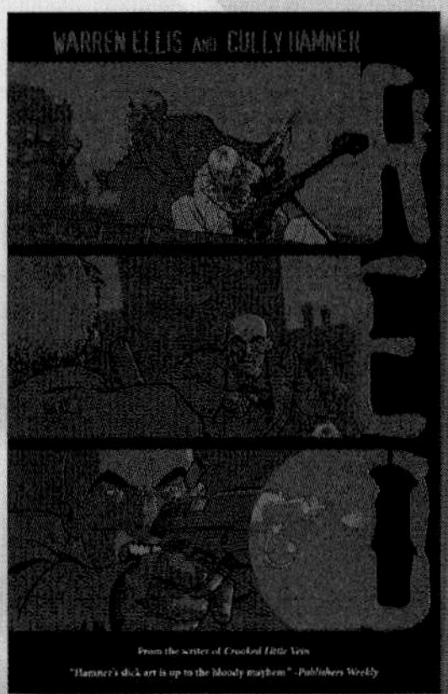
WARREN ELLIS AND CULLY HAMNER

Ellis • Hamner

TERRA

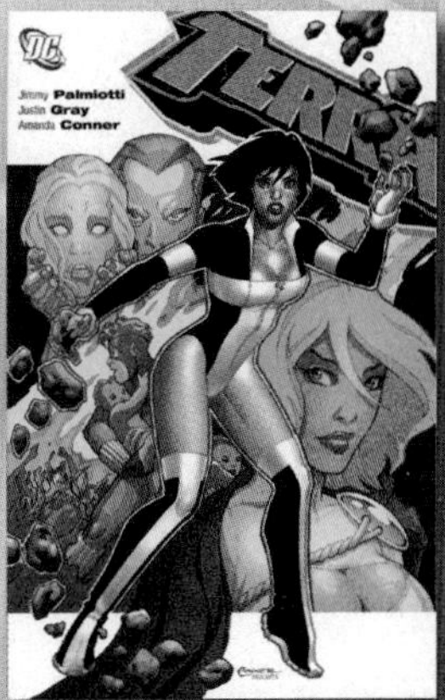
Jimmy Palmiotti
Justin Gray
Amanda Conner

Gray • Palmiotti Conner

SEARCH THE GRAPHIC NOVELS SECTION OF **WILDSTORM.COM** FOR ART AND INFORMATION ON ALL OF OUR BOOKS!

More fun one-volume stories!

KILLAPALOOZA

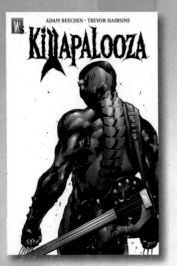

Beechen • Hairsine

MYSTERIUS THE UNFATHOMABLE

Parker • Fowler

NORTH 40

Williams • Staples

SECRET HISTORY OF THE AUTHORITY: HAWKSMOOR

Costa • Staples

VICTORIAN UNDEAD: Sherlock Holmes vs. Zombies

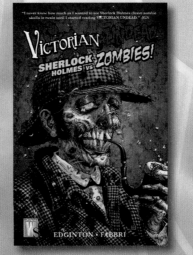

Edginton • Fabbri

THE WINTER MEN

SUGGESTED FOR MATURE READERS

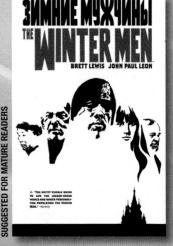

Lewis • Leon